D0402921

A CRISIS
of PEACE

A CRISIS
of PEACE

George Washington, *the* Newburgh Conspiracy,
and the Fate *of the* American Revolution

DAVID HEAD

PEGASUS BOOKS
NEW YORK LONDON

A CRISIS OF PEACE

Pegasus Books, Ltd.
148 W 37th Street, 13th Floor
New York, NY 10018

For Andrea, Carolina, Camila, and Andrew.

Contents

A Note on 18th-Century Writing

Writers of the 18th century were wonderfully idiosyncratic in things we now consider standard, like spelling, capitalization, and punctuation. To reveal something of an author's personality and education as well as the circumstances of composition, quoted materials reproduce the originals exactly—strange spellings and all—with only a few silent corrections for clarity.

Introduction

On a cold morning in March 1783, the officers of the Continental Army read a letter that was circulating through their cantonment along the Hudson River. The officers considered the letter's call to do something soldiers weren't supposed to do: meet to discuss how to send an ultimatum to the civilian authorities in Congress.

Some 10,000 soldiers, the bulk of the Continental Army, stood duty in the region known as the Hudson Highlands, a strategically vital area overlooking the spot where the river narrowed. Most of the men lived in log huts constructed in the farmland to the west of New Windsor, nestled among places with such appealing names as Snake Hill and Murderers Creek. A dozen miles south, a garrison guarded the fort at West Point, while other units were scattered another dozen miles beyond at Stony Point and Verplanck's Point. The commander in chief, General George Washington, was headquartered in a Dutch-style stone house along the river in Newburgh, two miles north from the main body of his men. The American victory at Yorktown in October 1781 had bloodied the enemy and driven the British ministry to the bargaining table, but British forces in North America remained formidable, above all in New York City. If the British decided to renew the war and resurrect their old strategy of dividing the colonies along the Hudson, the American army was nearby.[1]

The Highlands was also a place of sylvan solitude, conducive to contemplating life, and as the days slipped by and the drudgery of winter quarters dragged on for the eighth time in the war, the officers' thoughts turned to all they had sacrificed and the scant rewards they had enjoyed for it.

For eight years, the army was paid sporadically, and when it was, compensation was delivered in a mess of notes, certificates, and cash that had so depreciated that it was nearly worthless. In the wake of mass resignations and the treachery of Benedict Arnold in 1780, the officers had forced Congress to promise them pensions, but the treasury was empty—worse than empty: the nation was deeply in debt and the only way out, new taxes, was deeply unpopular.

When the officers looked outside their ranks, they saw greedy civilians snug by their firesides. Civilian government employees were paid reliably, while soldiers hunkered down in the snow. The officers believed in the cause. They believed in independence. They believed in republican government and creating the world anew. But they also saw themselves as gentlemen, and gentlemen needed to live a certain lifestyle, surrounded by certain fine things, to display their status. For the men with families, serving during the prime of life had taken away their chance to earn a genteel living and impoverished those who depended on them. For younger men, devotion to the army had delayed family formation and the entrance into full adulthood. An officer's title might help their prospects, but if a captain, major, or colonel proved penniless who would want him?[2]

The officers felt ignored and even suspected. Many civilians looked askance at them—and felt justified in their misgivings. The army were liberators, yes, but the republican ideology of the 18th-century Anglo-American world taught that a professional army was a favorite tool of the tyrant. Pensions were another. Pensions preferred some men to others, and made them dependent on government largesse taken by taxing the virtuous. Marry the two, and for many Americans, alarm bells sounded.

None of the officers' complaints were new. Earlier in the revolution, the urgency of the war had overcome the worst of the mutual suspicions harbored by soldiers and citizens. But as 1782 turned to 1783, treaty negotiations, long stalled by British domestic politics and the entanglements of the Franco-American alliance, moved forward. It was only a matter of time before peace was brokered and the people decided to break up the army, with or without a final financial settlement.

Sensing time was not on their side, in December 1782 the officers sent a delegation to Philadelphia with a memorial to Congress documenting their hardships and asking for a speedy resolution to their claims for justice. As the delegation lobbied Congress in January and February 1783, they sent news back to the army with a taste of encouragement—most congressmen were sympathetic to the army's plight—mixed with a heaping lump of delays, obfuscations, and the excuses that had long embittered Congress's relationship with the army.

By March, patience wore thin. When the anonymous letter appeared, the officers passed it around, distracted from the morning routine by its flashing rhetoric. The letter's author, whoever he might be, knifed into each of the officers' sore points.

Announcing himself "a fellow soldier whose interests and affections bind him strongly to you," the anonymous author declared himself disabused of his faith in Congress. Nothing would come from their memorial. It was naïve to expect otherwise. He saluted his fellow officers as the deliverers of the republic. "Yes, my friends, that suffering Courage of yours, was active once, it has conducted the United States of America, thro' a doubtfull and a bloody war," he wrote. "It has placed her in the Chair of Independency." But to what end? For the benefit of the country and its people? "Or is it rather a Country that tramples upon your rights, disdains your Cries—& insults your distresses?"[3]

Though unknown at the time, the letter was the work of Major John Armstrong, Jr., a twenty-four-year-old aide-de-camp to General Horatio Gates, a one-time rival to Washington who'd once hoped to parlay his victory at the Battle of Saratoga into overall command of the war. Armstrong was one of several young staff officers living at a New Windsor house that served as Gates's headquarters, and together with his friends, he composed the letter on the night of March 9 and prepared copies for distribution.[4]

Warming to his theme, Armstrong raised a vital question: what should the officers do? Send a new message to Congress, he answered, no longer asking but demanding, and making clear the consequences of more delays. "Carry your appeal from the Justice to the fears of government," he implored. "Change the Milk & Water stile of your last Memorial—assume a bolder Tone, decent, but lively, spirited, and determined." By meeting the following day, they could choose "two or three Men, who can feel as well as write" to tell their civilian leaders that this was their last chance, that "the slightest mark of indignity from Congress now, must operate like the Grave, and part you forever." Armstrong concluded by reminding the officers of their options. If peace came, they didn't have to comply. They could refuse to disband. If the war continued, they didn't have to fight. They could leave the country to fend for itself.[5]

When news of the letter reached General Washington in Newburgh, he projected calm firmness. In the next day's general orders, he forbade the officers from meeting that day. "His duty as well as the reputation and true interests of the Army requires his disapprobation of such disorderly proceedings," the orders read. Perceiving that clamping down too hard might cause a worse outburst, the general diffused the pressure by rescheduling the meeting. Washington set the time and place—"12 o'clock on Saturday next at the Newbuilding," a newly constructed social and meeting hall in New Windsor often styled "The Temple." Washington also set the agenda. "After mature deliberation," he directed, "they will devise what further measures ought to be adopted as most rational and best calculated to attain the just and important object in view," meaning Congress's handling of their grievances, and "report the result of the Deliberations to the Commander in Chief," indicating he would not attend.[6]

At headquarters, surrounded by his staff, or "military family" as he liked to call them, Washington was vexed by the anonymous letter. He knew the mood in camp could be surly because he knew the privations that were part of life in the Continental Army. He knew that men marched in worn out shoes and in threadbare clothes, hardly cutting the elegant figure he demanded. He knew that the states, the locus of power in the nation, put their own interests first and that a hamstrung Congress could not equip the army efficiently. He knew that cunning suppliers sent rancid beef and foul whiskey and charged sky-high prices because inflation was through the roof and the nation's credit had cratered long before. By any measure, Washington was a wealthy man, but even he felt the pressures of a thin wallet, his farms never meeting expectations in his absence. He ate better than others and dressed better than others, but, fatigued by constant paperwork and bearing the burden of ultimate command, he knew the physical, mental, and emotional toll taken by the war.

But he never thought the army was in crisis until now.[7]

Washington was not at his best in the heat of the moment. On the battlefield, he could be hesitant when boldness was needed, and impulsive when the occasion called for restraint. Even in his larger conduct of the war, Washington fixated on some objectives—he was obsessed with attacking New York City—only to be dissuaded by his officers and allies.

Washington's true talents as a general were his organizational abilities, relentless attention to detail in administration, and deft sense of the war's politics, skills he learned as a Virginia gentleman planter-politician. Washington's true genius as commander in chief of the Continental Army in the American Revolution lay in his rock-solid commitment to the ideals of the cause, his unwavering deference to civilian authority, and his unshakeable belief that the Revolution would succeed. He was the right man, in the right place, at the right time, for the kind of war that the Americans fought.[8]

As the week wore on and Washington kept up the appearance of boring camp life, he worked to confront the officers' anger head-on. Consulting his staff and trusted advisers, Washington prepared to take the unhappy officers by surprise. He would address them as a group—the first time he would do so, at that late date in the war. His words, carefully chosen, would call them back from the precipice.[9]

As it turned out, words weren't enough.

—⁓—

The events of that week in March 1783 marked the culmination of what is often called the Newburgh Conspiracy, a mysterious episode in which nationalist-minded leaders in Philadelphia such as Superintendent of Finance Robert Morris, his assistant (but not relative) Gouverneur Morris, Congressman Alexander Hamilton, and others supposedly combined with disgruntled officers led by General Gates to pressure Congress and the states to approve new taxes and strengthen the central government—and maybe even replace Washington in command. The label "conspiracy" poses a problem, however. It prejudges the event's core question: Was there really a plot between Philadelphia nationalists and angry officers to achieve their political goals with the threat—or reality—of violence?

People in the 18th century loved conspiracy thinking; for them it was inconceivable that events unfolded by anything other than design. People today also love conspiracy theories, with varying degrees of devotion. They can be a fun source of debate, or a debilitating pathology for individuals and whole societies. My research has made me skeptical that a true conspiracy unfolded at Newburgh, and the following pages will explain why. I ask readers to set aside their assumptions about conspiracy thinking: join me in the 18th century and look with fresh eyes at how the American Revolution really ended.

As we'll see, regardless of whether it was a conspiracy, the events at Newburgh represented a pivotal moment at the end of the American

Revolution that exposed the tensions between the states and the central government and between the army and civilians that had simmered throughout the war. In the two years from the October 1781 victory at Yorktown, often thought to have ended the war, and the official announcement in America of the Treaty of Paris in November 1783, the prospect of peace actually made the tensions among Americans worse as the logic for hanging together—fighting the war so they would not all hang separately as rebels—dissipated and the nation was left to decide what the Revolution was for. It was a crisis of peace, a time when the Revolution still might have failed, and the crisis at Newburgh was an hour of grave danger.

A CRISIS
of PEACE

ONE

The Road from Yorktown

O n October 19, 1781, the American and French armies lined up along the road outside Yorktown, Virginia, and prepared for a soldier's most gratifying duty: witnessing the surrender of the enemy.[1]

The Americans stood on the left side of the road, the regulars mostly arrayed in blue, the Virginia and Maryland militia behind them in drab hunting shirts. Across the road the French army formed up, their white coats accented by red, white, and green facings. A band played as they paraded into place, and the jingle of a tambourine, an unusual instrument for a military ensemble, produced "a most enchanting effect."[2]

Several thousand spectators—men, women, and children—turned out to witness the surrender on that warm midautumn afternoon. They watched from fine carriages and rough wagons, from horseback and on foot. Many were locals, while others, including a group of Oneida Indians from New York, had traveled from far away to share the moment. Camp followers and sutlers, women and men who cooked and cleaned for the troops and hawked them goods, watched alongside planters who came to reclaim property—horses and enslaved people—that the British had seized as they raided across Virginia earlier in the year.[3]

Around two o'clock the British army, in brilliant red, tramped out of Yorktown, joined by the blue-clad Hessians, the German mercenaries rented early in the war to subdue the colonists. Together they were led by Brigadier General Charles O'Hara, a beefy Irishman known for his wit and charm. The British commander, General Charles, Earl Cornwallis, was ill, probably with an acute case of humiliation, but possibly he had a fever. His absence disappointed Americans eager to see the haughty British general get his comeuppance.[4]

As the defeated army advanced, a drummer beat a melancholy English march. Tradition says it was "The World Turn'd Upside Down," but there's no evidence such a name was attached to any tune at the time. Riding forward, O'Hara approached the allied commanders. Assuming the French army was preeminent, he proceeded to General Jean-Baptiste Donatien de Vimeur, Comte de Rochambeau. General Rochambeau directed O'Hara to the man next to him, the commander in chief, General George Washington. Sitting atop his charger, Washington wore a blue coat with buff facing, a buff waistcoat and matching breeches, and black leather boots. A tricorn hat covered a head of gray hair; the stress of war had made powder unnecessary for the forty-nine-year-old.[5]

O'Hara's mistake must have been deliberate, because George Washington emanated command on and off the battlefield. He was tall and powerfully built, athletic but also graceful. Standing about six feet tall, though some sources said six-foot-two or -three, he tipped the scales at 210 pounds. Famous for his horsemanship and feats of strength, Washington lit up the dance floor with his light footwork and easy manners. But it wasn't Washington's physique alone that fixed the gaze of those who saw him. Other men were as tall or taller, and in an age of strenuous farm labor and hard military living, Washington wasn't alone in his strapping musculature. Likewise, dancing was a vital skill for the genteel, and dancing lessons were *de rigueur* for the elite and those who aspired to fit in among them.[6]

There was something special about Washington, though, something ineffable that seized the attention of others. His superb military bearing, his devotion to his appearance and fashion, his iron self-control forged through lifelong battle against his raging passions all radiated an image of heroism perfectly suited to the age. Washington exuded the ultimate virtue of 18th-century leadership: the ability to deny the self for the good of the country.[7]

Once O'Hara found the right man, he removed his hat and offered Cornwallis's apologies. Washington, punctilious about protocol, indicated that General Benjamin Lincoln, equal in rank to O'Hara, would then conduct the ceremony. Lincoln guided the surrendering army to a large meadow for the grounding of arms. Regiment by regiment, they entered the field, and man by man they tossed away their muskets, swords, and cartridge boxes. After discarding their weapons, the British and Hessian soldiers, now prisoners of war, marched back to Yorktown, ending the ceremony. The American victory was complete.[8]

That evening, the general officers of the American and French armies marked their triumph with what looks to modern eyes like a bizarre ritual: they dined with the British officers. Having surrendered, the British officers were now gentlemen in distress and other gentlemen were honor bound to relieve their anguish. A gentleman didn't notice unpleasant things like the fact that the hosts caused their guests suffering. General O'Hara, in fine spirits, regaled his enemies as if old friends.[9]

Washington took a break from planning the army's next moves to enjoy an evening dining with fellow gentlemen. He was under no illusion that the surrender would end the war, however. The British had some 30,000 men under arms in North America. They occupied New York City; Charleston, South Carolina; Savannah, Georgia;

Wilmington, North Carolina; and some forts in the West; while garrisons stood duty at Halifax, Canada, and St. Augustine, East Florida. The Royal Navy remained formidable, and the war had spilled into the West Indies, the Mediterranean, and even India. Britain wasn't leaving America anytime soon. [10]

Whether the United States could sustain the war was another question, which was still in doubt despite the victory. The Franco-American conquest of Yorktown resulted from an astonishing alignment of the military stars. Cornwallis stationed his army in a coastal tobacco port confident he'd never be trapped. The French navy moved north from the Caribbean to escape the hurricane season at precisely the right moment to prove Cornwallis wrong. The American and French armies marched from New York's Hudson Valley to Virginia with remarkable celerity, covering more than 400 miles in a month, even though, for the Americans, supplies were scanty and some soldiers verged on mutiny because pay was so scarce. Only a timely French loan—doled out to the Continentals from barrels of silver coins—kept them marching. From beginning to end, the campaign was a miracle, its financing the most miraculous of all. [11]

—⁓—

In the weeks after Yorktown, General Washington supervised the army packing up and boarding ships to carry them across the Chesapeake on their way north to winter quarters in the Hudson Highlands. Washington planned to ride overland with his aides so he could spend a few days at his beloved Mount Vernon and then proceed to Philadelphia to wait on Congress, which received Washington's official notice of the British surrender on October 24. A celebration ensued in Philadelphia, kicking off at noon with cannon fire, continuing with a solemn procession of dignitaries to hear a sermon of thanksgiving, and finishing at night with an illumination, as citywide, patriots placed candles in their windows to light up the dark with American military pride. Patriot mobs, well lubricated by whiskey and British tears, smashed Loyalists' darkened windows. Typical Philadelphia. [12]

On November 5, Washington left Yorktown, and after thirty miles he entered Eltham, Virginia, where Jack Custis, Martha Washington's last surviving child from her first marriage, was recovering from camp fever, a form of typhus he had contracted while visiting the siege and serving as a civilian aid. Custis, twenty-six, had been a feckless boy and was still sophomoric, though he was the father of four surviving children. Despite fever, cough, and nausea, he insisted on staying at Yorktown to witness the surrender. When Washington arrived in Eltham, Martha and Jack's wife, Eleanor, were already there and Jack was in his last hour. Martha was inconsolable. She had outlived all of her children. George, though often at odds with Jack, felt the loss as well. He was, according to one observer, "uncommonly affected by his death." [13]

Six days later, Washington departed for Mount Vernon. He stopped in Fredericksburg to see his often-difficult mother, Mary Ball Washington, who, to the general's relief, wasn't at home, and then attended a party for French and American officers given by the city. He reached his Potomac mansion on November 13 and passed a week receiving congratulatory visitors and inspecting his farms. [14]

On November 20, Washington hit the road with Martha and his aides, and after events in Alexandria, Annapolis, and Baltimore, he entered Philadelphia on the afternoon of November 26 as more celebrations broke out. Washington took up residence in a townhouse on Third Street between Walnut and Spruce, owned by the lawyer Benjamin Chew. The Washingtons occupied the front half, while the Spanish ambassador lived in the back. George and Martha knew the neighborhood. While visiting the city in January 1779, they had marked their twentieth anniversary at a ball next door, at the home of Samuel and Elizabeth Willing Powel. [15]

After two days of rest, Washington appeared before Congress. Meeting in the Assembly Room on the first floor of the Pennsylvania

Statehouse (now Independence Hall), Congress was far from the august body of patriotic lore. True, it did important things like sign the Declaration of Independence and create a government from scratch during a war, but serving in Congress was a burden, not an honor. Delegates were chosen by their states, and voting in session was done by state, with each state receiving one vote. There was no standard size for a delegation, but each state needed at least two members present for its vote to count. Rounding up two men at the same time was a challenge, and the total size of the body fluctuated between twenty and forty, depending on who attended. Georgia, the most distant state and occupied by the British since 1778, was seldom represented at all. Many delegates envied the Georgians. They hated serving in Philadelphia and tried to get home as soon as possible to their state legislatures, where the real action was.

At one o'clock, the general was ready to make his entrance. He was escorted inside to a room familiar to him from his own time in the Second Continental Congress, when he received his commission as commander in chief. The Assembly Room is small, lacking the grandeur of its reputation as the birthplace of American liberty. But as a conference room for a working group of a couple dozen men, it fulfilled its purpose. The delegates sat in Windsor chairs at tables covered in green baize cloth and arranged in a semicircle before the president's table, which was raised slightly from the floor. The president, actually more of a presider, sat in the "rising sun" chair, later made famous at the Constitutional Convention when Benjamin Franklin made its half-hidden sun decoration an allegory for the new nation's bright future.[16]

Once inside, Washington stood as the congressmen remained seated, a silent affirmation of their civilian supremacy over the military. President John Hanson, of Maryland, spoke first. "Sir," he said, "Congress, at all times happy in seeing your Excellency, feel particular pleasure in your presence at this time, after the glorious success of the allied arms in Virginia." Hanson continued by promising to press the states for more resources for the army. He also asked Washington to stay in town to assist a committee on army affairs and invited him to "enjoy a respite from the fatigues of war."[17]

Washington's reply was brief, dignified, and politically astute. "Mr. President," he began, "I feel very sensibly the favorable declaration of Congress expressed by your Excellency." No one yet knew Washington as "Mr. President," but he was already famous as "your Excellency," and his use of the terms demonstrated his grasp of the ritual. He stood there to signal his respect for civilian authority. Washington agreed to remain in Philadelphia, and he liked the sound of pressing the states. "It is with peculiar pleasure I hear that it is the fixed purpose of Congress to exhort the states to the most vigorous and timely exertions," he announced. "A compliance on their parts will, I persuade myself, be productive of the most happy consequences." With that, Washington departed, and Congress went back to hearing committee reports.[18]

Washington's speech to Congress emphasized the message he imparted to everyone who wrote to congratulate him on the army's accomplishment: the war wasn't over yet and if they expected to win, people needed to support the army to the fullest. "I thank you for your kind Congratulations on the Capitulation of Cornwallis," he wrote to a former aide. "It is an interesting event and may be productive of much good if properly improved, but if it should be the means of relaxation and sink us into supineness & security it had better not have happened." He wrote the same to an Alexandria official and to a Maryland official, to fellow generals and retiring officers, to congressmen, and to state governors. The message was the same: vigor would produce ultimate victory; relaxation would prolong the war. He believed, he said, in the old Roman maxim "that the only certain way to obtain Peace is to be prepared for War."[19]

Washington was right to worry. At the same time he arrived in Philadelphia, the news of the British defeat at Yorktown was hitting London. Lord George Germain, secretary of state for American affairs, heard the news first. He told the prime minister, Frederick North, the Lord North, whose stomach turned. Devastated, North walked the floor of his Downing Street home. He stopped suddenly, threw up his hands, and shouted "Oh God! It is all over!" He then continued pacing, saying again and again "Oh God! It is all over!"[20]

In the long run North was right, but in the moment, King George III expected to keep fighting. The news of Cornwallis's defeat arrived on the eve of the king's annual speech to open Parliament. Surely, advisers said, the part where he predicted ultimate success in America would have to be rewritten. Why, the king wondered. The rebellion must be suppressed.[21]

—⁊⁊—

Back in America, Washington enjoyed the uncommon quiet of the winter season. He went foxhunting, and he attended dinners and passed evenings at the theater with Martha. Washington was always the center of attention. On one occasion, the Washingtons were guests of the French ambassador for the premier of an oratorio, *The Temple of Minerva*. Written by composer (and Declaration of Independence signer) Francis Hopkinson, the piece was an allegory of the Franco-American alliance and ended with the grandiose lyrics:

> Now the dreadful conflict's o'er,
> Now the cannons cease to roar,
> Spread the joyful tidings round.
> He comes, he comes, with conquest crown'd.
> Hail, *Columbia's* godlike son!
> Hail, the glorious WASHINGTON!

If Washington wasn't blushing—"godlike son!"—he was furious. This was the complacency he was warning everyone against.[22]

In between enduring encomiums, Washington followed political affairs in Congress and in the states, because if the army was headed back to the field in the spring, Congress and the states had to provide the money and the manpower. Though without an official role in the nation's governance, Washington's expertise and prestige couldn't be ignored, and in December he began attending weekly gatherings of the heads of the government's executive departments. Held every Monday night at six o'clock, the meetings were the idea of Robert Morris, the superintendent of finance. Responsible for every area of government touched by money, which is to say all areas, Morris was the most powerful man in Philadelphia.

Known as "the financier," Morris was born in Liverpool, England, in 1734, the son of a tobacco factor who left his family for Maryland's Eastern Shore when Robert was a boy. Robert joined his father in Maryland at the age of thirteen, learned the rudiments of math and Latin, and was apprenticed to a Philadelphia merchant named Charles Willing. Morris graduated from sweeping floors to copying correspondence and mastered the business along the way. At sixteen, Morris's father died (a victim of celebratory cannon fire from one of his own ships returning from a successful voyage) and left his son a £2,500 inheritance. A few years later, Willing also died, passing along the business to his son Thomas, who was by then close friends with Morris. Forming Willing Morris & Company, the two amassed a fortune trading throughout the Atlantic, pushed by Morris's appetite for risk. In 1769, Morris married Mary White, called Molly, the daughter of a wealthy English-born lawyer. He was thirty-five, she was nineteen.[23]

As the 1770s began and tensions with Britain flared, Morris was an affluent merchant with a young and soon-to-be growing family. Though he might have preferred to concentrate on business, Morris entered politics and served in the Continental Congress (1775–1778), where he lent his commercial expertise to buying supplies in Europe through the Committee of Secret Correspondence, and in the Pennsylvania legislature (1778–1781). Morris made enemies during his Secret Committee days by mingling his private business with public transactions, in part to conceal arms shipments from Europe, in part because his personal credit was needed to make deals, and in part to keep up his network of contacts and make money. Conducting private and public business together, Morris was dogged by charges that he lined his own pockets with the nation's money.[24]

Forty-seven in 1781, Morris was six feet tall and thick around the middle. A 1782 portrait shows Morris seated and filling every inch of an armchair while wearing a blue suit over a bulging blue waistcoat. He looks serious, stern, no nonsense. In person, however, Morris is outgoing and sociable. He and Molly loved to entertain at home, and they were fixtures of the Philadelphia ball scene.[25]

Morris was accompanied to the Monday night meetings by his personal assistant in the Finance Office, Gouverneur Morris, a former Congressional delegate from New York. Gouverneur, twenty-nine, was born to an old Dutch family and raised on a sprawling Long Island estate called Morrisania. He graduated from King's College (Columbia) and joined the bar as relations with Britain deteriorated and divided his family. Gouverneur Morris entered politics, supported a middle position in the New York Provincial Assembly as independence was declared, and represented the state in Philadelphia from 1777 to 1779. Six feet tall and trim, Morris was a charmer, full of bonhomie, despite suffering severe bodily disfigurement on two occasions: a scalding at age fourteen that left his right arm and side scarred and a 1780 carriage accident that broke his left ankle, leading to an amputation below the knee. Morris wore a peg ever after. The injuries did not detract—and perhaps even enhanced—Morris's reputation as what the 18th century called a "rake," an incorrigible ladies' man. (A story that Morris broke his ankle leaping from a married woman's second-story window is, alas, too good to be true.)[26]

Gouverneur caught the elder Morris's eye when he came to Congress in 1778. At first sight, Robert called him a man of "first rate abilities," but also "a little too whimsical." Robert learned that he was right about the first, wrong about the second. At the Finance Office, the two made a dynamic pair. Gouverneur was intellectual but pragmatic, especially in politics, and a hard worker, going from four in the morning until eight at night; Robert was a man of business but as innovative as any philosopher and prone to keep similar hours. Together, they strategized, brainstormed, and game-planned ways to address the nation's crisis, churning out letters and reports to explain, defend, and advocate their rescue measures. "Gouverneur and myself are great Slaves," Robert told a friend in Europe. "Our confinement is constant, our attention unceasing and my Anxiety great, but our Spirits carry us through."[27]

Three other men rounded out the Monday evening club. Robert Livingston, a New York lawyer and member of the powerful Livingston clan, represented the Foreign Affairs department, while Benjamin Lincoln, a Massachusetts general, attended as secretary at war. To make sure Congress didn't suspect any shenanigans, Charles Thomson, the body's secretary, tagged along. The final department, Marine Affairs, was also led by Robert Morris, and the group met at the Marine offices on Front Street. No one at the time called it a cabinet, and the government wasn't set up that way—the departments reported to Congress and there was no chief executive. Still, the group was a cabinet in embryo with Robert Morris as its leader.

Over wine, the men most often discussed the condition of the nation's finances and what they could do to improve them. The answers: "terrible" and "not much." By 1781, the nation's fiscal health was fading fast, assailed by four comorbid maladies: the war's enormous cost, inflation, debt, and an inability to tax.[28]

The cost of fighting the war beggared all expectations. Consider the food bill. At the start of the war, Congress decreed that each man should receive the following daily ration:

> 1 pound of beef, ¾ pounds of pork, or 1 pound of salted fish
> 1 pound of bread or flour
> 1 pint of milk
> 1 quart of spruce beer or cider

Weekly, they were to also receive:

3 pints of peas, beans, or "vegitables equivalent"

1 half pint of rice or cornmeal

Between Lexington and Concord (April 19, 1775) and the surrender at Yorktown (October 19, 1781), there were 2,376 days. That means an army of 10,000 would have consumed approximately 50,000 cows, 123,000 pigs, 3 million gallon jugs of milk, and 63 million bottles of beer.[29]

Rations rarely materialized as promised, however. Soldiers' complaints about their poor food and shelter flew as thick as a musket volley. Washington nagged Congress on their behalf. More than once he warned that if they didn't get more beef or bread, the army would disappear. Still, the Continentals ate and drank a staggering amount. During the Valley Forge winter of 1777 to 1778, when the army was starving, the men consumed over 2 million pounds of beef, more than 2 million pounds of flour, and almost 16,000 gallons of rum and whiskey (that's more than 1.3 million shots).[30]

To carry out its vast buying needs, Congress created its own currency, the Continental dollar. Printed in denominations ranging from one dollar to thirty dollars and designed by Benjamin Franklin, the notes were physically small, measuring 2¾ inches by 3¾ inches (about the size of a modern one dollar bill if, looking at the front, you fold the left side over to the last "A" in "The United States of America"). Franklin emblazoned the notes with patriotic imagery, such as a four dollar note that featured a wild boar, an animal that, like America, minded its business unless provoked into ferocious self-defense.[31]

Congress emitted $2 million in June 1775, followed by another $1 million in July, and $3 million more by the end of the year—six months before declaring independence. As expenses mounted, Congress printed more, and more, and more. At first, new issues came every month, then every two weeks, then every week. Millions of dollars churned off the presses, burly printers straining to keep up with the pace. By fall 1779, Congress gave up, and authorized no new

Continentals after November 29, 1779. All told, Congress printed $199,990,000 worth of paper currency. Values plummeted with each new sheet. The wild boar was helpless to fight off the depreciation. In January 1777, $1.25 in paper equaled $1 in specie. By April 1781, it took $167.50 in paper to get $1 of specie, a 13,300 percent increase. The Continental dollar, now a waste of perfectly good blank paper, stopped circulating the next month. [32]

Congress's love of paper money wasn't as reckless as it sounds. Paper money in the 18th century worked differently than it does today, when the US dollar is a fiat currency sustained by faith in the US government and the certainty that if you accept a dollar as payment today, someone else will accept it from you as payment tomorrow. In colonial times, paper money was more like a security. It was backed by something of value, such as specie, land, or taxes, and operated as a kind of loan to the government. Some currency paid interest.

In its simplest form, paper currency worked like this: governments printed paper money and used it to pay for goods and services. The recipients could then generally exchange the paper for specie or use it to pay taxes, which was useful because taxes otherwise had to be paid in hard coin. The paper currency thus returned to the issuing government. The notes would then be taken out of circulation—or "retired"—often by public burning. If the notes were not used for taxes, they could pass from hand to hand as a media of exchange, promoting commerce. Though governments were always tempted to issue just a few pounds more, taxes and public burning forced them not to overdo it. [33]

What went wrong with financing the Revolution was partly the enormous cost of the war (see above) and partly the inability of any government to collect sufficient taxes (see below). But another aspect of the problem lay directly with Congress and its mismanagement of retiring Continental dollars. When first issuing the currency, Congress planned to assign each state an amount it was responsible to collect through taxes of its choice and turn the Continental dollars over to Congress for burning. Congress, however, kept changing the redemption schedule and requirements and even instituted *ex post facto* laws that went back in time to affect earlier emissions, so the states did not know how much they were supposed to collect and whether Congress would change the amount later anyway.[34]

Congress was responsible for inflation in one additional way. Inflation worked as a hidden tax that extracted resources from citizens when the government had no power to tax. Simply for the cost of paper and ink and the labor of a printer, Congress bought the army supplies. As depreciation kicked in, people who sold their goods lost the paper value they'd received in exchange. Congress pocketed the difference for the war effort as surely as if it had been transferred by force.[35]

Even with all the paper money floating around the country like an unwanted ticker tape parade, Congress was still far short of meeting its expenses, and it looked for other sources of funds, including loans both foreign and domestic. The result: a canyon of debt. The problem started small. Early in the war France and Spain aided the United States with secret loans of military supplies funneled across the Atlantic. After allying with the United States, France loaned money openly, and the Spanish crown and Dutch investors chipped in as well, bringing total assistance to some $3 million in specie. Following the collapse of the Continental dollar, Congress became ever more dependent on foreign loans.[36]

Congress also borrowed money from Americans in the form of bonds called loan office certificates. Congress set up offices in each state to sell the bonds, which when first issued in 1776, promised 4 percent interest and maturity in three years. The bonds sold poorly, so a few months later Congress upped the return to 6 percent with no maturity date. Requiring a minimum investment of $200, the certificates were an investment for the wealthy. The certificates could also be profitable, at least if purchased early when Congress paid interest in bills of exchange secured by a French loan, meaning the payments were almost as good as gold and protected from depreciation. The owners of loan office certificates formed an important interest group as the war ground on. Collectively, they were known as "public creditors" or "civil creditors," and they had loud voices, loud enough to command action in Congress and state legislatures.[37]

A second type of domestic loan wasn't much of a loan at all. It was an IOU, called a "certificate of indebtedness," offered to compensate owners of property seized for use by the army. The practice of expropriating private property for military use was called "impressment," just like the naval system of forcing sailors into service. Though supposedly an emergency measure, impressment was widely practiced. Before 1781, Congress issued certificates with a face value of $95 million. Backed by nothing but Congress's vague promises of future payment, the certificates made for a poor investment and rapidly lost value.[38]

To deal with the challenge of financing a war, a mature fiscal-military state like Great Britain would have raised revenue through taxes. But the United States was not mature and more to the point, the conflict was rooted in an objection to British tax policies. Citizens of the new republic understandably didn't want Congress to tax them and bring on the tyranny they believed would inevitably follow.

Congress itself had no ability to tax on its own. None. No money went straight from any American to Congress for its use. Instead, the body made requisitions on the states, with the total amount divvied up by population as an approximation for wealth and ability to pay. States rarely provided the requested amounts, however. As of September 1, 1779, for example, the states had delivered only about $13 million in paper money value when nearly $200 million in Continentals had already been issued.[39]

The states weren't deadbeats as it might appear. Their fiscal health was no better than the nation's. They also paid to fight the war. They issued at least as much paper currency as Congress did. They impressed private property with IOUs. To help the cause, states raised taxes above normal levels, and they accepted depreciated Continentals at more than their value. Each state felt aggrieved when Congress sent down its requisition each year, and each state had its reasons for protesting that its share was too much. Often, they had a point, especially those states occupied by the British or which saw their productive capacity wasted by battle. Whatever the reason, however, the result was the same: Congress had too much money going out and not enough coming in; the army suffered and the war effort faltered.[40]

—⁂—

As bad as fiscal conditions were in the winter of 1781 to 1782, they could have been worse, because throughout the war Congress's finances were a lot worse—until Robert Morris took office as the financier the previous spring. The position of superintendent of finance was created in February 1781 as part of Congress's effort to streamline its executive functions. Congress began the war by trying to handle everything itself through committees, then tried to lighten its burden by employing administrative boards compromised of both congressmen and outside officials. Finally, Congress handed off daily administration to departments headed by civilians who were not members of Congress.[41]

Over the summer of 1781, Morris developed an extensive fiscal program with several interlocking parts that moved toward remedying what Morris saw as the nation's central problem: the lack of public credit. For Morris, credit was more than a financial issue, since it said something vital about the stability of the nation, its people and government and tied the various states and their varied people together in one nation capable of surviving and thriving in a world of monarchies hostile to a new republic.[42]

Some of Morris's credit-building methods are easily recognizable. He rationalized the operation of his office, reduced expenses, and sought additional revenue. Morris's principle method, however, seems strange today. He planned to use private credit, often his own, to substitute for public credit until the nation's finances were resuscitated and the government could function on its own.

Morris did not take office officially until June 27, as he kept his seat in the Pennsylvania legislature to help fight a new state paper currency emission. He failed, and so did the emission, which predictably sunk in value. In the meantime, Morris hit the cobblestone streets running. In late May, he proposed that Congress charter a national bank. To be called the Bank of North America, it would be the second bank in the country, following the example of the Bank of Pennsylvania, founded in 1780 with Morris's involvement.[43]

As a private institution, the Bank of North America had its own president and board of directors elected by its shareholders, though the government was a shareholder and a customer and Morris kept the right to inspect its books. The bank's lifeblood was conservative, short-term commercial loans distributed in bank notes that also circulated as media of exchange. Morris demanded that the notes be accepted at par with specie for taxes. In effect, then, Morris wanted private investors to create a new currency whose value would depend on the bank's credit alone.[44]

The bank encountered opposition, including from James Madison, a Virginia delegate and otherwise a Morris ally. Previewing his later bruising contest against the Bank of the United States in the 1790s, Madison thought Congress lacked the power to charter a corporation. Despite Madison's misgivings, Congress gave Morris the go-ahead.[45]

Morris set up shop in a rented space on Front Street next to his home and began reforming operations. He hired a comptroller, treasurer, register, two auditors, and several clerks, and then convinced Congress to add two more staff, outside of its original approval of the department: a cashier, brought over from Morris's counting house, to help segregate new obligations from old ones, and a personal assistant, Gouverneur, to help with correspondence and reports.[46]

—⁂—

A lean finance office staffed with talented men might save time and money, but its operations paled in comparison with the spending and logistics of the administrative leviathan, the army. At first, the financier vowed to stay away from military supply, but already in May 1781 he was drawn in by one of Washington's periodic warnings that the army was about to dissolve for want of provisions, this time flour. Morris scrounged up 1,000 barrels and arranged transport, pledging his personal credit to ensure prompt delivery. [47]

In August, Morris rode up to New York to meet Washington and discuss cost savings. Washington balked. He wanted more resources, not fewer. While the two met, news arrived that the French fleet was available for action in the Chesapeake, and Morris suddenly had a major campaign to help finance, which he did through creatively shifting paper resources under his control, the timely arrival of a French loan in barrels of silver, and the extension of his own credit in the form of so-called "Morris Notes" that he issued through his cashier at the finance office, once more merging public and private functions. [48]

Morris also introduced an innovation in army supply known as the contract system. Pennsylvania had appointed Morris its agent for supplying its troops, and during the Yorktown campaign, he rejected the cumbersome specific supply system, in which states sent goods directly to their troops, in favor of hiring contractors, via sealed bid, to provide what the army needed. The system promised significantly reduced costs and simpler logistics as private merchants assumed the burden of acquisitions and transportation. After Yorktown, Morris expanded the system. Time, however, would reveal dire shortcomings. [49]

Amidst starting a department, founding a bank, and supplying an army, Morris also addressed the nation's debts. For once, there was good news. France was generous bordering on prodigal with its financial assistance to the United States in 1781. It lavished the country with a free gift of 6 million livres and a loan of 4 million livres, and then followed up by effectively cosigning a 10-million-livre loan from

Dutch investors. All told, 20 million livres, worth $3.7 million in specie, flowed to the United States. There were strings attached, of course. Most of the money was spent by American agents in Europe, and the loans would need to be repaid, but for the moment, French money was a godsend. [50]

The condition of the domestic debts, by contrast, was bleak. Basic questions such as how much was owed to whom seemed impossible to answer, since the debts were ensnared in a thicket of poor record keeping, white lies, and depreciated currency, not to mention the complex system of state credits toward requisitions offered under the specific supply system. Nevertheless, Morris pushed to untangle the debt and come up with firm numbers. Otherwise, the states would claim they were unjustly burdened and refuse to pay. [51]

To facilitate proper accounting and distinguish his department from the earlier Board of Treasury, Morris forswore responsibility for any debts incurred before he took office and stopped making payments. It was not a repudiation, however, and Morris did believe the debts should be paid one day. He planned to roll the old debts into a new category of "public debt" composed of certificates of indebtedness, loan office certificates, and foreign loans that would be Congress's responsibility to pay, not the states', though the states would still be responsible for paying, by requisition, the costs of the war incurred via the ordinary spending by Congress on the states' behalf. [52]

The problem, of course, was that Congress had no revenue of its own with which to service a public debt. Which brought Morris to the final piece of his program: national taxes. The idea was not invented by Morris. In February 1781, even before the Articles of Confederation were in effect, Congress approved an amendment to create an impost, or tax on imports, of 5 percent with the proceeds dedicated to paying war debts. The revenue generated would be small, but that was OK, because the impost's purpose was not to liquidate the debt, but to provide security to attract future foreign loans. The impost amendment would take time to wind its way through the states, however. It was an amendment to the Articles, which required the assent of all thirteen states, whose legislatures would want to debate it, slowly, in detail.[53]

Washington and the department heads helped Robert Morris as much as they could, but as their Monday evening conversations revealed, their powers were limited because each man, including the commander in chief, reported to Congress, and Congress depended on the states. Any serious reform needed to reshape the fundamental relationship between the people and their government, when the proper relationship with their government was what inspired Americans to grab their guns and go shoot redcoats.

In the winter of 1781 to 1782, Congress was still in its first year working under the Articles of Confederation, which, though drafted in 1777, went into effect on March 1, 1781. A dispute between Maryland and its neighbors over western lands delayed ratification. Congress under the Articles was dysfunctional, though mere dysfunction was an improvement on its prior experience: barely controlled chaos guided by no formal plan of government.[54]

Early in the war, all Congressional responsibilities were administered by committees made up of delegates, which considered a particular issue and reported back to the whole assembly. Then, the full body decided on the committees' recommendations and passed them along to the appropriate military or civil officials, who figured out implementation.[55]

Foolishly, the committee system failed to triage the many demands on Congress. Some delegates worked on important matters, such as the military, finance, or drafting the Declaration of Independence, while others devoted their energy to trivial matters, like assessing the supply of ticklenburg linen in Philadelphia. Regardless of the importance of the matter at hand, congressmen loved to wrangle over procedural questions, and debates about process derailed discussions of substance.[56]

The burden of committee administration weighed heavily on congressmen, especially the dependable, respected ones who found themselves nominated for numerous committees and subcommittees.

Workhorses, like John Adams, rose early to attend meetings that started at seven, before heading over to the Pennsylvania Statehouse, where sessions usually began at ten. Congress stayed in session through the late afternoon. After dinner, more meetings, from six to ten. A few hours' sleep, and they were off to a new day of meetings. The workload was particularly unfair because the manpower available fluctuated. There was no set number of congressmen. The states appointed different sized delegations, and those men appointed by their states didn't always show up for duty (or at least not on time). Congress sat in session six days a week, with only Sundays off. It was bad for the delegates' health. William H. Drayton of South Carolina died while attending Congress. Though he suffered from a "putrid fever," an obituary blamed the "incessant attention to business for near two years' attendance on Congress, which his constitution, though naturally strong, was unable longer to sustain." Drayton was thirty-eight.[57]

Congress revamped itself several times during the war. It tried to throw off some of its burden to administrative bodies of various configurations. But there was no savior to give them rest. The executive departments, launched in 1781, lightened Congress's load, but at an ideological price. They looked like executive centralization, the aggrandizement of distant authority over free citizens, the *bête noire* of true patriots. Ultimately, Congress moved slowly because the people wanted it that way. They liked their government lethargic: too sluggish to oppress them.

By the dawn of 1782, Washington, the Morrises, Livingston, and Lincoln rejected the hardline anti-Congress stance of the radical republican elements in the states. From hard experience recruiting the army, feeding the army, and leading the army, they knew a weak central government was the source of many evils, and if the country hoped to survive long enough to enjoy the sweet fruits of independence, then Congress needed more authority. It needed to be something more than a body to intermediate among thirteen wary partners forced together by the need to coordinate resistance to British policy and fight a war. Congress needed to be a true national government.

Their thinking marked a shift in politics after Yorktown, when a movement emerged that envisioned the United States as a strong, united nation with a central government capable of administering the nation's business rather than relying on the states. Men influenced by this nationalist spirit were later dubbed "nationalists," with the Morrises, Livingston, Lincoln, some members of Congress, Washington, and other officers counted among their number.[58]

These nationalists, however, were not a political party in the 1780s, although some nationalists later became the architects of the Constitution, identified as Federalists during the ratification debate, and led the Federalist Party of the 1790s. In the 18th century, "political party" was synonymous with conspiracy against just government, but even adjusting for the difference in meaning, the nationalists were not a party because they lacked the organizational cohesion of a modern political party. Moreover, they would have described themselves not as nationalists but as "Continentalists" or "men who thought continentally," a subtle indication that shared geography shaped their thinking about the states' destiny together as much as did abstract ideas about nationhood. The term "nationalist" also has limited utility for explaining the positions of so-called nationalists on particular issues. For example, Benjamin Lincoln opposed Robert Morris's plans to consolidate the different kinds of war debt into one public debt to be paid with revenue from a new tax. "Nationalist," then, is shorthand to describe political leaders who, despite their differences over policy details, shared a sense that greater union among the states was vital because otherwise, with the war waning, the most important tie that bound the states together would go slack and endanger the future of every citizen in every state.[59]

—m—

Washington was as hot for independence as anyone else, but his role as commander in chief made him a confirmed nationalist. Individual states could not meet the army's needs, and his men suffered. Nevertheless, reforming the nation's political structure was the responsibility of civilians, and he had an army to lead. As winter thawed and his business concluded, time came to return to the field. [60]

Washington appeared before Congress at 10:30 A.M. on March 21, when he was again escorted into the chamber for a ritual affirming civilian preeminence. President Hanson had "nothing particular" to tell Washington; Congress, he said, "appointed this audience only to assure you of their esteem and confidence, to recommend you to the protection of Divine Providence, and to wish you happiness and success." Washington's reply was even briefer. He thanked Congress and "declared that nothing in his power should be wanting to promote their views and insure success in the operations of the ensuing campaign." Then, Washington left the room. [61]

He couldn't escape Philadelphia that easily. Another round of celebrations ensued, there was one more meeting with Robert Morris, and then, finally, on March 23, Washington left for the Hudson Highlands, escorted out of town by a troop of light horse. A new campaign—possibly—awaited. [62]

TWO

The Insipid Campaign

Washington was on the way to the Highlands, and Colonel Hugh Hughes, the officer in charge of preparing headquarters for the general, was freaking out. "I am afraid the Commander in Chief will be at Newburgh before I can possibly be ready for him," Hughes worried. "I wish to see him [but] dread his appearance." The trouble started in the fall. While Washington tarried in Philadelphia, Hughes discovered that the general's previous headquarters, the Thomas Ellison House in New Windsor, had been occupied when the army moved out for Yorktown. A backup location, a home owned by New York governor George Clinton, was also unavailable. The tenant didn't want to move, and the governor didn't want to evict him.[1]

Hughes's search wasn't easy. Small towns dotted the region; Newburgh and New Windsor together had a population of about 2,500 people. From that small stock, only a few homes could possibly satisfy Washington's needs. He required tight security, since Loyalists prowled the area and kidnapping officers was standard in 18th-century warfare.

Washington was also attended by his "military family" of aides, young officers such as David Humphreys, Jonathan Trumbull, Jr., and Benjamin Walker, who hefted his mountainous correspondence, as well as various servants, including his enslaved valet, Billy Lee, who did everything from arranging Washington's clothes and tying his hair in a queue with a silk ribbon, to delivering messages, and taking care of his personal papers. As a military headquarters, the house would receive a stream of visitors every day, and Washington expected to host meals for dignitaries, civil officials, and other officers. The young aides didn't need much space and the servants were used to cramped quarters, but so many people coming and going meant the house had to have stables for horses, a warehouse for supplies, and expanded "necessaries" for, well, for life's necessary moments. Plus, barracks for the guards and a powder magazine. And it couldn't be too rustic either, since Martha Washington, a woman of taste and sensibility, planned to join her husband. General Washington was a burdensome housemate. [2]

Hughes at last zeroed in on the best option: a Dutch farmhouse in Newburgh owned by a widow named Tryntje Hasbrouck. Perched on a hill 400 yards from the Hudson, the location was strategically ideal. With clear views for miles up and down the river and an easily defensible position, Washington would be safe. A nearby ferry and a wharf on the property linked the house to the other side of the river, and to New Windsor and West Point. [3]

The house itself was a plain stone structure, two stories, with a sloping roof. A Dutch-style stoop led into the main room, which featured a low ceiling with exposed beams, a wooden floor, and, strangely, seven doors but only one window. A large jambless fireplace, again typical of Dutch architecture, sat open to the floor. A bedroom for the Washingtons was off the main room, and a workplace for the staff, a small office for the general, a kitchen, and other quarters completed the first floor. Upstairs, there was space for storage and more make-do places to sleep. [4]

Hughes expected the widow Hasbrouck would be agreeable since she had boarded officers before. But she balked at welcoming General Washington. Hughes unwisely delegated the task of coaxing her out to a Captain Mitchell, a timid fellow afraid of delivering bad news. He tried to play salesman and pointed out all the lasting advantages of the temporary inconvenience: the army would build a stable, renovate the kitchen, fix the wharf. Think of the boost to her property value! But Hasbrouck wouldn't budge. She sat silent, fuming, while her family berated Mitchell. Resigned to the inevitable, Hasbrouck at last spoke, telling the captain that "General Washington & her could not both live in the House." So the family packed their things and went to stay in New Paltz, never to share a night under the same roof with the father of their country.[5]

Once the Hasbroucks were out, construction started, and despite the inevitable nail biting over all the renovations, Hughes met the deadline. The house was ready in time for Washington's arrival at the end of March. The frantic preparations would be the most activity in camp until fall.

—␣—

Washington settled into his new headquarters in April and commenced whipping the men into shape for the new campaign season. In his first general orders, Washington saluted his army for guarding "the Country so successfully against the depredations of the Enemy during the absence of the General" and announced plans to review all the troops, brigade by brigade. Up first: Massachusetts, the largest line, followed by Connecticut. Inspections commenced two days later.[6]

The orders were typical of Washington's leadership style. He coupled praise with high expectations in the belief that soldiers were inspired to excellence by the example of their officers and the pressure of their peers. Reviewing the troops not only provided Washington with information about the quality of the men he led, but it also played to the men's love of military display and made them feel like soldiers. Reviews also touched on the natural competitiveness of young men and pushed each unit to outdo its neighbors as they sought the prize: a good word from the commander in chief.

On returning to the field, Washington was especially concerned about the army's appearance, and he admonished the officers to ensure their men had proper, well-fitting uniforms. "The General is exceedingly concerned to observe the distressed State of Several Corps for the want of clothing," Washington announced in general orders. "Nothing can be more essential than this to the good appearance of the Troops and nothing more detrimental than the want of it."[7]

Washington, of course, realized the real problem lay outside the army, with suppliers and ultimately with the states and Congress, and he complained up the chain of command. "It gave me equal surprize & concern," Washington revealed to Secretary at War Lincoln, "to find that several Corps had not been able to get the new Cloathing compleated, so as to be delivered to the Soldiers, & that the Men were actually in the most naked & distressed situation that can be conceived." The army also lacked shoes, and even worse to the commander in chief, adequate hats, "thro' the want of which," he continued to Lincoln, "the beauty & uniformity of the other Articles will be in a great measure lost . . . and the Troops can never make a military appearance." Washington's concern with military appearance was more than fussiness. An army's look expressed the power of the government it served, and the more smartly dressed, the more awed civilians would be. Likewise on the battlefield, impressive-looking soldiers signaled their military prowess: if they could polish all their buttons and wear their hats just so, imagine what they could do with a bayonet![8]

One of the general's greatest obstacles was complacency. Everything the soldiers saw told them combat was over. Washington proclaimed the opposite: get ready to fight. In further general orders, he directed repairs be made to better secure West Point, and he commanded the men to prepare to march, "for the purpose of affording an equal Opportunity to every Corps for perfecting itself in discipline and Maneuvres." The soldiers were no doubt thrilled that everyone would get a chance to march. [9]

Washington cracked down on other temptations to disorder. He curtailed furloughs, which led to excessive absences, and he ordered officers to better regulate the men's alcohol consumption. Washington was no teetotaler. He liked to drink and hailed alcohol as "salutary" and "designed for the comfort and refreshment of the troops." But too many men drank too much and couldn't handle it. To restrict access, Washington recommended officers keep a "liquor Roll," a list of who was and who was not allowed to receive a drink, and he decreed an end to "the vile practice of swallowing the whole ration of liquor at a single draught." No detail was too small for the commander in chief, and he expected that the same exacting standard be upheld by his officers. [10]

The inspections ended in mid-June, and the result pleased Washington. He praised the army, noting "the present laudable disposition and pride of Corps which seem to be diffused throughout the Army." Only one thing was lacking: constant practice, "that frequent and repeated Exercise [that] is absolutely necessary to constitute the perfection of Discipline." [11]

All generals believe in discipline, but for Washington, training men in discipline was more important than usual because of the kind of army he led: a republican army made up of independent-minded men, guided by inexperienced officers of uncertain social status, in the service of a people weakly attached to each other and suspicious of an army's danger to liberty, regardless of what uniform the army wore.

Throughout the war the soldiers of the Continental Army were overwhelmingly young, poor, and unattached to local communities; the kind of men 18th-century elites called "rabble" and assumed should be supervised. Though condescending and mean—on first meeting the Massachusetts troops, Washington called them "an exceeding dirty & nasty people"—the belief wasn't exactly wrong. Their hygiene, for example, was terrible, even by 18th-century standards. Soldiers didn't like to wash their clothes—that was women's work!—or wash themselves, because who needed the trouble? Rinse the hands and face, smooth the hair, and their morning routine was done. Nor did they like to dig latrines, and even when latrines were dug and sited at the proper locations away from the water source, soldiers didn't like using them. They "eased themselves" wherever they pleased during the day, and when nature called at night, rather than stumbling somnambulant for the little soldier's room, it was so much easier to roll over and commence, as the saying went, "pissing abed." Camp hygiene improved during the war, and in 1782, it wasn't nearly as bad as in the early days, but soldiers still needed regular admonishment to keep themselves clean. [12]

Though professionalism grew, the army was still a threat to itself. With so much time on their hands, soldiers found themselves easy prey for "Barrel Fever." Symptoms: black eyes and bleeding noses. Cause: excessive alcohol intake. Alcohol alone wasn't to blame for soldiers fighting each other, however. Shared achievement—and suffering—helped bond the troops, but old habits of looking down on men from outside their state died hard. According to one account, a young Noah Webster visited camp that spring and witnessed a shocking number of fights, which he blamed on the babel of accents he heard among the troops. How could they, or any Americans, live together if they couldn't understand each other? The experience helped inspire Webster to write a new American spelling book to unify the rising generation. [13]

Another source of division among the soldiers was the unequal terms of service. Improvising, Congress and the states instituted no uniformity in how long men were expected to serve for. Through the war some men signed up for periods as short as a few months—in 1775, for example, enlistments expired on December 31, emptying out the ranks as the calendar turned—while other men contracted for longer stints, such as three years. In a different category were the men who enlisted "for the duration of the war," a designation created in 1776 when the war still had seven years to go. Open-ended commitments chafed against liberty-loving purists, who felt short-term contracts preserved soldiers from oppression. But brief enlistments were wildly impractical, even dangerous, for an institution in which experience saved lives. [14]

To instill discipline, Washington knew the model he wanted followed: the army of the enemy, Great Britain. It made sense to follow their example. Colonists such as Washington had served in the British Army throughout the empire's 18th-century wars, and they were familiar with its methods, procedures, and values. Also, the British Army was really good, victorious time and time again across the globe. Many factors explained Britain's military success, but at its heart the army won with iron training that turned soldiers into fearsome weapons wielded by gentleman officers. [15]

Washington faced several problems copying the British practice of discipline, however. British soldiers enlisted for long terms, twenty years or more, while Americans on short-term contracts could easily opt not to re-up and anyone could easily desert, as nearly a quarter of soldiers did. More abstractly, Britain proclaimed a subject's duty to a sovereign king, while the United States was a free country—at least that's what the recruiting rhetoric said—and although soldiers knew they gave up some freedom upon enlistment, it was a fine line between necessary restriction and tyranny. Officers knew they could only go so far or risk undermining the rationale for taking up arms. As a result, for example, physical punishment in the Continental Army was limited to 100 lashes, and though harsh to modern ears, it never matched British practice (where 1,000 was the max) or met the desires of American commanders (Washington wanted 500). [16]

Unable to flog his men into submission, Washington relied on another aspect of the British model: namely, inspiring discipline by reproducing inside the army the social hierarchy of the civilian world, with officers as the gentlemen elite who kept soldiers subordinate. In the 18th-century way of thinking, gentlemen and commoners were different beings: the few and the many, the refined and the vulgar, the leaders animated by ambition for greatness and the unthinking herd, designed to follow and be forgotten. The insults tripped easily off the tongue of every elite. Surprisingly to us today, ordinary people often internalized their inferiority as well.[17]

Society in the 18th century was also corporate, in the sense that everyone belonged to one body, or, to switch metaphors, everyone belonged to one family, with the king as the head, or father, and everyone else some lesser body part, or the children. Whatever the metaphor, society was hierarchical as well as enveloping: everyone had a place, but everyone had someone both above them (except for the king) and below them (except for enslaved persons). Authority flowed down and obedience up, though respect, according to one's station, was supposed to be mutual.[18]

The Revolution disintegrated that social model and ushered in the individualistic, democratic society we know today—but not because General Washington countenanced those values in his army. Washington wanted social hierarchy to reinforce military hierarchy, the system of social rank to buttress military rank, and a rigid social order to reproduce disciplined military order, while a robust sense of honor drove the army forward. And so the officers of the Continental Army had to be gentlemen.[19]

Pinpointing what exactly made a man a gentleman was not easy, however, since no one test revealed a person's true status. It was not a matter of birth. Though coming from a good family helped, gentlemen were not aristocrats, the titled nobility born to their station. It was also not a matter of wealth. Again, wealth helped, but there were down-on-their-luck gentlemen who held onto their status despite poverty and prosperous merchants and planters who never made the cut. Gentility was more a complex of manners, behavior, education, taste, fashion, and feelings. You were a gentleman because you looked like a gentleman, acted like a gentleman, spoke like a gentleman, and treated others like a gentleman should.[20]

Beyond the definitional challenge, Washington's plan to staff the officer corps with only gentlemen faced a serious demographic problem: even under the most expansive criteria, there simply weren't enough gentlemen to go around. The small number of men of property from respectable families with a liberal education, agreeable manners, and independent means snapped up commissions for the upper ranks. That left the junior ranks empty. With what made a gentleman uncertain, ambitious young men embraced the opportunity to enhance their social status. The sons of farmers and shopkeepers before the war, they reversed Washington's formula and aimed to become officers so they could be seen as gentlemen. It was a feat of social climbing if it worked, but it left young officers nervous about their true identity and fearful of being unmasked as frauds. [21]

The result of trying to instill discipline through social hierarchy and limited physical punishment was always imperfect, and Washington's general orders teemed with court-martial notices for infractions both petty and grave. The orders for June 5, 1782, alone featured multiple notices of courts-martial, including two cases of desertion, three instances of fraudulent reenlistment (deserting then signing up again to get an extra signing bonus), a captain beating a soldier "without sufficient cause to Justify such correction" (the captain was later acquitted because he'd caught the soldier stealing), and a corporal "exciting Mutiny" in his corps. The last offense, mutiny, represented the most glaring failure of discipline; despite their gravity, mutinies erupted throughout the war. Almost 6 percent of all courts-martial involved mutiny, though overcharging insubordination as mutiny juiced the numbers somewhat. But organized rebellion happened, too, in every theater of the war, from among troops attacking Quebec in 1776 to soldiers occupying South Carolina in 1783. Soldiers mutinied because they didn't like their officers or their orders. Because they didn't like their terms of service and wanted discharges. Because they didn't like the punishments meted out. Because they didn't like their food (or there wasn't any food). Because they didn't like their pay (or there wasn't any pay). Because they didn't receive their liquor ration. Because, ultimately, something was lacking in what the soldiers, as free men, felt was their due.[22]

It turned out another factor was critical to inducing soldiers and officers to give their all: self-interest. Officers and enlisted men alike expected to be paid. "There's nothing [that] reconciles being shot at," one British officer quipped, "so much as being paid for it." Americans would have agreed. In addition to wages, enlisted men received signing bonuses, or bounties, in the form of cash or land from their states and from Congress, the amounts varying from place to place and time to time, depending on how generous—or desperate—a state or community was in meeting its recruitment quota. Later enlistees often got a better deal, to the irritation of men who'd served longer. Enlisted men also expected clothing, food, and liquor, or, if not provided, an equivalent cash compensation. Officers received wages and also counted on compensation for rations not delivered as promised, as well as reimbursement for expenses, such as forage for their horses and the cost of maintaining a hospitable dinner table.[23]

Washington understood. "A Soldier reasoned with upon the goodness of the cause he is engaged in and the inestimable rights he is contending for, hears you with patience, & acknowledges the truth of your observations; but adds, that it is of no more Importance to him than others," he observed. "Nothing but a good bounty," he continued, "can obtain them upon a permanent establishment."[24]

Paying the officers was even more important, and though Washington himself served without pay as a gesture of his elite magnanimity, he did not want similar volunteers, finding them excessively independent and unwilling to take orders. Officers needed good pay, Washington argued, in part because they were more likely to have families to support and property to lose, so their sacrifice was greater than the soldiers. More so, however, officers needed money so they could display "the character of a gentleman."[25]

Today, "character" is a private virtue—it's what you do when no one's watching—but in the 18th century that made no sense. Character was public, acted out before others and confirmed by others. The character of a gentleman, then, was something a man performed while everyone watched: he was honest in his dealings and polite in his manners, showed integrity in the face of temptation and bravery on the battlefield. In a word, a gentleman possessed honor. Considered a man's most valuable possession, honor, like character, rested on the opinion of others, which is why even petty insults were grounds for a duel: the insult-giver was a thief who attempted to steal the insult-receiver's honor, a case of aggravated robbery that a gentleman saw as a deadly threat to be resisted with his life.[26]

Strictly speaking, the honor of a gentleman might be displayed without money, but in practice a gentleman had to look the part in how he dressed, how he lived, and how he moved about in the world. It was a rank-ordered society in which everyone constantly scanned for the social status of others to know how to interact in everyday life. And unless you wanted to doff your cap to the wrong person at an insufficient distance or with inadequate gusto, you learned to interpret how a man presented himself as a window into his soul.[27]

To command respect for their status, officers spent to keep up appearances. In the field, officers' dress rarely matched the fashionable ideal, but not for lack of trying to drape themselves in velvet, ensconce themselves in silk, and flaunt fine lace, the frillier the better. Officers expected to have servants, either enlisted men or personal servants or enslaved persons brought from home. To avoid physical hardships beneath their station, officers rode horses rather than marched, rented lodgings in private homes rather than camped with the men, and when sick, they appealed to the hospitality of friends or arranged a room in a private home instead of going to the hospital. All that was expensive, but officers, especially the ones of uncertain status, cringed at scrimping, lest their masks slip and they be exposed as not truly genteel.[28]

As much as they expected money, officers and soldiers alike rarely received any pay at all. As Washington told a complaining Maryland general in spring 1782, "no pay has been lately given to the Troops of any State." He could have said the same at virtually any other point in the war. Before Robert Morris took charge, the states were responsible for paying their lines, but with no better resources than Congress, the states instead offered—sporadically—IOUs, certificates promising full payment, plus interest, at a future date. Unable to wait, soldiers and officers sold their certificates to speculators who offered steep discounts in exchange for immediate cash.[29]

Many enlisted men at least had land bounties to look forward to, but the officers had no such security. They felt their poverty keenly because it cut down their claims to gentleman status. As the war continued the officers burned through their patrimony or borrowed and sank into debt. The prospect of peace only increased their dread. More and more, officers talked about being unfit for civilian life not because army service had left them injured (though sometimes it had) or because the civilian economy had moved on without them and their skills weren't transferable (also sometimes true), but because having tasted the life of a gentleman, they didn't want to go back to being common. They couldn't bear to be seen as just another farmer, merchant, or tradesman.[30]

Denied pay, some officers resigned their commissions and returned home. The number spiked in 1777 through the Valley Forge winter into 1778 when, according to Washington, 200 to 300 officers left the service "and many others [were] with difficulty disswaded from it." It got so bad, a Connecticut surgeon heard, that the commander in chief feared "being left Alone with the Soldiers only." To make sure he had company, Washington pushed Congress to offer the officers pensions. The promise of money after the war would compensate the officers for their sacrifices, help provide for their families, and steer them back into civilian life, their minds calm with their status secure. Happily for Congress, the cost could be put off to the future while the benefit of a stable officer corps would be realized right away. "If some generous expedient is not embraced to remove their discontent," Washington warned Congress, "so extensive a desertion of the service will ensue, and so much discouragement be cast upon those who remain, as must wound it in a very essential manner." Washington's appeal worked. In May 1778, Congress approved pensions of half pay for seven years for officers who served out the war.[31]

But as campaign followed campaign and one year turned to the next with no end in sight, officer discontent swelled. Half pay for seven years wasn't enough, and more resignations followed, some 150 through the fall of 1780 alone. Washington again appealed to Congress. The officers needed something more generous: a lifetime payment. "Supported by a prospect of a permanent dependence," Washington assured Congress, "the officers would be tied to the Service and would submit to many momentary privations and to the inconveniencies which the situation of public affairs makes unavoidable." With Benedict Arnold's September 1780 treason fresh in mind as a specter of what a bitter officer could do, Congress approved pensions of half pay for life. Morale stabilized, but the underlying issue—disciplining an army with gentlemen officers who weren't paid enough to maintain their gentleman status—never went away.[32]

In May 1782, one veteran officer proposed a stunning solution to the officers' predicament: after the war, they should found their own state in the west and acclaim a king as their ruler. The idea was the brainchild of Colonel Lewis Nicola, a sixty-five-year-old immigrant from Ireland who'd spent a quarter century in the British army, mostly in obscure administrative posts in his native isle. In the mid-1760s, with his career at a dead end and his family growing, Nicola decided to start fresh in Philadelphia and make a go of the dry goods business. Finding limited success, Nicola joined the patriot cause and presented himself for service in 1776, when he became the city's barracks master. Later he established the Invalid Corps, a unit of soldiers not healthy enough for active duty but not sick enough for discharge. They usually performed guard duty to free physically fit soldiers for combat. [33]

Nicola unveiled his plan in a letter to none other than the commander in chief. Writing from his headquarters in Fishkill on the eastern shore of the Hudson, Nicola claimed to speak for a number of officers and enlisted men upset about "injuries" to their "pecuniary rights." He blamed the "schemes of economy in the legislatures of some States" that would leave the army with the "dismal prospect" that "the recompence of all our toils, hardships, expence of private fortune &c. during several of the best years of our lives" would amount to nothing. "To those who cannot earn a livelihood by manual labour"—that is, all gentlemen—Nicola predicted one fate awaited: "beggary." [34]

Nicola was an intellectually curious man who had written scientific papers on fish, helped found the American Philosophical Society, and translated military texts from French for Continental Army use. He expanded on his complaints with an analysis of the problems of government that undergirded the army's poor treatment and reached a diagnosis: the excesses of "Republican bigots." The treatment: a constitutional monarchy, modeled on the British system (with its worst aspects reformed, of course). Nicola concluded that if Congress agreed to discharge its debts to the army in western land, the veterans could form their own state, with their own constitution, and their own monarch. Contrary to legend, Nicola did not expressly invite Washington to be king, nor did he ask directly for Washington's support. Nicola was venting, exploring an idea to see where it might go. [35]

Shocked, Washington stomped on Nicola's plan. "With a mixture of great surprise & astonishment I have read with attention the Sentiments you have submitted to my perusal," he replied. "Be assured, Sir, no occurrence in the course of the War, has given me more painful sensations than your information of there being such ideas existing in the Army as you have expressed, & I must view [them] with abhorrence, and reprehend with severity." *Translation: Are you crazy?* Washington continued the ink-and-paper lashing. "I am much at a loss to conceive what part of my conduct could have given encouragement to an address which to me seems big with the greatest mischiefs that can befall my Country. If I am not deceived in the knowledge of myself, you could not have found a person to whom your schemes are more disagreeable." *Translation: You think I'd go along with this? You ARE crazy!* Washington ordered Nicola to drop the scheme immediately. "Let me conjure you then, if you have any regard for your Country, concern for your self or posterity—or respect for me, to banish these thoughts from your Mind, & never communicate . . . a sentiment of the like nature." *Translation: I'll do us both a favor and forget the whole thing.*[36]

Nicola's letter was born of frustration, not malice, however, and though poorly thought out, it wasn't crazy given his experience of suffering at the hands of self-styled and loudly proclaimed republican partisans. At the same time, Washington's smack down was entirely warranted, given his sensitivity to civilian suspicions of the army and the ideology of liberty that started the Revolution in the first place.

Every army enters into a covenant with the people it serves, with the soldiers pledging to give up some freedom and risk death for the benefit of their country, while civilians agree to support their soldiers, mitigate their suffering whenever possible, and show gratitude for their sacrifice. By 1782, from the perspective of Nicola and other officers, the civilians had broken the agreement.

The execrable state of supply throughout the war was the most obvious offense. The bloody-foot-prints-in-the-snow winter at Valley Forge is the best remembered hardship, but it was hardly unique. Worn-out clothes were the customary uniform, rotten food the usual fare. Morris's contract system, introduced in the fall of 1781, failed to improve conditions. By spring 1782, everything was in short supply, down to an insufficiency of "metal to make Buttons for the Soldiers Cloathing." Food was delivered late, in scanty quantities, and distributed at locations distant from many soldiers, who had to walk as far as three miles to get their provisions, which were likely spoiled anyway. At one point, General William Heath informed Washington he had 200 barrels of rancid food on hand, "some so bad as to be nauseous and must be buried."[37]

In late May, Washington lit into the contractor, a Long Island merchant named Comfort Sands. "Why Sir are the Troops without Provisions?" (It was always a bad sign when Washington called someone "sir" like this.) "Why," Washington continued, "do you so pertinatiously adhere to all those parts of the Contracts as are promotive of your own Interest & convenience . . . and at the same time disregard the most essential claims of the public?" Washington, a businessman himself, lectured Sands. "There are two parts to these contracts and that while you seem so well disposed to exact, with great rigidness, the fulfilment of the one, it becomes my duty to look to the performance of the other." For the rest of the summer, Washington wrangled with Sands and implored Morris to make changes. The army ate what it could, each disgusting meal a reminder of how little civilians cared about them.[38]

With their current conditions barely tolerable, officers looked to their pensions for security for the future. But it turned out their pensions were no sure thing. The trouble started in October 1780, when, at the same time Congress approved pensions, it also reduced the size of the army by sixteen regiments in a bid to economize. Hundreds of officers left the field, or, to use the now unfortunate-sounding term employed at the time, they were "deranged." Though eligible to begin receiving half pay according to the pension resolution, no money materialized. Congress, as was its style, neglected to provide funds for payment and failed to decide who would be responsible for the pensions, Congress or the states.

The deranged officers' clamors peaked in the summer of 1782. A contingent of veterans from Connecticut traveled to Philadelphia and knocked on the financier's door asking when they could expect their money. Morris, who didn't have money for current salaries let alone pensions, encouraged them to petition Congress, which they did and touched off a testy exchange in late July and August. Some delegates tried to relitigate granting pensions altogether in hopes of canceling them. Their effort failed, but Congress was stuck and decided to punt and delayed further debate until the following January, in five months' time. Officers in the Highlands watched, unimpressed by their civilian leaders and with no reason to believe they'd be treated differently when they turned in their commissions.[39]

Many civilians, however, were not sympathetic. They felt the army was lucky to get the pay and provisions they received, and for every soldier or officer who whined that they were the only ones to sacrifice for the cause of liberty, there was a farmer forced to sell his cow to a commissary agent, a merchant who discovered his shipment pilfered by soldiers, and a mother of young children left alone while her husband took up arms. Ordinary Americans supported the cause but feared their own army. And for good reason. Wherever the army camped, its thousands of men instantly made it a large city by 18th-century America's standards, and with its poor sanitation, diseases like camp fever struck outside a cantonment as well.

Soldiers stole and vandalized. They broke down fences, sometimes for firewood, sometimes just to smash things. They filched corn and apples and carried off pigs, sometimes to eat, sometimes for fun. Occasionally soldiers abetted by officers plundered houses and burned them to the ground to hide the evidence of their crimes. Armed and well-liquored, soldiers bullied civilians for the thrill of it, or beat and robbed them for money. Smart civilians buried their valuables when the army marched by. Soldiers were notorious for their dissolute morals. Even boarding your son and his friends for a night could be intolerable, since you couldn't trust them to keep their hands off your daughters. With no sense of shame, soldiers "eased themselves" everywhere, just as they refused to use latrines in camp. Pity the farmer waking up to milk the cows only to discover Bessy wasn't the only one making manure in the barn.[40]

For civilians, life near an army posed not only a physical threat but an existential one as well, because the longer the war continued and the more the Continental Army grew in size and professionalism, the more it resembled a standing army. And 18th-century people knew standing armies crushed liberty.

Revolutionary-era Americans lived in a mental universe suffused by republican ideology that explained how the world worked with a story. The republican story featured an unending battle between two forces: power, the lust of men to dominate others, and liberty, the ability to exercise one's natural rights. In the story, liberty was fragile and required unblinking vigilance to protect. Power was rapacious, scheming, and never missed a chance to expand itself. The best protection against the assaults of power was an army of citizen-soldiers, men of property, and therefore independent, who leapt to the defense of their country and then returned home, enemy vanquished and liberty intact. [41]

According to the story, a standing army—that is, a permanent force of professionals—was a weapon wielded by a malevolent ruler against his own people. A standing army was simultaneously a symptom and a cause of the decay of liberty on which power feasted. A people who relied on a standing army revealed they were decadent, so unwilling to defend themselves that they hired landless, desperate men to do their fighting instead. At the same time, a standing army imposed a heavy burden to maintain, so taxes were levied and force employed to collect them. A man lost control over his property as a result, and tax by tax he lost independence. Without independence, it was a short road to slavery. Standing armies. Taxes. Slavery. One naturally led to the other, according to the story of power and liberty. [42]

For American patriots, history abounded with real-life examples of how a standing army corrupted liberty, from the fall of the Roman Republic in antiquity, when the army followed Caesar instead of Rome, to the New Model Army of the 17th century English Civil War, when Parliament's force pursued its own interest, turned against the people, and installed Oliver Cromwell over the body of a headless king. American patriots also had their own lived experience of standing armies. They served alongside British regulars in the imperial wars of the mid-1700s, and suffered their insults as hapless "Yankee Doodles" who couldn't fight. American patriots also witnessed the military occupation of Boston in the late 1760s, when red-coated regulars arrived, ostensibly to restore order. In reality, they beat up townspeople, brawled with dockside laborers, and raped old ladies reading the Bible. Samuel Adams published a newspaper documenting every abuse, so colonists knew it was true. When the Boston Massacre happened, anyone versed in the danger of standing armies could have predicted it was only a matter of time before armed soldiers spilled innocent blood. [43]

Early in the war some revolutionary leaders indulged the belief that America would not need a regular army, that militia fresh from the field, equipped only with their patriotism and a trusty fowling piece, could turn back a European army. The fantasy didn't last long, however, and civil officials conceded the country needed a regular force. But the suspicion that it would grow into a dangerous standing army never subsided. When the army was idle—like throughout the summer of 1782—well, people thought, what was the point of having an army? Except, maybe, to plot a way to prolong the war and force hardworking civilians to support lazy soldiers in the field, or worse, give time for some would-be Caesar to cross the Delaware and conquer Philadelphia. [44]

For civilians schooled in the machinations of power, the officers posed the gravest threat. They set themselves up as a distinct class, with interests of their own, and insisted that ordinary people salute their sacrifice as somehow better than the sacrifices of civilians. Offices were aspiring aristocrats, in this view, men trying to raise themselves on the backs of free people fighting a war against aristocracy. Good thing Nicola heeded Washington's advice and kept his officer monarchy plan to himself.

Popular antipathy toward officers broke open in the debates over pensions because pensioners, like standing armies, were villains in the story of power and liberty. Pensioners were a source of corruption. They were dependent on the government and therefore no longer independent. They were tools of arbitrary power with no will of their own and ready to carry out whatever malignant scheme a ruler concocted. Even if a pensioner were personally benign (for the moment), he still lived on money raised from taxes on honest people, and the more pensioners, the higher the taxes, the greater the coercion to collect them, and it was the taxes-lead-to-slavery cycle all over again. To give officers pensions, then, ensured the people's enslavement.[45]

General Washington mediated between civilians as represented in Congress and the army, and it's a testament to his political skill that he kept a lid on the mutual antagonisms as much as he did. But hostility always simmered. Common ground was impossible because both soldiers and civilians alike shared in another worldview endemic to the 18th century way of thinking: a love of conspiracy theories.

Conspiratorial thinking was everywhere in the 18th century. The Revolution began in no small part because patriots interpreted the British policies as conspiracies and justified their resistance as heroically disrupting a cabal. British officials denounced the colonists' response to their policies as a rebellious covin and authorized force to put it down. Paranoia wasn't confined to the deteriorating colonial relationship. British politicians, Whig and Tory alike, invoked conspiracy thinking to analyze every maneuver of their opponents on every question, and in foreign policy, British ministers were sure the nation's enemies were scheming against them. The Spanish thought the same way. So, too, did the French, whose own revolution would be triggered by fears of plots by the king, plots by aristocrats, plots by the clergy, plots by the bourgeoisie, plots by *sans-culottes*. Plots within plots within plots. Every right-thinking person understood that all actions were calculated. An outcome you didn't like was intended by your enemies. It had to be. Only an idiot believed in accidents, mistakes, blunders, or plain old bad luck.

Conspiracy thinking flowed from sources both religious and philosophical. Christianity has always evoked the perfection of God's divine plan for the world and each person in it, but the Protestant reformers of the 16th century and their descendants in the 17th century intensified the focus on God's providence in an effort to eradicate the magical, occult beliefs that for many people lay side by side with Christian practice. If everything were under God's control, then there were no accidents. The Scientific Revolution of the 16th and 17th centuries and the Enlightenment of the 18th century that applied scientific principles to society likewise upended notions of chance. Isaac Newton unmasked the mysteries of the physical world and brought to light a mechanical universe of clear causes and effects. Social theorists adapted his insights to society and government: just like in the movement of the stars, there were no uncaused effects in the affairs of men.

In the 18th century both strands of thought, religious and philosophical, braided together to imbue events with moral meaning, and people reasoned backward from the outcome to the intention of the agent. According to colonists, then, a policy with negative effects—say, the Stamp Act of 1765—could not have resulted from the joint decision of a mix of wise and foolish policymakers trying to pay down Britain's debt who misjudged the temper of millions of people an ocean away. No, the damnable effect—the extinction of liberty—was without a doubt the plan all along.[46]

With conspiracy the standard mode of interpretation, the army, its officers, and the civilians they ostensibly served had no way to look innocently on each other's faults. As a result, officers saw civilians' reluctance to support them as a deliberate plan to dishonor them. Civilians saw officers' demands for pay and pensions as a stratagem to make themselves lords and masters of the new republic. And each stayed eagle-eyed for the slightest sign of the other's nefarious plot. Because, everyone knew, that's how the world worked.

—ɯ—

Washington was as suspicious as any of his contemporaries, and though the British were quiet throughout the summer of 1782, he was sure it was a trick and a prelude to a new offensive. In early May a new British commander, Sir Guy Carleton, disembarked in New York City to take over the Crown's operations in North America. The Irish-born Carleton was a veteran of colonial wars in Quebec and in Cuba and had previously served the king as military governor of Canada, where he deftly steered the colony away from aligning with the rebels to the south. The vicissitudes of army politics had sidelined Carleton for the previous few years, but back in the king's good graces in 1782, he was called from his country estate to wind down the war in America.[47]

Shortly after taking command, Carleton wrote Washington to inform him of the British disposition toward peace and offer his commitment to restraining violence against civilians. He urged Washington to do the same, presuming he was "alike interested to preserve the Name of Englishman from Reproach." When Washington read the letter at the Hasbrouck House, he raised an eyebrow. British overtures, he thought, were a ruse to lull American defenses. News of the Royal Navy's victory over France at the Battle of the Saints in the West Indies confirmed the general's misgivings. Surely, the British would fight on in North America, too. For Washington, the best way to bring peace, as ever, was to prepare for war. "If they are only playing the insidious game," Washington told Robert Livingston, "this will make them think of Peace in good earnest."[48]

Washington held out hope for a summer or early autumn attack on New York City, or, as a second choice, Charleston. An expedition into Canada was also on the table. But any operation depended on France. He needed the French army's numbers and, if New York or Charleston were the objective, French naval support as well. In spite of their joint achievement at Yorktown, neither ally lived up to the expectations of the other. The Americans thought France should concentrate on fighting in North America, not the Caribbean. The French wondered why they did so much of the heavy lifting when so many American men refused to enlist to do their own fighting and the states failed to pay for their own defense.[49]

Diplomatically sensitive, Washington cultivated a positive relationship with French officials through public displays of respect, even when the full symbolism didn't quite make sense for the United States. In late May, Washington hosted a party at West Point to honor the birth of King Louis's baby boy, Louis Joseph, the dauphin, the heir to the throne of France. Some 500 guests assembled under an enormous bower decorated with French and American flags for festivities that included dinner and the traditional thirteen toasts, each one announced with thirteen cannon blasts. Washington savored a toast raised to "a new edge to our swords, until they shall have opened the way to independence, freedom, and glory; and then may be converted to the instruments of peace." No wonder they quaffed so many toasts: by the time such wordy salutes were finished, everyone was sobering up. [50]

Afterwards, the American army executed a *feu de joie*, a rapid sequential firing of unloaded muskets. This display was extra elaborate, with troops stationed in a giant circle around the fort on both sides of the river. Thirteen more cannon blasts gave the signal to commence fire: flash, bang, flash, bang, flash, bang all around the line. Then they did it again, two more times. "The mountains resounded and echoed like tremendous peals of thunder," Dr. James Thacher marveled, "and the flashing from thousands of fire arms in the darkness of evening, could be compared only to the most vivid flashes of lightning from the clouds." The show concluded with the army shouting three cheers "of acclamation and benediction for the Dauphin"—a baby prince and next in line to the throne of a hereditary monarchy. The alliance was built on such compromises. [51]

In early July, Washington got the news he'd been waiting for. The French fleet was sailing north to avoid hurricane season in the Caribbean, and General Rochambeau was moving the French army from Williamsburg, where they'd been encamped in idleness since Yorktown, to the headwaters of Chesapeake Bay. Finally, action! Washington galloped to Philadelphia to confer with Rochambeau about their target. There wasn't a moment to lose.

Once together, Rochambeau proved less eager for battle than Washington. He declined the American's three aggressive options in favor of a fourth. The French army would march to the Hudson and take up a position north of New York City and see what developed. At the very least, the French army would supplement American defenses and force Carleton to keep men in the city rather than releasing them for service in the Caribbean. Unable to persuade his ally to something more vigorous than rearranging the pieces on the geopolitical chessboard, Washington acquiesced. He attended another bash for the dauphin, hosted by the French minister, and returned to Newburgh at the end of July to await the French march north. [52]

In the meantime, Carleton wrote again in August about "the pacific disposition of the Parliament and People of England toward the thirteen Provinces." Negotiations were underway, Carleton reported, and the king consented to acknowledge independence. The British commander was ready to start exchanging prisoners; no need to make them suffer any longer. Washington doubted. "The enemy talk loudly, & very confidently of Peace," he related to a French officer, "but whether they are in earnest, or whether it is to amuse and while away the time 'till they can prepare for a more vigorous prosecution of the War, time will evince." In September, Carleton acknowledged to Washington that he considered the recovery of America a lost cause. He foresaw no further engagements. "I must," he wrote, "frankly declare to you, that being no longer able to discover the object we contend for, I disapprove of all hostilities both by land and Sea." Washington softened, but he still smelled a trap. [53]

—⁂—

Wary of British designs, Washington prepared the army to move out at the end of August for Verplanck's Point, about twenty-five miles south on the eastern shore of the Hudson, where they would rendezvous with the French. "What our object will then be," one of

Washington's aides wrote, "must depend on the uncertainties of a month." At 5:00 A.M. on August 31, the army was up and ready to board boats for the journey downriver and what the commander in chief promised would be "that happy moment" when the Continentals "shall again unite our standards with those of our generous and gallant Allies in the face of the common enemy."[54]

For the next two weeks, the chores of setting up a new place to live disrupted the summer's ennui. Eager to impress his European counterparts, Washington assigned his men a course of drill, parade, and inspection, and he ordered the army to set up their tents with the "regularity" that is "extremely pleasing to the eye." Washington wanted bowers erected outside the tents to provide shade—and to look nice—and he wanted more bowers to hide the vaults "as much as possible from view." He would be watching. "By frequent passing along the line [the general] will have an opportunity of Judging which corps are most remarkable for their attention to regularity and even elegance." Offering his approval to spur public competition among the soldiery—the sentiment was vintage Washington.[55]

The army of King Louis arrived on September 14, and Washington led the troops out to honor General Rochambeau, who was suitably impressed. "You must have formed an alliance with the king of Prussia," Rochambeau quipped. "These troops are Prussians." Luckily, no republican zealots overheard the compliment. The French then bivouacked in Crompond, five miles to the northeast, and waited. More parades, reviews, and inspections followed, but it turned out the only common enemy the allies faced together was boredom. News filtered in that the British were abandoning Charleston; New York City was next, if the rumors were true. Washington's hopes for conquest faded.[56]

When October rolled around, the weather cooled and the army was back to its standard duty: sitting around doing nothing. Rochambeau had had enough. With further hostilities unlikely—and offering little reward with Britain poised to relinquish Charleston and New York—he decided to redeploy his force to the Caribbean. At the end of the month, the French broke camp and marched to Boston, where the navy would whisk them south for operations in warmer climes with their other ally, Spain. Before saying goodbye to Rochambeau, Washington completed one more grand review, dazzling the foreign officers and swelling his heart with pride. The campaign's "last Grand Manoevre," Washington said, saluting the troops, "surpassed every other exhibition of the kind that has been made in the American army." The campaign complete, the army marched north to New Windsor and winter quarters. [57]

For all the officers glowed in the commander in chief's praise, they grew sullen as the military season closed. Frustrated by the pointless expedition to Verplanck's Point, General Arthur St. Clair, a Scottish-born Pennsylvanian, called it "a very insipid Campaign." True, it could have been worse. The campaign was "a harmless one," according to General Henry Knox's aide-de-camp Samuel Shaw, since "nobody [was] killed or wounded." But that was the only positive. Battle at least offered officers the chance to show their courage and win honor. Policing soldiers' drunken antics and making sure they covered the latrines were necessary, but not honorable. "The campaign is now brought to a close, and no glorious deeds have been achieved," Dr. Thacher lamented. Even hanging out with French officers wasn't much fun because it revealed their inability to host in proper style. In the end, the 1782 campaign left the officers another year older and another year poorer. [58]

Washington understood the officers' affliction, and he warned Secretary at War Lincoln in Philadelphia of the brewing storm. The officers couldn't take much more. The lack of pay, the uncertainty of pensions, the deranging of officers, the poverty of their families, the burden of debt, and the "mortification" they experienced when they "cannot invite a French Officer, a visiting friend, or travelling acquaintance to a better repast than stinking Whiskey (and not always that) and a bit of Beef without Vegitables"—it was unbearable. In "these irritable circumstances, without one thing to sooth their feelings, or frighten [away] the gloomy prospects, I cannot avoid apprehending that a train of Evils will follow, of a very serious and distressing Nature."[59]

Even without battle, the war weighed heavily on Washington, as the collapse of the army from civilian neglect now threatened the republic more than British arms. Still, he was up to the challenge. A French officer who met Washington for the first time in autumn 1782 noticed the war's physical toll—and the general's determination not to fail. "He is tall, nobly built and very well proportioned," observed the Frenchman, a twenty-six-year-old named Charles Louis Victor, Prince de Broglie. "His face is much more agreeable than represented in his portrait. He must have been much handsomer three years ago, and although the gentlemen who have remained with him during all that time say that he seems to have grown much older, it is not to be denied that the General is still as fresh and active as a young man." Like so many other young officers, de Broglie was in awe. "One cannot fail," the prince gushed, "to give him the title of an excellent patriot, of a wise and virtuous man, and one is in fact tempted to ascribe to him all good qualities, even those that circumstances have not yet permitted him to develop." De Broglie was perceptive. The looming officers crisis would soon call on Washington to show some rarely seen skills.[60]

THREE

The Officers' Grievances, the Financier's Frustration

The army went into winter quarters, and Dr. John Cochran, director of the military hospital, was furious with Timothy Pickering, the quartermaster general. Responsible for finding a site for a cantonment, Pickering was also in charge of securing private houses for officers like Cochran. Pickering selected 1,600 acres of farmland west of New Windsor for the soldiers, but in a tight local housing market, procuring officers' quarters was always a struggle.

Cochran didn't care. He was tired of his temporary quarters, a room in the home of John Ellison, a handsome stone house built with one side in Georgian style and the other in Dutch colonial. He wanted his own house. Now. When Pickering responded that he thought Cochrane would make arrangements himself, the doctor exploded and accused the quartermaster of "illiberality," "Ignorance of your Profession," "inebriety," and "Partiality in Favor of those immediately under your own Inspection." The abuse concluded with a not-so-subtle challenge. "Should you conceive your Feelings injured by this reply to your scurrility," he wrote, "I am ready to give you any satisfaction you may demand, where Pen, Ink and Paper are not concerned." Easily irritated, Pickering was not one to suffer quietly, but morally opposed to dueling—he called it an "absurd and barbarous practice"—he stifled any reaction to the "scurrility" remark.[1]

Then, another officer jumped in, this time a senior one, General Horatio Gates. Gates was staying in temporary quarters of his own and wanted into the John Ellison House, which he would take over with his military family. "The Season is late, and it is time, I should be fixed in some Quarters," Gates lectured Pickering in November. But Pickering couldn't secure Ellison for Gates until Cochran moved out, which he refused to do until Pickering located a place for him. The quartermaster was stuck.[2]

Gates couldn't be ignored. Second in rank after Washington, he commanded the army's right wing: the regiments of New York, New Jersey, and Connecticut. Gates was a complex man at the end of a tortuous wartime journey. No one had more military experience when the war started. Born in Essex, England, Gates first came to North America in 1749 to fight for king and empire. A competent administrator, he was also a battlefield commander who led the American victory at Saratoga, New York, in 1777, besides Yorktown the only other time a British army surrendered to the Americans. Gates's record was uneven, however. His singular triumph was counterbalanced by a humiliating defeat, the disaster at Camden, South Carolina, in 1780, when the outnumbered British under Cornwallis smashed the American lines and Gates fled the scene, galloping 200 miles in three days.[3]

Despite the failure, Gates was popular with his men, soldiers and officers alike. Solicitous of their well-being, he smelled the smoke of battle and led from the front (except the time he skedaddled from Camden). He affected a simple, down-to-earth manner and loved to swear. The men called him Granny Gates, because of his prematurely aged appearance. Gates, who was fifty-four in 1782, walked with a stooped posture, had receding gray hair, and wore spectacles perched on the end of his nose.[4]

Gates had an uneven relationship with Washington. The two first crossed paths during the ill-fated Braddock Expedition of 1755 when Captain Gates, the British regular, and Washington, the upstart colonial colonel, followed General Edward Braddock into a French and Native ambush in the Pennsylvania backcountry. Gates was wounded; Washington, rallying the troops, became a hero. Years later, Gates's relatively low-prestige birth put a ceiling on his ascent in the British army, similar to the limitations on the colonial Washington's ambitions. When Gates decided to relocate to start anew in America, he consulted Washington about buying land in Virginia—who else knew more?—and in 1772 Gates purchased a 600-acre plantation in the Shenandoah Valley. He called it Traveller's Rest.[5]

Gates joined the war early and served as Washington's adjutant at the Siege of Boston (1775), but he was a restless subordinate throughout the war. Once he had a command, he feuded with other generals over seniority, dragged his feet detaching troops for Washington's use, planned an invasion of Canada without Washington's input, and, worst of all, angled to replace Washington as commander in chief. Gates's Saratoga moment coincided with a string of defeats for Washington and the loss of Philadelphia, and when some congressmen wondered if the army needed a new commander with a winning record, Gates didn't discourage them. Fanned by the indiscreet letters of a general named Thomas Conway, Gates's ambitions and Congress's natural second-guessing of Washington at such a low point struck the commander in chief's partisans (all conspiracy theorists, of course) as a cabal. It wasn't, but hard feelings lingered.[6]

Gates was one of a minority of officers who didn't like Washington. Most officers venerated the commander in chief, but a few like Gates resented his fame. To them, the godlike Washington had two feet of clay: indecision on the battlefield and excessive sensitivity to criticism. They could've done just as well—no, better!—if they'd only had the chance.

By 1782, however, Gates was a different man. He'd passed the previous two years on the sidelines at Traveller's Rest pending a court-martial investigation of his conduct at Camden. In time Congress gave up the inquiry, and Gates reported for duty in October 1782, determined to regain his reputation by doing something useful for the cause. It's a mark of Gates's charm that Prince de Broglie, who usually swooned for the commander in chief, came away from a meeting with the two most impressed by Gates. "Mr. Washington treated Mr. Gates with a politeness which had a frank and easy air," he remembered, "whilst the other responded with that shade of respect which was proper toward his general, but at the same time with a self-possession, a nobility of manner and an air of moderation." De Broglie thought Gates deserved better. "Mr. Gates was worthy of the successes he had gained at Saratoga," while his defeats "only rendered him more worthy of respect, because of the courage with which he bore them."[7]

Gates was correct in his deportment toward Washington and carried out administrative tasks as assigned. He saved his anger for Pickering, who couldn't figure out a way out of a most frustrating game of musical chairs and find a place for every quarrelsome officer to live. Gates asked Washington to intervene. "Your Excellency's Dog-kennel, at Mount Vernon, is as good a Quarter as that I am now in," he complained. "The season will be soon severe—and every reason that is disagreeable, induces me to desire the Quar. Master Genl may receive Your Excellency's positive Orders to fix me at Ellison's, which is upon every account my proper Quarter."[8]

In the end, Cochran relented. He moved into a house across the river, and vacated Ellison for Gates, though he couldn't resist one last swipe at Pickering. "It is a little unfortunate for us both," he wrote Gates, "that Colonel Pickering was either unacquainted with his Duty or that certain Prejudices prevailed too much, to permit him to execute it." Everyone in their own place, the crisis was averted.

While the officers squabbled about their quarters, the enlisted men and noncommissioned officers had no choice about their accommodations. They were ordered to construct log hunts according to Pickering's design. Featuring some 1,100 square feet of living space, the size of a two-bedroom apartment today, the huts were divided into two large rooms with a door on one end and a chimney and window on the other. Each hut could house sixteen men. One French visitor described them as "spacious"—because nothing says "spacious" like sharing a modest apartment with fifteen other men. Officers, naturally, enjoyed somewhat larger accommodations and they shared with fewer men. Their huts also had kitchens, either attached to the main house or constructed as an outbuilding, and they had two windows, for extra natural light in the dreary New York winter. General Washington, always fastidious about appearances, had high expectations. He exhorted the men "that *regularity, convenience,* and even some degree of *elegance* should be attended to in the construction of their huts."[9]

Each company was required to build two huts, and as November began, they beavered away, felling trees, cutting logs, and putting up small houses. The generals were impressed. "Our men are becoming so adroit and perfect in the Art of Hutting," General Gates wrote, "that I think they will be more comfortable and better Lodged, in the Quarters they build for themselves than in Those any City in the Continent would afford them." General William Heath of Massachusetts called the cantonment "regular and beautiful" a place where "the army spent the winter very comfortably." Washington, the sternest of critics, never complimented the men publicly, though he did privately hail the huts as the "most comfortable Barracks . . . that the Troops have ever yet been in." As the generals would soon learn, however, the junior officers didn't agree.[10]

—∞—

The fuss over housing was so testy because in that eighth winter of the war the army was irritable, with everything still so uncertain. Was the war over? Would they ever be paid? If they were paid, would the money be worth anything? Would the officers receive pensions? Would they be humiliated by civilians who laughed at their pretensions to gentility? Or chastised as layabout pensioners? The answers were all outside the army's control and still seemed nowhere near resolution.

The officers were not inert, however, and they organized themselves to push state authorities and Congress to pay attention to their claims. The Massachusetts officers led the way. In June 1782, they began drafting a memorial to ask for redress of their grievances. Officers petitioning civil officials happened throughout the war. Individual officers wrote to their state governors about their hardships, and in 1779, twenty-six generals had written a memorial to Congress demanding increased pay. Ignored, the generals sent a new memorial the next year asking for additional compensations of pensions and land. This time, however, the effort was broader, a state's entire officer corps seeking relief together.[11]

For leadership, the officers looked to their highest-ranking member, General Henry Knox, commander at West Point. Knox was a hulking man, six-foot-two and 280 pounds. A 1784 portrait reveals a broad-chested figure in uniform with a large, oval face and a prominent double chin—growing into a triple chin—as well as rosy cheeks and a friendly smile. Hair powdered gray makes Knox look far older than his age: only thirty-two in 1782.[12]

When the war began, Knox was selling books, a trade he'd followed since being apprenticed to a bookstore owner at the age of nine, after his father, deep in debt, ran off to St. Eustatius, and left behind Henry, his mother, and a younger brother to fend for themselves. Too young for the French and Indian War, Knox dreamed of battlefield glory and eagerly joined the militia, where he helped build up its artillery, his specialty throughout the Revolution. Knox's deep, booming voice cut through the roar of cannon fire, and he looked as solid as a mortar—both reassuring to troops under his command. Like many leaders of the Revolution, Knox was a voracious autodidact. He learned the art of war from books both ancient and modern, and from talking shop with the British officers who stopped by his store. [13]

Naturally outgoing, Knox attracted friends easily and won the respect of his peers. His wife, Lucy, matched his personality and physique. The daughter of a Boston Tory, she had dark eyes and a glowing face, and although her notion of fashionable dress and *au courant* hairstyles invited frowns from republican purists, she was vivacious and a favorite dance partner of General Washington. [14]

Henry Knox first met Washington during the siege of Boston in 1775, when his organization of artillery convinced the Virginian that contrary to his expectations, some Massachusetts soldiers knew their business. Knox fought alongside Washington through every major engagement, culminating at Yorktown, when the artillery performed its glittering best. [15]

Washington appointed Knox commander of West Point in August 1782. The fort's garrison faced many of the same issues as men in the main cantonment. "The Soldiers are thickly stowed in both Hutts & Barracks," one inspection revealed, and "in addition to other Evils an inveterate Itch is general among the Troops." Knox had relocated his family to the fort and its insalubrious climate. In September, tragedy struck. Henry and Lucy lost their little boy, nine-month-old Marcus Camillus, Washington's godson. Devastated, General Knox lost his usual effervescence just as he plunged more deeply into the depressing issues of delinquent pay and unfunded pensions. The war was Knox's ladder to rise socially, from a bookseller—a tradesman with an intellectual side, but still a tradesman—into an officer and a true gentleman. But with a taste for fine living and a large family to raise, Knox needed a pension as much as anyone. [16]

To advance their case, the Massachusetts officers first had to decide whom to address: Congress or their state legislature. Initially, they planned to send their memorial to Congress, but learning that Congress had tabled discussion of pensions until January 1783, the officers chose an indirect strategy. They would first petition their own state legislature, which they knew probably wouldn't work. The New England states were fiercely antipension. But starting with Massachusetts would prevent Congress from brushing them off with orders to try their state first. The state legislature might surprise and say yes, but if it didn't, the officers would save some time and be able to put extra pressure on Congress when the time came to escalate. [17]

A delegation of officers left camp in September, and in Boston they weathered the usual legislative delays—reports, meetings, committees, more reports, meetings, and committees—until November when the antipension faction pulled a fast one. They made public a private letter from one of the state's congressmen, the Boston merchant Samuel Osgood, that said if Massachusetts settled with its officers independent of Congress, it would not get a credit toward its share of war expenses, and the state would end up paying twice. Besides, Osgood informed, Congress was set to discuss pensions in the new year and there was no reason for Massachusetts to act first. [18]

With a way to tell the officers no without actually saying no, the legislature tabled the memorial, killing it for the moment and probably for good. When Major Samuel Shaw heard how the Massachusetts legislature treated the respectful, democratic petition of Massachusetts men, he was dejected. "The treatment the application to our State, in behalf of its troops, has met with from the legislature occasions universal discontent," the doleful Shaw told his father. So much, he concluded, for "Public faith." [19]

The Massachusetts officers regrouped, again with Knox leading a committee, and prepared to take their case to Congress. Meeting on November 16, they decided to turn up the volume of their petition. First, they invited the other states' officers to join them. Representatives from Connecticut, New York, New Jersey, and New Hampshire responded positively and sent representatives to form a new, expansive committee, again with Knox at its head. The Rhode Island line, stationed at Albany, joined in later. Second, the Massachusetts officers solicited grievances from their line's individual regiments. [20]

The soldiers didn't need to be asked twice to complain, and over the next few days, the officers of each regiment met and drew up reports, pouring their bitterness onto Knox. Some reports were lavishly formal and deferential, others blunt and heavy handed. Some officers wrote long narratives of their suffering, while others offered tight, bullet-point-like lists. Some wrote in a beautiful hand, others in a near-indecipherable scrawl. Most grievance reports focused on the officers' needs, but a few included the enlisted men, especially the "veteran soldiers, who have served with fidelity thus far thro' the hardships and dangers of the present contest." The officers blamed Massachusetts for their problems just as often as they accused Congress. They despaired for their families, which "are either already suffering the utmost extremes of poverty or hastening with a quick step toward it." They resented civilians "swimming in luxury" and deplored them as ungrateful. They demanded action but seemed resigned to yet more failure. And the huts. They hated the huts. Deeply. Passionately. Ferociously. No matter how regular, how convenient, how elegant. The "art of hutting" was a black one. [21]

The grievances of the Third Massachusetts were typical. The officers pointed to arrearages in pay, stretching back "for almost two years past." When they were paid, they received depreciated Massachusetts notes, which they were "obliged to part with . . . for less, than one quarter of their real Value." The consolidation of units and dismissal of officers frightened them. "The frequent deranging of Officers, from the Army, without any kind of Settlement, or Compensation, for their past Services, we look upon, as a very capital injury," the grievance read. Then, in a passage more intense than any other, the huts. "Our being under the disagreeable necessity, after quitting the Field, year Succeeding year, of building Hutts for ourselves, in the severe or most extreme parts of the Season" the report said, "is a hardship, and cruelty to the Army, which cannot be too firm, & warmly pointed out, as a grievance." Finally, pensions. The regiment wanted Congress to either "make such permanent provision, as will beyond all doubt ensure it when due, or recommend it to the State, to make such settlement."[22]

Turning to what Knox's committee should do, the officers wanted their feelings expressed to Congress in "a spirited Address," a "very Spirited address," a "free & spirited representation," or "a memorial and [a] humble, but *spirited*, petition." The Fifth Regiment, lacking a new way to say "spirited," instead wanted their communications to go through General Washington or the secretary at war "that he may give them all possible official sanction." Though only mentioned by one regiment, asking Washington to take charge would reappear at a crucial moment in the future.[23]

The grievance reports struck few notes of optimism. Some tried to set deadlines for an affirmative response—January 1 or February 1 or March 1 or even, for an installment of pay, by July 1—but more often the officers said what they would have to do when a negative answer came back: resign their commissions. "We are fully convinced," the Fourth Massachusetts officers wrote, that without a firm commitment from Congress "we shall be under the disagreeable necessity of returning our commissions to that power from which they originated, that we may then fall upon some plan to obtain a comfortable support in life for ourselves and families."[24]

Despite the raw emotion aired in the grievances, most units protested within the system of civilian supremacy over the military and threatened to play the one card allowed by the system: resignation.

The Sixth Regiment went further and turned the language of revolution against civil authority. "We believe," the grievance read, "we engaged to serve the public not as slaves at discretion for life, but as free men upon contract for a definite period." The officers bewailed the penury that surely awaited them. "We shall be like asses of burthen who after having drudged through the heat, to save expense, are turned out to graze the streats for support, till their masters see fit to make use of them again." If not paid, the officers concluded, they considered their contract broken and would "seek support in the honest callings of domestic life and whatever the consequences may be, the world will judge." [25]

Here were the electrifying words of republican ideology: freedom and slavery, liberty and power, social contracts kept and broken, with the justice of the officers' actions submitted, like the Declaration of Independence, to a candid world. Except now Congress and the people were the British and the officers alone were the true patriots.

—⁘—

In late November and early December, the multistate committee led by Knox convened at Horton's Tavern in New Windsor, and over a series of meetings the officers shaped their grievances into a memorial. Two drafts survive in the Henry Knox papers and show how the officers' strategy gained focus, purpose, and rhetorical power. [26]

The first draft started simply, asking permission to address Congress "in plain & respectful Language," on behalf of the officers and soldiers of the army. The draft then framed its message in contractual terms, a traditional New England way of understanding military service as an inviolable agreement between the soldier and his community. The officers had kept their end of the bargain while Congress had not. "There does not lye on the Army, any Imputation of unfaithfulness," it announced. "Its unexampled Perseverance & fidelity under accumulated Hardships & Wrongs, have excited the Astonishment & applause of strangers." [27]

The proposed text followed the introductory section with a detailed account of how Congress had fallen short of its obligations: Continental money "palmed off upon the Army," payment in state securities sold at 70–80 percent discounts, inadequate rations, and undelivered clothing with no compensation to offset the shortage, accounts unsettled and "scarcely thought of but by the Army." [28]

The draft was as drafty as a poorly constructed hut. It lacked organization, failed to note the predicament of the retired officers until the very end, and never discussed pensions. Huts were never mentioned, either, though that was a wise choice, since Congress couldn't do anything about it. When it came time to state what the officers wanted, the draft was uncertain. The officers asked for Congress to settle their accounts as much as possible immediately and have "the Remainder put on Such a Footing as will restore Chearfulness to the Army."[29]

Overall, the draft's language was plain and respectful, as promised, but also uninspired and unfocused—as blah as a New York December day. The second version made a vigorous improvement.

Recorded by Major Shaw, though likely composed by committee, the draft deleted the opening about contracts and substituted an emotional appeal showing the effects of the officers' indigence. "We have Struggled with our difficulties, year after year under the hopes that each would be the last; but we have been disappointed," the introduction proclaimed. "We find our embarrassments thicken so fast and have become so complex, that many can go no further."[30]

The new draft ended its introduction on an ominous note. "Our distresses are now brought to a point," it warned. "We have borne all that men can bear." Their own money long ago spent, "our private resources are at an end, and our friends are wearied out, and disgusted with our incessant applications." With nowhere else to turn, the officers said, "We, therefore, most seriously and earnestly beg, that a supply of money may be forwarded to the army as soon as possible."[31]

In case Congress failed to grasp the point, the text continued with an alert about the enlisted men. "The uneasiness of the soldiers, for want of pay, is great and dangerous; any further experiments on their patience may have fatal effects." Though often misinterpreted as the officers threatening "fatal effects" if they were ignored, the reference was to "soldiers." The officers had already implied their reaction if Congress failed to act. "Unable to go further," they would resign.[32]

With the climactic close to the introductory section—sure to grab the attention of even the sleepiest of congressmen—the second draft incorporated the first draft's material on rations, clothing, and the plight of retired officers, now moved up to a more logical position in the argument. Shaw left a large blank space in his paper where the material from the first draft should go and the final version seamlessly entwined the two.[33]

Then, the draft addressed pensions head-on. It condemned the "odious point of view" that discountenanced pensions. On the contrary, the officers proclaimed. "We regard the act of Congress respecting half-pay, as an honorable and just recompense." The officers now offered a deal. In lieu of half pay for life, they would accept from Congress full pay for a limited number of years or a lump sum payment to discharge the obligation once and for all.[34]

Here was the spirited representation of grievances that the officers wanted, though it was also respectful. Obeisance to Congress sweetened the text with assurances that the address, "with all proper deference and respect," was offered to "your august body," in hopes of finding relief from "our head and sovereign."[35]

After circulating for comments, the second draft was approved on December 5, with minor edits, most notably a new last line urging Congress to act without delay "to convince the army and the world that the independence of America shall not be placed on the ruin of any particular class of her citizens." Two days later, the committee gathered one last time at Horton's Tavern, and fourteen men (four generals, eight colonels, a major, and a surgeon) signed their names to the document.[36]

—⚏—

As the officers pulled together to pry open the public purse, the financier's program suffered a devastating blow in November when a single state, Rhode Island, voted down the impost, the key new source of revenue for Congress and the cornerstone of Robert Morris's fiscal plan. Conditions worsened when it turned out that Rhode Island wasn't alone in opposing the new tax.

The defeat of the impost was a stunning reversal from earlier in 1782 when the government's finances had shown signs of life. The Bank of North America opened for business in January 1782, and its notes were holding their value while Morris secured $300,000 in bank loans for the government. The funds were short term and only allowed Morris a few weeks of breathing room at a time, but the bank was doing its job: smoothing the government's transactions in tempestuous days.[37]

Good news arrived from France in April. The king approved a new 6-million-livres loan ($1.1 million specie). More good news from abroad arrived in May: Lord North's government had fallen, breaking open treaty negotiations and promising to reduce military expenses. Even more good foreign news: July reports announced that the United Provinces of the Netherlands had recognized American independence and Ambassador John Adams was negotiating with Dutch merchants for a 5-million-guilder loan worth $2 million specie. Domestically there was good news, too: by July the impost amendment was approved by every state except two, Georgia and Rhode Island.[38]

But bad news was never far behind. The army's contract system struggled. The French loan came with heavy strings attached, more like binding ropes. This loan was it, the French minister warned, and France would end its prior practice of covering the interest payments on US loan office certificates, which owed their attractiveness to French backing. At the same time, the existence of the foreign loans and the sight of peace on the horizon relaxed the pressure on the states to fulfill their requisition payments. By the end of June, a requisition of $8 million had brought in $29,925.43—that's 0.37 percent of the goal. Only three states sent money at all.[39]

At first, Morris didn't want to tell Congress about the foreign loans, fearing the states' lassitude could be worse still. Privately, Morris wondered if peace was really a blessing. "I wish most sincerely and ardently for Peace that I may get rid of a most Troublesome Office," he confided to a friend in Europe. "But was I to confine myself to the Language of a Patriot, I should speak in another manner and tell you that a continuance of the War is Necessary until our Confederation is more strongly knit."[40]

With his office tethered to everything the government did, Robert Morris stood at the center of every storm. The demands never stopped. Morris often started work before breakfast and ended after midnight (good thing he lived next door—a short commute). In the summer, he blocked out two hours, three times a week for people to come harass him for money he didn't have. The French loan was spent as soon as it was announced, Morris's personal credit was devoted to supplying the army, and state requisitions were low as always, and there was no new revenue coming in.[41]

In June, Morris rolled up his sleeves to twist arms. In reaction to France pulling its subsidy for loan office interest payments, Morris recommended Congress stop paying interest on the certificates until it received adequate revenue from the states to make the payments without foreign assistance. Their income in doubt, bondholders erupted in protest, as Morris knew they would, as Morris hoped they would.

On June 28, a group of Philadelphia merchants accosted Morris at his office demanding to know why their interest payments were being suspended. Morris assured the merchants he wanted to pay. He owned certificates, too, and he considered prompt payment a matter of honor "as essential to the Interest, happiness, freedom and Glory of the United States, as it is also to the interest and Justice due to Individuals." But it wasn't up to him. Congress, and more so the states, were the real culprits because they would not produce the necessary revenue. If they wanted payment, Morris concluded, "the public Creditors should unite and use their Influence" on Congress and their state legislatures.[42]

The merchants did their part. Forming a committee, they sent a petition to Congress in July that painted a vivid picture of their unquestioned patriotism—they were "among the earliest Promoters of the glorious Revolution in America"—and colored in dark tones the agony of "the Widow, the Orphan, the Aged, and the Infirm" whose one "screen" from "the most wretched Poverty" was their income from loan office certificates. In their private meetings, the merchants were furious and ready to fight. Morris tried to talk them down. He cautioned them to "avoid the language of Threats" and stay focused on making "common Cause" among the nation's creditors "to have influence on all the Legislatures in the several States." Not everyone bided Morris's counsel, however. Again darkening the financier's door on the evening of July 9, several merchants addressed him "very warmly" and "declared great Dissatisfaction."[43]

Then Morris did his part. At the end of July, he sent to Congress a long report on public finance that urged the United States to quit depending on France to secure American credit and instead take responsibility for its own commitments by generating new revenue to make the interest payments on the certificates. In addition to the impost, which Morris assured was so certain of approval that "this Revenue may be considered as being already granted," Congress should prevail upon the states to enact new land taxes, poll taxes, and excise taxes on "all distilled Spirituous Liquors." Aware of the objections to taxation, Morris walked through the effects of each measure, arguing that the burden would be surprisingly light. In the end, Morris made a moral claim. The nation's debts must be paid. The government that did otherwise, Morris contended, "shews a flagitious Contempt of moral Obligations, which must necessarily weaken, as it ought to do, their Authority over the People."[44]

Morris's power made him many enemies. The financier's keenness to harness private interest to public good abraded republican notions of pure self-sacrifice, which his collaboration with merchants and imperious tone in demanding payment from states reinforced. A businessman, Morris moved fast. Legislators, jealous of their power, were more deliberate. In the summer of 1782 one Morris enemy was new to Philadelphia, a delegate from Rhode Island named David Howell. A professor and lawyer, Howell, thirty-five, entered politics to fight the impost. Born in New Jersey and educated at Princeton, Howell came to Providence in 1766 as one of the first faculty at

Rhode Island College (Brown), where he taught natural philosophy, math, French, German, and Hebrew. At the same time, he earned a master's degree and joined the bar. In 1770, Howell married into the Brown family, the mercantile dynasty after whom the university would be named. When the war left him without students to teach, Howell served as a judge.[45]

In the spring of 1782, as pressure mounted on Rhode Island to approve the impost, merchants like the Browns opposed the tax as detrimental to commerce. The state's peculiar geography meant the Browns often engaged in the reexport trade and the impost offered no drawbacks to offset the cost of landing goods and paying the tax before sending them somewhere else. What's more, refusing to pay taxes levied by a distant authority meddling in their trade was what the Revolution was about.[46]

Rhode Island newspapers crackled with attacks on the impost, some written by Howell. Rather than defend the merchants' interests, however, Howell's articles riled up the backcountry farmers with 180 proof, straight power-and-liberty republicanism. Once the new tax passed, Howell averred in one article, the loss of liberty would be permanent. "Whatever may be our wishes or prayers afterwards," he warned, "it will be like *Adam's fall*, unalterable, and affect not only ourselves, but all our posterity." If the Biblical allusion wasn't enough, Howell added a classical one. The impost "will be like *Pandora's box*, once opened, never to close."[47]

Elected to Congress, Howell took his seat in June. When called upon to explain his state's reluctance to approve the impost, Howell put away the ideological rhetoric. He stressed Rhode Island's outsized contribution to the war, problems with national officers collecting the tax rather than state ones, the deleterious effects of the tax on commerce, and that new western lands should be sold for the benefit of all, producing revenue for common debts, and not added to an individual state. The objections were surmountable, Howell implied. Then in letters back home, he denounced the corruption of the evil impost.[48]

Talkative and eager for political prominence, Howell was at first lonely in Philadelphia, not knowing anyone and often at odds with most other delegates. Howell's spirits perked up after a few months when Rhode Island sent another anti-impost delegate to Congress, Jonathan Arnold. Howell also moved to a house on Fourth Street, closer to the political action.[49]

In the meantime, Howell cast the ultimate source of his loneliness—his singular opposition to the tax—as a virtue, and he scratched out letter after letter in a grandiose sense of mission to save Rhode Island and liberty. "In New-England alone have we pure & unmixed Democracy," he boasted to a friend from home, and in Rhode Island "it is in its Perfection." It was all up to "our little State," he continued. "Preventing the 5 per Cent [impost] from taking effect," he bragged, "would be to us an additional gem."[50]

In fall 1782, the deteriorating army supply contract forced Morris to redouble his advocacy for the impost. The contractor, Comfort Sands, never delivered quality—or quantity—but he charged affordable prices and accepted the government's credit on attractive terms. Still, the army couldn't take it anymore. Morris relented and canceled Sands's contract. Stringing together a replacement exposed the government's inability to pay all over again and endangered army supply for 1783. Morris needed the impost as soon as possible, as much for the shot of confidence in the government's resources as for the actual revenue.[51]

To help push things along for Morris, on October 10, Congress passed a resolution calling on the two delinquent states, Georgia and Rhode Island, "for an immediate definitive answer whether they will comply with the recommendation of Congress." Howell lacerated the impost anew. "Should the Impost be adopted, which God forbid, I should no longer suppose myself the Representative of a Sovereign & Free State," Howell lashed out. "This is but an entering wedge," he admonished, and "others will follow—a land tax, a pole tax & an Excise." Howell mocked the shallow reasoning offered by the impost's supporters. They were "linsy woolsy politicians" who offered nothing but "the *single,* tho *dreadful* word *necessity,*" and hoped to triumph "by the *hocus pocus,* magic charm of—NECESSITY."[52]

In his less excitable moments, Howell admitted that Congress must pay its debts for the sake of justice and to establish its credit. However, Howell believed that the impost was inferior to requisitions on states and loans from foreign government. Contrary to today's conventional wisdom that government debt unfairly burdens our children and grandchildren, Howell lauded loans for that very feature: pushing out repayment to a time when he assumed the country would be more prosperous. Loans would, he assured Nicholas Brown, "enable us to transmit our debt to posterity without inconvenience."[53]

Convinced that the Dutch loan was sufficient, Howell went beyond impassioned argument. In October, he wrote a private letter to the publisher of the *Providence Gazette.* The contents: secret diplomatic information and reports from the minister to the United Provinces of the Netherlands, John Adams, carefully massaged by Howell to make it look like European support was much stronger than it was. "The national Importance of the United States is constantly rising in the Estimation of European Powers, and the civilized World," Howell revealed. "Such is their Credit, that they have of late failed in no Application for foreign Loans." The only trouble, according to Howell, was that too much money was available. Howell's dispatch, naturally, found its way into print.[54]

Rhode Island's day of decision came on November 1, and the state's "immediate definitive answer" was no. Howell was ecstatic. "The rejection of the Impost by *the independent 54,*" he wrote in reference to the nay-voting legislators, "will eventually redound to the credit of our State & I hope to the benefit of the whole Union." The "approaches of Tyrannys," he enthused to a Rhode Island friend, were defeated. "Long may the Independent 54 be remembered as the incorruptible Patriots of 1782!"[55]

Morris wasn't giving up. Determined to change Rhode Island's vote, he deployed a weapon of his own: Thomas Paine. Earlier in the year, Morris had hired Paine, the pamphleteer extraordinaire, as a staff writer to produce articles promoting Morris's projects. It was a surprising partnership. Paine, the radical, had once raked Morris over the newspaper coals for his habit of mingling public and private ventures, but seeing the army's suffering up-front had turned Paine into a nationalist sympathizer. Morris knew the writer's skills and arranged for him to receive a regular salary, much needed by the penurious Paine, drawn from the secret service budget of the Foreign Affairs department. Eager to cross pens with the enemy, Paine drew up plans in November to write a series of articles for the Philadelphia papers that would then be reprinted in Rhode Island. Paine imagined his task grandly. He not only wanted to defend the impost, but to show the benefits of a stronger union among the states. "At present," he opined to Morris, "we hang so loosely together that we are in danger of hanging one another."[56]

Stung by the rejection, Morris's allies in Congress pitched in. On December 6, Congress selected a delegation to travel to Rhode Island and personally press the legislature to reconsider. Though "a subject of considerable debate," in the end only the Rhode Islanders refused. The delegation delayed—Congress always did—to await Rhode Island's official explanation of its rejection of the impost and then Congress drafted a response. Finally, on December 22, the delegation left Philadelphia for Providence.

Only a few miles out of town and gabbing to pass the time, one member of the delegation, Abner Nash of North Carolina, mentioned he'd read a letter with a piece of information they might find interesting: Virginia's legislature had reversed its approval of the impost. Dumbfounded—he couldn't have said something before they left?—his companions sussed out his source, found it reliable, and rode back to Philadelphia.[57]

Now, two states had given definitive negatives. Virginia's action was astonishing because it was so mysterious. The state's representatives were at a loss to explain it, even to other Virginians such as James

Madison and George Washington. In the end, lingering anxiety about the impost's effects on state sovereignty and resentment over how Virginia's western land claims were treated by Congress had been turbocharged by the arrival of Arthur Lee, an implacable enemy of Morris, to Virginia from Philadelphia. Along with his brother Richard Henry Lee, he engineered the change to cut the financier down to size.[58]

With the delegation back in Philadelphia, Congress awaited official confirmation of Virginia's about-face. When the letter arrived on December 24, it made for a gloomy Christmas. "The most intelligent members were deeply affected," one Virginian wrote, "& prognosticated a failure of the Impost scheme, & the most pernicious effects [to] the character, the duration, & the interests of the confederacy."[59]

Frustrated congressmen took vengeance on leaky Howell. First alerted to a suspicious article circulating in New England in early December, the impost's supporters demanded an investigation, clearly hoping that the state's vote could be reversed as the illegitimate result of a dastardly disinformation campaign. Howell, "visibly perturbated," initially kept quiet, but a week later, he not only admitted that he was the source, but proclaimed it with pride. He was keeping his constituents informed, Congressional policies of secrecy be damned. What did Congress have to hide, Howell wondered? Hostility to a free press? A desire to be independent of the people? Jonathan Arnold provided cover, boasting that he had written similar letters. He had a fresh one ready to send, he crowed, and would send more in the future. Only the people of Rhode Island could judge Howell. In early January, Howell left Philadelphia, his mission accomplished, suffering the "universal indignation" of his colleagues in Congress but hailed at home for his "meritorious service" in the "cause of freedom."[60]

—⁓—

With no idea what they were getting themselves into, the officers in the Highlands continued preparations to send their memorial to Congress.

Deciding they wanted the message delivered in person—the better to keep up the pressure, answer questions, and, if need be, negotiate over pension terms—the officers chose three men to represent them: Major General Alexander McDougall of New York, Colonel John Brooks of Massachusetts, and Colonel Matthias Ogden of New Jersey. [61]

McDougall, an experienced politician, military administrator, and businessman, was the unanimous choice to lead. Born in Scotland in 1732, McDougall's family migrated to New York when he was six and settled on Manhattan, where Alexander grew up on a dairy farm—only the island's southern tip was city—before hearing the call of the sea as a teenager and pursuing a salty life that saw him rise to become a shipmaster. McDougall commanded privateers during the French and Indian War, and afterwards he turned ship owner, merchant, and speculator in Hudson Valley land. He owned at least one slave, a young woman he gave to his second wife as a wedding present. McDougall bought the trappings of gentility—fine clothes, a snuff box, books, a College of New Jersey (Princeton) education for his sons—but he never lost the rough edge of life on the farm and at sea. [62]

An early radical, McDougall joined the New York Sons of Liberty. He specialized in enforcing the colonists' nonimportation agreements among weak-kneed merchants, and when New York had its own Tea Party in April 1774, he supervised the "Mohawks" dumping tea into the East River. McDougall won respect as a polemicist when he was twice jailed for libel, as a result of his broadside *To the Betrayed Inhabitants of the City and Colony of New-York*, which condemned the Quartering Act. ("In a Day when the Minions of Tyranny and Despotism in the Mother Country and the Colonies, are indefatigable in laying every Snare that their malevolent and corrupt Hearts can suggest, to enslave a free People," it began, like a movie trailer, and continued with similar verbal pyrotechnics.) Following Lexington and Concord, McDougall helped organize New York's Provincial Congress and began raising a regiment for the state's defense, which was brought into the Continental Army a year later. [63]

During the war, McDougall's body retained the muscular frame of his early years, but surviving portraits from the period show a middle-aged man with a hairline that is beginning to recede and jowls that are starting to droop. He looks at the viewer with a mixture of determination and liveliness expressed in a slight smile and clenched jaw. On meeting McDougall for the first time, John Adams described him as "talkative" with a "thorough Knowledge of Politicks" as well as a "very sensible man, and an open one," who "has none of the mean cunning which disgraces so many of my countrymen." McDougall's health, however, failed constantly, with bouts of rheumatism and "a Complaint of the Stone" (recurring kidney stones) rendering him unfit for a field command. Still, he was a capable administrator and oversaw the Highlands, including the construction of West Point.[64]

McDougall knew Philadelphia politics firsthand. In 1780 he traveled there to represent the generals lobbying Congress for better pay, and in 1781 he served as a delegate from New York, while keeping his military office, much to the annoyance of some congressmen. McDougall was equally suspicious of civilians. "Can the country expect Spartan virtue in her army," he once asked General Greene, "while the people are wallowing in all the luxury of Rome in her declining state?" From McDougall, the officers could count on a zealous representation, adroit politicking, and enough classical allusions to keep pace with the most educated lawyer.[65]

Ogden, twenty-eight, commanded the First Regiment of the New Jersey line. Born in Elizabethtown and raised in the same house as Aaron Burr (both had lost their parents early in life), Ogden was a student at the College of New Jersey (Princeton) when his buddy Burr convinced him to join the army encamped outside Boston in 1775. They arrived just in time to set out on the expedition against Canada, in which Ogden was later wounded in a battle outside Quebec City. Recovering, he continued to serve in the Continental Army, rising to colonel in 1777.[66]

Five years later, Ogden helped manage the spy networks operating in New York City. On learning that King George's seventeen-year-old son, William Henry, a Royal Navy midshipman, was in the city and only lightly guarded when onshore, Ogden hatched a plan to kidnap the prince. Kidnapping enemy officers was a standard part of 18th-century warfare, and to bag a prince would be a major coup. Washington, impressed by Ogden's "spirit of enterprise," gave the go-ahead, but before the plan could move forward—it called for forty men rowing from New Jersey to Manhattan on a rainy night, landing secretly, breaking into William Henry's quarters, and possibly fighting their way out—British spies caught wind of the idea and Ogden called it off. Like many field officers, Ogden had spent his twenties in the army, and although he came from a prominent family, he knew the anxiety of their circumstances. [67]

Brooks, thirty-two, was a doctor and militia captain in Reading, Massachusetts, when the war came to his door. He was a minuteman who turned out to the shot heard 'round the world on April 19, 1775, and led his fellow citizens in sniping the British retreat to Boston. Brooks again saw action at Bunker Hill, and after he was incorporated into the Continental Army in 1776, he became a battlefield commander surrounded by smoke at the major engagements in the Northeast: White Plains, Fort Stanwix, Freeman's Farm, and Bemis Heights. Brooks was also at Valley Forge and witnessed the shivering starvation of his men. [68]

Colonel Brooks later took on administrative responsibilities, first as adjutant to General Charles Lee, and then in the inspector general department. In 1782, Brooks was back in the field, commanding the Seventh Massachusetts, whose grievance report threatened resignation should Congress "by a tedious procrastination evade the justness of our claims." Brooks already knew tedious procrastination: he represented the Massachusetts line to the state legislature in Boston earlier in the year. Brooks was married before the war and already had two children, with a third on the way as he set off for Philadelphia. When the officers complained about how much they'd risked and how much their families had suffered by their absence, he could offer his own life as testimony.[69]

With their representatives chosen and the memorial finalized and signed, the officers' committee delivered its charge to McDougall, Ogden, and Brooks. "We wish you to inforce our Address in the most modest terms—yet in that steady manner that is expressive of the character of Officers, and the justice our requisitions demand," the instructions read. The emphasis on modesty cut against the urge for spiritedness found in the grievances. The officers, ambivalent about the proper tone, still had not decided how aggressive they should be toward Congress. The problem would flare up anew as Congress took its time responding.[70]

The officers had one last piece of business before McDougall, Ogden, and Brooks could mount their horses for Philadelphia: how to pay for the trip? The officers took up a collection, but because they were so short of funds—that was the whole point of the memorial!—it took more than three weeks to get the money together. Finally, on December 21 the general and two colonels departed the cantonment, the officers' futures as civilians resting with how Congress reacted to their spirited, but respectful, appeal.[71]

General Washington understood the mood of his men, and he feared what might happen if they didn't like Congress's response. Back in the summer, Washington had given the Massachusetts line his blessing to meet; then, he stayed out of their deliberations. But as the officers passed the hat for the delegation's travels, Washington wrote ahead to Philadelphia, sending a letter to Virginia delegate Joseph Jones, a friend from Fredericksburg, to let Congress know what was coming.[72]

"The temper of the Army is much soured," Washington wrote, "and has become more irritable than at any period since the commencement of the War." Washington had decided against returning to Mount Vernon for the winter, though he longed to see its majestic view of the Potomac, because he dared not leave the army in its current state. Washington reported that many officers had been planning to resign, but instead channeled their discontent into the memorial, giving Congress one more chance to make good. He urged Jones to pursue "soothing measures" for the officers. It was the officers who clamped down on the ordinary soldiers' anger, and it was the officers who "quelled, at the hazard of their lives, very dangerous Mutinies." Without them, Washington warned, "I know not what the consequences may be."[73]

FOUR

The Delegation to Philadelphia

After a wintry week on the road, McDougall, Ogden, and Brooks dismounted their horses in Philadelphia on December 29. As they moved into the Indian Queen tavern on Fourth Street, between Market and Chestnut, the officers discovered that the snow wasn't the only adverse condition they'd have to plow through. With Rhode Island intransigent on the impost and Virginia a surprising negative, other states, whose approval was contingent on unanimous adoption of the amendment, wavered. The officers plunged ahead anyway. They had no choice.[1]

Congress was adjourned for the New Year, but McDougall, Ogden, and Brooks got to work lobbying the financier and delegates alike. During meals and meetings, at breakfast and through the long night, with friends and allies and enemies and opponents, the officers pressed their case to make sure, as McDougall reported to General Knox, that "Minds might be fully possessed of the Nature and importance of the Subject, of our errand."[2]

Nationalists already had their minds attuned to McDougall's subject. James Madison, an unusually long-serving delegate from Virginia who was beginning his third year in Congress, welcomed the delegation. "I am told [the petitions] breathe a proper spirit and are full of good sense," he shared with a fellow Virginian. Madison, a thirty-one-year-old lawyer, was a quiet, canny politician and perceptive chronicler of debates. Though a nationalist generally, he seldom wandered far from the interests of his home state. But on the impost, he agreed with Virginia's original stance, and hoped that the officers' memorial might help bring the measure back to life.[3]

Gouverneur Morris was more effusive in sharing news of the officers' delegation. Writing on New Year's Day to Matthew Ridley, a colonial agent in France, Morris sensed a providential opportunity. "All Things says St Paul work together for Good to those who fear the Lord," he puffed. "I shall not be sorry to see some Things which may draw forth general Attention to our Affairs."[4]

Writing that same day to John Jay, also in France, Morris was even bolder. He assured Jay that the army was stable. But there was no money. Even if Congress would promise to pay the army, Morris lamented, there was no means to raise the revenue that would put actual coins in the hands of actual soldiers. Pension payments for officers were also doubtful. Morris then switched to a cipher, used to conceal sensitive information from the notoriously peeking eyes of French postmasters, to deliver his next lines. "The army have swords in their hands," he wrote. "You know enough of the history of mankind to know much more than I have said and possibly much more than they themselves yet think of." There was no crisis yet. But it was coming. "I am glad to see Things in their present Train," Morris divulged, switching out of the cipher. "Depend on it good will arise from the Situation to which we are hastening."[5]

Morris's writing was often vivid, sometimes sensational, but here he descended into the obscene—smiling at a revolt in the army. A civilian with no military experience, Morris, for all his sophistication, didn't grasp what made the army tick. Officers were steeped in American liberty and suffused in notions of honor. For them to transgress civilian authority and risk the Revolution? No good could come of it. Morris's lurid lines were fantasy, the product of exhaustion at work and New Year's cheer more than a well thought-out plan. Jay was one of Morris's oldest friends, from their days as young gentlemen in New York, and though Jay was considerably more straightlaced than his rakish pal, he enjoyed Morris's ribald antics. Even if Morris's letter wasn't meant in earnest, it was still reckless. He should have kept his pen out of the ink.[6]

Congress was back in session on January 6; McDougall, Ogden, and Brooks entered the Assembly Room of the Pennsylvania State-house and officially presented their memorial. The delegates were impressed by the gravity of the officers' situation, and as a "mark of the important light in which the memorial was viewed," Congress appointed a grand committee comprised of one member from each state. The grand committee met that night at six o'clock, and achieved the important result of scheduling another meeting, with Robert Morris, the next morning.[7]

Morris confirmed that the officers' hopes were indeed grim. The country had no money to pay them. Not present pay, not back pay, not pensions. Morris further warned the committee against making promises it couldn't keep, and in any event, it was unwise to let the army think that their memorial had worked. Morris didn't want anyone else following their example, thinking they could persuade Congress or his office into paying.[8]

At the same time, Morris revealed that he had been working on the problem, though he wasn't ready to clue Congress in on the details. The committee would have to trust him. The meeting then broke down as, according to Madison, "Much loose conversation passed on the critical state of things, the defect of a permanent revenue, & the consequences to be apprehended from a disappointment of the mission from the army."[9]

"Trust me—I have a plan . . . but I can't tell you," sounded fishy, but Morris really did have a plan to leverage the Dutch loan, whose proceeds would not be available for some time, into something with more immediate utility. In the fall, he had sent a ship to Havana, partly as a private venture and partly to sell $200,000 worth of bills of exchange against the forthcoming Dutch loan, in effect using one borrowed asset to finance another. The outcome was still uncertain, however. It was January and there was no news from Havana.[10]

Two days later, Morris interrupted Congress's debate with another cryptic message. He wanted a committee to advise him on a confidential matter. Morris said no more, but he had a bombshell to drop and he wanted it to explode quietly. Congress balked at appointing a committee without knowing the topic they were to discuss, and they took umbrage at the superintendent's opinion of their ability to keep a secret, but they did eventually appoint a committee. After the day's session, the committee met Morris. The news was devastating. The United States had overdrawn its loan from France, and not by a little, either. It was 3.5 million livres to the bad, roughly $650,000.[11]

Morris doubted France would do anything rash, like cut off its insolvent ally. After all, he reasoned, France would not want to see the United States defeated if the war should continue in the spring. To stop spending was also unthinkable. The only choice, Morris concluded, was to overdraw the loan, to go further into debt, beyond even the sizable credit France had already extended. One congressman objected, saying that this was a shabby way for the United States to treat a friend. Morris said it was the only way. Otherwise, "our credit would be stabbed abroad and the public service wrecked at home." The United States was a deadbeat, overdrawing its line of credit and abusing its friends, paying off debt by taking on more. It was only a matter of time before everyone knew.[12]

That same day, January 9, McDougall reported to General Knox for the first time since his arrival in Philadelphia. The congressmen were "rather pleased than otherwise" with their memorial, he observed. But, the money. "*The great difficulty,*" he wrote, "is Cash for present Wants" and a source of funds for the future, meaning pensions. McDougall had taken the pulse of Congress, and despite the "*great* Majority" being "seriously disposed to do everything in their power" to help, at least six states would never go along. New York and Massachusetts would probably promise to pay but wouldn't follow through and collect the money for a pension, McDougall estimated, while New Hampshire, Rhode Island, Connecticut, and New Jersey would not "pass even vague Laws to recognize those debts."[13]

McDougall then mentioned an idea picked up in his informal conversations. What if, he asked Knox, the army advocated not only the end—pay and pensions—but also the means to secure revenue? What if the army joined with other groups in a similar situation? "What if," McDougall wrote, "it should be proposed to unite the influence of Congress with that of the Army and the public Creditors to obtain permanent funds for the United States which will promise most ultimate Security to the Army?" McDougall was floating a strategy similar to Robert Morris's advice to the public creditors when he stopped interest payments: organize yourselves and send a message to Congress and the states.[14]

The next evening, in weather of "extreme badness," the grand committee again convened with Morris at the statehouse for a meeting with the army delegation. McDougall, suffering from a bout of rheumatism, had Ogden and Brooks ask if the committee could gather instead at his lodgings in the Indian Queen tavern, located two blocks from the statehouse. One congressman objected, however, to a grand committee waiting on the officers' delegation. It was highly irregular and "derogatory from the respect due to themselves." They declined McDougall's request—it was cold outside and the weather had prevented several members from coming, anyway—and rescheduled for the following Monday. What was another weekend in Philadelphia for the officers when tramping two blocks in the snow would derogate the dignity of Congress?[15]

In the Highlands, the officers awaited the result of their memorial, and in the meantime, they kept up their drills and discipline. General Washington made sure of it. "I was hurt yesterday at the appearance of the Detachment under your Command," Washington rapped one major who fell short of the mark. "Dirt & Trash . . . of every denomination, was so liberally strewed—even upon your Parade, and immediately before the Doors of your Hutts; that it was difficult to avoid the filth" (and by "filth" he didn't mean dirt or garbage but a certain foulness of human origin). For Washington, the commanding officer made the difference between "a fine Regiment, and an indifferent one." It was the officer, Washington pronounced, who gave "health, comfort, and a Military pride to their Men; which fires and fits them for every thing great and noble."[16]

When the officers weren't on duty, domestic thoughts preoccupied their minds. Some officers did more than pine. They left camp for home, not deserting but on furlough, though more than a few overstayed their approved leave, and invited Washington's wrath. Winter was not vacation time for a soldier, the general instructed. Some officers might feel "there was nothing or at least very little to be done in Winter Quarters," but Washington would have none of it. "For my own part, I must confess, I have never found it so, but on the contrary have frequently had as much business to be done by myself & Aids in that Season, as in any part of the Campaign."[17]

Timothy Pickering, the quartermaster general, felt Washington's lashing tongue in December and hustled back to the Highlands in January after a six-week absence to care for his wife, Rebecca, and their three boys in Philadelphia. He returned just in time to get arrested for debt, the result of his official duties buying supplies with Congress's deteriorated credit. One night in Newburgh, after hosting the Washingtons and General Edward Hand and his wife, Katherine, Pickering was accosted by the Ulster County sheriff, who rode up and served a warrant in front of everyone. A local merchant had bought up army certificates at a steep discount expressly to sue Pickering, whose signature was on all the IOUs, for the full value. "None but men who deserve worse names than I choose to give them would bring such vexatious suits," Pickering told his wife. The suit was legal, however, because although Congress had urged the states to enact laws protecting army officers in the discharge of their official duties, New York never complied. "With equal justice upwards of ten thousand such suits might be brought against me," Pickering admitted.[18]

Thirty-seven in the winter of 1782 to 1783, Pickering was the son of a deacon from a well-established family in Salem, Massachusetts. Despite the advantages of family and a Harvard education, Pickering's talents were often overwhelmed by his obstreperous personality and indecisiveness in executing the demands of his post. Almost six feet tall, but gangly and prematurely balding, Pickering was a late bloomer socially, marrying at the age of thirty in the midst of the Revolutionary upheaval that had cleared out Salem's old elite and opened a lane for Pickering to enter into politics, secure a judgeship, and gain a command in the militia.[19]

When the war came, Pickering hesitated to fight, not from cowardice so much as from moderation and a belief that somehow he could espouse radical opinions without action. When Pickering reluctantly marched to war in December 1776, Rebecca was six months pregnant with their first child. The next spring he accepted a position on Washington's staff, against Rebecca's wishes, then moved on to the Board of War later in the year. Thanks to his attempts to choke graft out of army supply, Pickering was appointed quartermaster general in 1780, but whatever the department gained from honest dealing, it lost in efficiency as Pickering could not keep up with the workload and refused to ask for help. While on the Board of War, Pickering relocated his family to a farm outside Philadelphia and began planning a new future as a merchant, if only he could leave the army with a pension for his service.[20]

Unhappy to be in Newburgh, the prickly quartermaster relieved the day's cares by penning sweet letters to his wife. "By what names of endearment, my Dear Beckey, shall I address thee?" he began one on a cold Sunday night. "My faithful friend! My soft and sweet companion! My pride! My present joy! My future consolation! My fond, my affectionate wife! How shall I love thee sufficiently? How shall I find words to express that love? Dear are thou to me as my own life: more tenderly than ever do I love thee." In the stillness of his Newburgh house, he imagined her coming to join him. "I have indeed several times figured to myself the sleigh coming down the hill, and you entering my quarters, all fresh and blooming as May." But it was all reverie.[21]

As the winter dragged on, Pickering ruminated on the future, writing dear Beckey about finding a new house, something away from "traders with their crowds of customers" so they could enjoy "tranquility, better water, better air, and perhaps have a cheaper rent." The quartermaster's prospects were uncertain. He asked his brother for help. "Are there any offices in the state which I may obtain, which will give me more than a scanty subsistence? Or shall I, when the war ends, and my best years are wasted, be driven 'to seek my fortune' elsewhere?"[22]

Across Newburgh in the Hasbrouck House, Washington had the good fortune to be joined by Martha in December, as was her custom throughout the war during winter quarters and beyond. In fact, according to one estimate, Martha spent between fifty-two and fifty-four of the war's 103 months with her husband or nearby. She eased the general's cares and brought a splash of genteel sociability to the drabness of daily life, hosting visitors and making the rounds to visit other officers and their wives.[23]

General Washington's other recreation was managing Mount Vernon from afar, and over the winter he dispatched long, exacting letters to his cousin Lund Washington, the plantation's manager, who knew to send detailed responses. Washington wanted to know everything: the yields of his wheat and corn crops; updates on horse sales; the status of stable repairs; the availability of barrels; the prospects for his grapevines, yams, and apple trees; and, of course, the progress of land deals, especially for a coveted parcel between the Dogue and Little Hunting Creeks. Washington also sent along precise instructions for planting "Shrubs & ornamental & curious trees," which he wouldn't see for some time if the war continued. The general's letters reveal his frequent annoyance at not being on hand to supervise personally. But he found the exercise deeply meaningful. He transported himself to Virginia, momentarily forgetting the weighty responsibilities in New York.[24]

Washington was a wealthy man, but he was rich in land and had limited liquid assets. He enjoyed expensive living and loved to shop. Like his officers, then, he worried about his finances. "I want to know before I come home (as I shall come home with empty pockets whenever Peace shall take place) how Affairs stand with me—& what my dependence is," he lectured Cousin Lund. Any man with a commission might have said the same.[25]

At the other end of the hierarchy, young officers compounded their financial worries with anxieties about their status. Everyone knew Washington was a gentleman, but the junior officers couldn't be so sure of how they'd be perceived out of uniform. Some officers had served since 1775, joining up as teenagers. Now in their late twenties and knowing little of the life of an independent man, they were ambivalent about letting go of the army, the institution that had been their home for eight years.[26]

Benjamin Gilbert, a twenty-seven-year-old lieutenant from Brookfield in Western Massachusetts, lived out those anxieties. At nineteen, Gilbert had turned out for Lexington and Concord, serving as a militia fifer. He'd been in the army ever since, rising from an enlisted man to receive a commission and lead a light infantry unit. In September 1782, Gilbert opened a shocking letter: Patience Converse, his *amour* from a recent furlough home, was pregnant and said he was the father. Converse was the daughter of a well-respected family, and the community expected the couple to marry. Gilbert didn't want to. For the moment, army duty was his salvation, a respectable reason not to form a "matrimonial coalescence," as he put it.[27]

At the same time, Gilbert fretted about his financial prospects. He wanted out of Brookfield. Because of Converse's pregnancy "Scandal is such a prevalent evil" and the town was full of "excreable miscreants, who have made scurrility their Topical head of discourse." Instead, Gilbert eyed a move to New York, where he expected the legislature would approve the confiscation of Tory lands around Albany. Gilbert wanted in on a scheme to scoop up the land at a bargain price. What better spoil for a long-suffering officer to begin life fresh?[28]

Despite his problems, Gilbert enjoyed the diversions of camp life—drinking, dancing, carousing with his fellow officers, self-styled playboys all. "Doctor Finley, Lieut. Warren, and I went to Newburgh in the afternoon," Gilbert recorded in his diary, and "we acted the part of proper Helions all Night." Some entertainments were innocent. One night, Gilbert recalled, he and his friend Jonathan Wing "dined at his Excellencies." The next day, a gentleman visited the cantonment with his wife and three daughters and Gilbert and the boys "drank Tea in company with them" before, he said, "they came to my Hutt where we moved a number of Country Dances."[29]

More often, however, Gilbert's interest in the ladies was less wholesome. "We have established a Seraglio [brothel] at a place Vulgarly called Wyoma where we have super fine Kippen [prostitutes] Issued immediately on application," he bragged to a brother officer. "We draw on separate orders, I make my returns once a week and receive a full ration without giving a receipt for the same." Buying sex on credit—for Gilbert, being an officer had its perks.[30]

—⁂—

In Philadelphia, McDougall, Ogden, and Brooks finally had their audience with the grand committee on January 10. McDougall had recovered enough from his aching joints to walk to the statehouse,

Congress's honor now unthreatened by an unseasonable fieldtrip. McDougall spoke first. In a thick brogue disrupted by his habitual stutter, McDougall recited the officers' position. The whole army needed current pay and back pay, and the officers needed half pay pensions, although, he reiterated, they were willing to accept a lump sum payment instead.[31]

The general then narrated the history of the army's service—its achievements and hopes in the cause, its disappointments and misery in the face of so much ingratitude. McDougall assured the committee he was not exaggerating. The army was in "actual distress," and they feared the impending peace would not be a blessing but would curse them with invisibility to the public eye. Their cries for justice would also go unheard. Throughout his speech, the general used "very highly coloured expressions," according to Madison; McDougall himself recalled that "truth and decency were the only bounds" he observed. Brooks and Ogden followed in turn, each adding more examples of suffering, discontent, and anger. Ogden swore he would not go back to Newburgh if he were forced to carry a message of disappointment.[32]

When the officers finished, a congressman asked just how bad things would really be if the army were not paid something right away. The officers were too polite to ask if he had been listening. They answered that it was impossible to say for sure; then, they hinted darkly about observing "sequestered consultations" among the sergeants and some of the privates. They did not know of any plots in the offing, but a mutiny was possible. Enlisted men mutinied throughout the war, and the officers could always be counted on to put them down and reassert discipline. But maybe not this time. The "temper of the officers" was so sour that they might not act with their customary "vigor."[33]

Questioned further by the committee, McDougall, Brooks, and Ogden dilated on the officers' complaints. They hated having to punish soldiers severely for even minor infractions when Congress, the states, and the people got away with violating commitments to the army. The officers resented civilian government officials who, they claimed, were always paid on time and in full. A committee member pushed back, pointing out that civilian officials had to pay for their food and lodging from their salaries while the army kept them fed, clothed, dry, and warm. Still, the officers looked askance at civilians, living in "ease not to say affluence," who nonetheless refused to pay taxes to equip the men who defended their liberty. Finally, the officers took umbrage at the way civilians resented them for wanting half pay pensions. Congress had promised them half pay for life as part of their compensation. It was a reasonable recompense for men who had risked their lives in defense of their country and who, by giving everything they had to their country—their time, talent, and treasure, their bodies and souls—would be unlikely to find good employment after the war. Men who had lent only money to the cause expected a return on their investment, a reward for what they had risked. The officers said they wanted a similar annuity for their investment of "blood and service to the public." Instead, though, the officers complained, "their reward had been industriously and artfully stigmatized in many states with the name of pension."[34]

McDougall castigated the weakness of the current federation. The Revolution itself was in danger, he said, from the "debility and defects in the federal Govt. and the unwillingness of the States to cement & invigorate it." Madison noted the general made these remarks "with peculiar emphasis."[35]

If anyone disbelieved the danger of the moment, McDougall and Brooks removed all doubts. "The army were verging to that state which we are told will make a wise man mad," McDougall said. Brooks warned that "they did not reason or deliberate cooly on consequences, & therefore a disappointment might throw them blindly into extremities."[36]

Having said their piece, McDougall and the colonels departed. The grand committee then appointed a subcommittee to consult with Morris and draft a report on the army memorial that made recommendations for Congress. The grand committee also agreed to pay the delegation's expenses. Then, they adjourned for the night.[37]

Since arriving in Philadelphia, McDougall, Brooks, and Ogden had done their job as best they could. They politicked behind the scenes, presented their formal memorial to Congress, and made their case in person, with passion and purpose, to the grand committee and the superintendent of finance. They had shown their zeal for the Revolution and their nation while standing firm that there were some sacrifices it would be best not to ask them to make. In their meeting with the grand committee, the officers gave little indication of a plan to unite themselves with the nation's other creditors, although McDougall had made a special point of criticizing the government's inability to raise permanent revenues. He wanted to hear back from Knox first.

Robert and Gouverneur Morris saw the army's potential for playing a role in national politics more clearly. Around this time the Morrises drafted an analysis of the country's financial problems and possible solutions to assist the French minister in Philadelphia, Antoine César, Chevalier de La Luzerne, in lobbying his government to continue extending credit to the United States. The report called for reform of the Articles to give the central government more authority over the citizens and the states, compelling them to do things like actually pay their yearly tax requisition. The Morrises knew that was unrealistic. More promising, however, was uniting the country through financial interest via a funded debt, a favored part of Robert Morris's long-term plan. The new wrinkle was the "Clamors of the Army." "If the Army can be kept together in a respectable Situation, without the immediate Collection of heavy Taxes," the report predicted, "their Influence (joined to that of the other Public Creditors) will probably obtain Funds for the Public Debts."[38]

With a strategy coming together, the financier worked on getting money to the army, at least to give them a month's pay. On January 14, Morris asked the paymaster general, John Pierce, to prepare an estimate of just how much one month's pay would cost. The next day Morris received a letter from Nathanael Greene, commander of the Southern Army, then in South Carolina. Greene announced that the British had evacuated Charleston, and, because good news could never come unalloyed, he also informed Morris that he had already committed to giving his army two months' pay. If McDougall and the colonels found out, the result was easy to imagine. The officers' words still fresh in his mind, and Greene forcing the issue anyway, Morris met with the army memorial subcommittee and decided to advance the Northern Army one month's pay. It was a big risk. The French loan was still overdrawn. There was still no word on the mission to obtain money against the Dutch loan in Havana. Morris was gambling on French forbearance and good luck in Cuba. Morris called McDougall to his office on Friday, January 17, to share the good news that money was on the way to the army.

Morris planned to stretch out the payment over time, however. One month's pay meant being paid for one month's worth of service, not being paid once in the month of their service. Soldiers and noncommissioned officers would receive their money a half-dollar a week until they had received the equivalent of the salary owed them for January 1783. Officers had a choice: they could accept their salary in Morris's personal notes, or they could wait until after the soldiers had received all of their money to get specie.[39]

Morris had two reasons for structuring payment this way. McDougall and Brooks had suggested withholding pay from the enlisted men; a pocketful of coins and they would go wild—drunken, riotous wild. Besides, once the soldiers were fed, clothed, and sheltered, what more did they really need? Morris agreed. "Considering what Kind of Men usually fill up the Ranks of an army too much would be rather pernicious than useful," he wrote.[40]

The superintendent's second reason was less condescending, but even more depressing. The longer he could stall the payment, the more time for his Havana ship to come in. Morris expected grumbling from the soldiers, and he counted on the officers to sell their men on his plan. McDougall and Brooks agreed. On the other measures dear to the officers' hearts—back pay and half pay—Morris could only ask for more patience while he looked for the money.[41]

Morris had been an ally to the army delegation, meeting with them on their arrival in December and throughout the following weeks. His initial judgment, that the nation's finances did not permit current pay, much less back pay or pensions, was not wrong. Still, Morris was willing to take the risk to meet their needs, and for the moment, at least, they were placated.

Then, another disappointment. "This Day I received a Letter from his Excellency the Minister of France," Morris recorded in his diary, "the Contents of which I regret &c. &c." The contents were more than regrettable. They represented a new crisis. La Luzerne told Morris to stop overdrawing the loan. "I do not see Sir any other course to take in the present circumstance" La Luzerne wrote, "than for you to religiously abstain from negotiating a single bill" more.[42]

Without French credit, Morris's options were dwindling. There was the Havana mission (possible) or Congress could open a new line of permanent revenue, such as a new impost (possible, but difficult), and the states would agree to collect it (a long shot). France had not ruled out a loan for 1783, though abusing their credit was an interesting negotiating technique. Morris stood by his commitment to the army, however. Even when the estimate for one month's pay arrived at more than $250,000, he forged ahead. He also stood by General Greene's promises, although he resorted to an accounting trick to keep the two armies' pay in balance, calling part of the money one month's pay with the rest allocated to offset the value of rations not provided to the army. Morris was doing everything he could for the army, but temporary measures couldn't satisfy the officers forever.[43]

—m—

For the moment the officers in the Highlands quietly went about their duties, and there was little chance they would cause trouble while Congress's response was still expected. The enlisted men, however, were different. Their usual petty crimes—illegally selling wood, plundering "the Country people come to the huts with marketing," killing livestock, "stealing Fowles," and "using insulting language"— might explode into mutiny. Washington needed to keep them busy. When Dr. Israel Evans, a Presbyterian chaplain in the New Hampshire line, suggested that what the cantonment really needed was a large new building for sermons, meetings, and receptions—something really nice to complement the elegant huts—Washington jumped on the idea. And so began, in the dead of winter, a new construction project.[44]

Throughout January, the army, once more working like a colony of frigid beavers, cut trees, lugged logs, and shaped them into a handsome hall. (Unlike beavers, the men received rum for their work.) Sitting on a bluff above the frozen Hudson, the new building measured 110 by 30 feet, with ten windows on each long side. Atop the shingled roof sat a small cupola with a flagstaff for signaling nearby troops. Inside, the main hall featured wood floors and log benches that could be moved aside for dancing. Several hundred men could fit beneath the room's arched ceiling. A platform fashioned a pulpit for sermons (or impassioned speeches to save the republic). Two fireplaces provided heat. Extending from the main hall at either end were offices for court-martial proceedings and for the quartermaster and commissary corps and rooms for storage.[45]

Generals such as Washington and Heath called the new building, unimaginatively, the "New Building." On the other hand, officers uneasy about their status as gentlemen, like Pickering and Gilbert, preferred the more flamboyant "Temple of Virtue," possibly after the Roman Temple of Honor and Virtue, where the Senate had met to recall Cicero, also once acclaimed the "father of his country," from exile during the First Triumvirate. Another possible source of inspiration was Masonic literature, where "Temple of Virtue" appeared in 18th-century works such as *The Temple of Virtue, a Dream* and *The Temple of Virtue, a Masonic Ode*. The grander name made a grander statement about the officers and their values.[46]

Whatever its name, the Temple, or New Building, opened on February 6, the anniversary of the US alliance with France. Washington invited "all the Gentlemen of the Army and other Gentlemen & Ladies who can attend with convenience." To kick off the festivities, the general reviewed the troops at noon, then the army executed a *feu de joie*. Washington also issued a pardon for prisoners and directed the soldiers to receive an extra half-cup of rum—after the firing show. The ladies and gentlemen repaired inside to hear Reverend Evans preach, then they enjoyed a cold collation, a light meal of cold meats and wine. Pickering, the resident Debby Downer, wasn't impressed. "I have returned from the 'Temple of Virtue,'" he informed Rebecca that evening. "Alas! How little will it deserve the name? For how little virtue is there among mankind?" The party was dull, he assured her. "You have lost nothing by being absent."[47]

—⸙—

Back in Philadelphia, the grand committee on the officers' memorial was ready to report to Congress, on January 22, a month after McDougall, Brooks, and Ogden rode south from Newburgh. To deliver its report, the committee chose a delegate recently returned to civilian life after a long stint in the army, a delegate not shy about sharing his conviction that Congress needed greater power. His name was Alexander Hamilton. In his late twenties in 1783, Hamilton joined Congress as a delegate from New York in November, not long after the tenth anniversary of his arrival in America from St. Croix. Born in 1755 or 1757 on the island of Nevis in the West Indies, Hamilton's upbringing was one storm after another. He was born illegitimate to unmarried parents, and when he was a child his father ran off, his mother succumbed to yellow fever, his guardian committed suicide, and his vindictive half-brother grabbed all of their mother's estate. Hamilton's salvation was a real storm, a hurricane that swept through the Caribbean in 1772, which gave Hamilton his shot. An account of the tempest he wrote for the *Royal Danish American Gazette* caught the eyes of local notables, who took up a collection to send the boy, then clerking at a merchant house, for an education in America.[48]

Hamilton attended a prep school, then enrolled at King's College (Columbia) in New York City, just as the colonial protests crescendoed. Hamilton added his voice to the clamor, his speaking and writing style already confident, learned, and aggressive. In the wake of Lexington and Concord (1775), Hamilton and his college friends formed a militia company called the Corsicans, and the next year Hamilton received a captain's commission in the regular army, thanks to the assistance of Alexander McDougall and John Jay. Hamilton formed an artillery unit, and his men boomed their cannon amid the smoke of battle at White Plains (1776), Trenton (1776), and Princeton (1777).[49]

During the New Jersey campaign, Hamilton came to the attention of General Washington, who at the time needed a writer more than an artillery commander. An explosion of correspondence threatened to bury the commander in chief. According to Washington, his circumstances "call[ed] loudly for Aids that are ready Pen-Men." But he needed "Pen-Men" of a particular kind: intelligent aides whom he could trust to draft letters and explain his directives without supervision. "It is absolutely necessary," Washington explained, "for me to have person's that can think for me, as well as execute Orders." Hamilton excelled at both. He spent the bulk of the war at Washington's side as aide-de-camp, indispensable to Washington's success. But Hamilton chafed against being a subordinate. The tension never subsided.[50]

Following Yorktown, Hamilton left the army and moved to Albany, the home of his wife's politically connected family, the Schuylers. While scrambling to complete his education and join the bar, in 1782 Hamilton became one of Robert Morris's tax collectors, and then, at year's end, a delegate to Congress, Hamilton's first political office. Always opinionated, Hamilton was a thorough nationalist. He wanted greater powers for Congress and greater efficiency in Congress. Taxes should not be feared but collected; centralized power should not be shunned but embraced to unite the states and warn off foreign enemies. "An extreme jealousy of power is the attendant on all popular revolutions, and has seldom been without its evils," Hamilton wrote in a series of newspaper articles under the pseudonym "Continentalist." "It is to this source we are to trace many of the fatal mistakes, which have so deeply endangered the common cause; particularly that defect, which will be the object of these remarks, A WANT OF POWER IN CONGRESS."[51]

Hamilton was not a physically imposing man like Washington. A touch below average height and trim, Hamilton nevertheless attracted attention with his handsome face, deep blue eyes, and auburn hair, which he wore powdered gray. A sharp, even flamboyant dresser, Hamilton cut a dashing figure in the latest fashions. He was a determined man of restless energy and evident self-confidence. "When he entered a room," one contemporary observed "it was apparent, from the respectful attention of the company, that he was a distinguished person." As soon as Hamilton entered the Assembly Room, he became one of its most vocal members.[52]

With the grand committee's report in hand, Hamilton rose to present four resolutions. First, the report called on Congress to provide current pay, as the superintendent judged expedient. Second, the report addressed back pay and recommended the states take responsibility for pay owed for service up to August 1, 1780, with the nation responsible for service after that date. Third, the report tackled the problem of pay depreciation. The resolution called on Congress to secure its notes with tax revenue, although the language was mealy-mouthed and weaselly. It promised that "Congress will make every effort" to obtain from the states "substantial funds" adequate for paying the US debt "and will enter upon an immediate and full consideration of the nature of such funds and the most likely mode of obtaining them." In other words, Congress would continue asking the states for money and hope that this time would be different. Finally, the report recommended half pay for officers, with the officers to choose whether they wanted to wait for a half pay pension for life or receive a lump sum payment equal to half pay for a period of years. Sensing the number would prove controversial, Hamilton left the space blank for the moment.[53]

Congress planned to debate the army memorial report on January 24, but before they began, another note arrived from Robert Morris. True to the pattern of his recent missives, Morris had a bombshell to drop. He was resigning as superintendent of finance, effective May 31. The letter made a "deep & solemn impression on Congress," Madison observed. The assembled members knew Morris's talent. A replacement would be hard to find, and the mere suggestion that he intended to resign would unsettle credit markets. Congress voted to keep Morris's note secret. This time, it was Congress that wanted the news to explode quietly.[54]

Morris kept his own counsel, so it's hard to know if he really wanted to resign or if he was playing politics and attempting to startle Congress from its deliberative pace. The stress of office was punishing, Morris's credit was stretched thin on behalf of the country, and his personal business suffered without his full attention. At the same time, Morris knew he was indispensable and threatening to resign is part of the bureaucratic department head's playbook.

Morris's letter cited several reasons for his decision. Although he had helped Congress finance the war and made progress on improving the nation's finances, work he considered the "last essential Work of our glorious Revolution," recent events had placed him in a "Situation which becomes utterly insupportable." Debts were mounting, while the prospect of revenue to pay them kept falling. Perhaps thinking of the army, Morris concluded by declaring "I will never be the Minister of Injustice." In his diary, Morris expanded a bit on his motives, mentioning "the warmest Attachment to the United States"; respect for "the Honor of Congress"; dedication to the "principles of Justice"; compassion for the public creditors; and "a lively feeling of what is due to my own Character."[55]

Still, Morris was a skilled politician, and the long lead time to actually leaving office suggests he hoped to be talked out of his decision.

Morris's explanation of the May departure date, though murky, implied it was conditional. "If effectual Measures are not taken by that Period to make permanent Provision for the public Debts, of every Kind," Morris wrote of his May deadline, "Congress will be pleased to appoint some other Man to be Superintendant of their Finances." Morris might have planned to bring Congress to an ultimatum—*you need me more than I need you*—and hoped they wouldn't call his bluff. And if they did, Morris would be released from service and free to build his business. Rescuing the nation's finances would be someone else's responsibility—and someone else's blame. [56]

With Morris's resignation hanging in the air, Congress debated the army memorial. The first resolution, recommending current pay, sailed through unopposed. The second resolution, on back pay, stumbled over the precise date upon which responsibility for payment should be divided between the states and the nation, with the New England states objecting that they had already paid their lines for service after August 1. Hamilton proposed changing the date to December 31, 1780, and the measure moved forward. [57]

Then the debate ground to a halt as Congress turned to a resolution calling on Congress to obtain revenue from the states. Theodorick Bland, Jr., a Virginian and former colonel in the Light Dragoons, wanted to discuss whether revenue would be raised strictly according to the Articles of Confederation (called "constitutional means" in the debate) or by some other method. He wasn't against an extraconstitutional method, he explained. He just thought they should try constitutional means first. Having wandered away from the topic at hand and into the fundamental issue of the structure of the government, Congress adjourned. [58]

Debate resumed the next day, and Congress took a step backward, reopening the question of the proper date for dividing responsibility for back pay. Hamilton and other delegates had met with Morris, who nixed the compromise date of December 31, 1780. It would upset his accounting of the debt. Tedious wrangling followed, with Morris's authority vis-à-vis Congress as the backdrop, until the delegates agreed to reinstate August 1, 1780, just as the original report recommended. After even more tedious discussions (about the meaning of "general" in the resolution), Congress finally got to the pensions and the fight over how many years' pay the officers should receive as a lump sum conversion from the half pay for life they had been promised. Hamilton suggested six years. Congress voted no. Believing Congress wanted to be more generous, Bland suggested six and a half. Congress voted no. Recently arrived back in Philadelphia, Bland clearly misunderstood the depth of New England's opposition to pensions of any kind. Rather than continue throwing out numbers, Congress created yet another committee to report on the matter before closing their business for the week.[59]

Congress finished January with everyone's favorite topic: national finance. The resolutions offered by the grand committee surfaced the perennial questions about debt, revenue, taxes, and the myriad issues—practical and philosophical—raised by any discussion of debt, revenue, and taxes. What kinds of taxes? How much would be owed? Who would collect them? How would each state's fair share be determined? Given the mutual jealousies of the states—and their wariness of centralized power—sending the officers to their individual states to collect payment was mentioned. The financier opposed that idea. He deplored the estranging effect on the union that would follow if some creditors received payment from their states while other creditors of the same class received less or nothing from their states. The officers also generally opposed settling with their states for the same reason. Some states would pay pensions in full, others partially, and some, opposed to pensions, not at all.[60]

The debate fluctuated between mind-numbing detail (how much revenue would a salt tax raise?) to grand statements on the character of the American people and the purpose of government, with James Wilson of Pennsylvania, observing that Americans lacked one thing only, "a cheerful payment of taxes," while Arthur Lee of Virginia warned that "no one who had ever opened a page or read a line on the subject of liberty, could be insensible to the danger of surrendering the purse into the same hand which held the sword."[61]

On February 4, Congress received the report from the committee on officers' half pay commutation (that would be the subcommittee of the grand committee appointed January 10). A delegate recommended that a lump sum equal to five-and-a-half years of salary be offered in lieu of a pension for life. The motion lost. Then five years was proposed. The motion lost. Too low? They tried five-and-a-quarter years. The motion lost again. The men from Rhode Island and Connecticut explained that they would vote no to any number; they were bound by instructions from their states to oppose any officer pensions.[62]

Madison and Wilson grew frustrated. The reason the debate on pensions had been delayed and referred to a committee was to appease the objections of states such as Rhode Island and Connecticut, and now their congressmen felt themselves unable to act independently of their states no matter what Congress proposed. "If such a doctrine prevailed," Wilson charged, "the authority of the Confederacy was at an end." With the fate of the republic once more invoked, Congress set aside the pension debate, unresolved. The army delegation had privately asked their allies not to push for a final vote if victory was in doubt, since they hoped new delegates expected from Delaware and Maryland could break the deadlock. Congress set the matter aside, awaiting the new delegates.[63]

As the pension debate foundered, Colonel Brooks prepared to return to Newburgh to report on events in Philadelphia and to deliver one month's pay to the army. Colonel Ogden packed for a trip to his home state of New Jersey, which like New England was a stronghold of opposition to pensions, to lobby for a change of heart. McDougall and his weary bones stayed put in Philadelphia. On February 5, Morris finally informed the officers that the pay was ready, and a few days later Brooks set out for Newburgh with just over $20,000 in cash, drafts, and three kegs of specie. He also carried a small package for General

Washington sent by David Rittenhouse, a Philadelphia astronomer famous for his skill in making optical instruments.[64]

As the officers of the delegation prepared to go their separate ways, the goals of their mission were entangled in the politics of the day, with no easy way to meet their needs without also deciding on the nature of the national government, its relationship to the states, and, indeed, the purpose of the Revolution itself. Like it or not, whether they planned it or not, the officers could not have the army's needs met alone. At the moment, the greatest danger for the army lay not in having their complaints ignored. Everyone agreed that their suffering was painful, that their requests were, in principle, just. Rather, the danger was that Congress would send the officers to their individual states for satisfaction of their claims. Each state would handle the matter differently. Or, just as bad, Congress would agree to convert their life pensions to a lump sum and then never receive the revenue to make good on its promises. Worse still, the moment might change. Peace could arrive, and they could be ignored, after all.

FIVE

Rumors and Gossip

Rumors of peace swirled in Philadelphia in February 1783. Brought by letters carried by ships that sailed in December from the ports of Europe for the islands of the West Indies, the news drifted over the Atlantic and then across the Caribbean at the speed of wind-filled sails. On February 11, the chatter quickened in the City of Brotherly Love. Word from Baltimore, via St. Kitts, said that the last anyone had heard from London, an agreement was only days away.[1]

In fact, a preliminary treaty was already two months old. The peace commissioners in France settled the framework of terms on November 30, 1782, and five days later, at the opening of Parliament, King George III confirmed the agreement's existence. Seated on the throne and robed in royal splendor, he acknowledged that the colonies were now "free and independent states." The war was inching toward an end.[2]

The text of the king's speech hit Philadelphia on February 13. Congress was in session when the message arrived, and it "produced great joy in general," James Madison noted. Elias Boudinot, the body's president since November 1782, was ignoring the debate to work on some correspondence when he stopped short. "Since writing the last Sentence the King of England's Speech is arrived," he told Nathanael Greene before hurrying back to his official duties. Goose feather quills fluttered as the delegates wrote home to share the good news.[3]

Alexander Hamilton was worried, however. Once Britain reached an agreement with France, the next step would be a cessation of hostilities, and the army would be disbanded. But if the army were disbanded before Congress acted on the officers' memorial, then the states would likely take responsibility for making their officers whole, and the nationalists would lose one of their strongest arguments for a stronger central government.

Also, it wouldn't be good for the officers—or the country. Republican ideology held that when a war ended, the men at arms should leave the battlefield as soon as possible, lest they menace the freedom-loving populace with standing army tyranny. If the order to disband came before Congress acted on their memorial, then the officers would have to make a decision: go home empty-handed and risk humiliation or stay in the field and risk a crisis that would forever change, if not destroy, everything they had fought for in the Revolution.

Writing to New York governor George Clinton, Hamilton shared a rumor. Peace might not be a blessing but "the prelude of civil commotions of a more dangerous tendency" because, it was said, "the Army will not disband, till solid arrangements are made for doing it justice." Though Hamilton's days on the battlefield were over, he continued to fight in the political arena where he deployed the weapons of an 18th-century politician: strenuous argument in oratory, crafty letter writing, and well-placed gossip. Fearing that the Congressional herd would not move decisively, Hamilton, and his fellow nationalists, searched for a strategy to spur them to a gallop.[4]

—·—

Congress, though, preferred its ambling gait throughout February. After setting aside the officers' memorial early in the month, the delegates devoted their energy to national finance and finding a way to raise sufficient revenue to pay the nation's debts. After daily battles, Congress advanced a plan to test the viability of the Articles of Confederation's funding mechanism of using land values to determine quotas of contribution. The states were asked to survey their lands and report back by January 1, 1784. Congress then renewed debate on establishing additional methods of revenue raising, such as a new impost, modified to meet the dissenting states' objections.[5]

On February 18, Congress combined the two issues explicitly when John Rutledge, a South Carolina lawyer, and John Francis Mercer, a Virginia lawyer, proposed dedicating impost revenues first to paying the army and then, if any funds were left over, to paying other creditors. Rutledge argued that discriminating among creditors would make the bitter pill of new taxes less gagging to swallow since the army's "merits were superior to those of other Creditors." Nathaniel Gorham of Massachusetts countered that paying the army first would make the impost less popular, since the other public creditors would perceive (rightly) that they stood a lesser chance of being paid at all. With different classes of creditors divided against each other, he alleged, the new impost would suffer the same fate as the old impost.[6]

And so the argument unfolded into the next day. Pro: meeting the army's needs first was good politics and good republican principle. "Distinct & specific appropriations of distinct revenues," Arthur Lee of Virginia proclaimed, "was the only true System of finance, and was the practice of all other nations who were enlightened on this subject." Con: discrimination wasn't good policy or principle. Pennsylvania delegate Thomas FitzSimons said his mercantile neighbors would never support being second-class creditors, and without them, the impost would surely fail in his state. It's unlikely Lee would shed a tear in that case; he felt the state quota system would provide sufficient revenue once the British quit the scene.[7]

When it was his turn to speak, Hamilton railed against discrimination. Calling himself "a friend to the army as well as to the other Creditors," he condemned any measure that would pay one group of debt holders but not another, announcing he "could never assent to such a partial dispensation of Justice." Hamilton, his anger boiling over, denounced the whole idea of trying to accommodate Rhode Island and Virginia, since their stated objections were "ostensible" only. Their real objections? Selfish. Rhode Island, he charged, simply wanted to collect its own taxes on goods that moved through its ports to Connecticut, whose geography gave its inhabitants little choice but to import through Rhode Island. Opposition from Virginia, Hamilton sneered, arose because relatively few creditors to the Continental government lived in the state. An impost, he accused, would make Rhode Islanders less rich while Virginians wouldn't get rich enough.[8]

Hamilton was not alone in bringing rancor into the Assembly Room of the Pennsylvania Statehouse. The bitter frustration of Congress's debates leaps from the pages of Madison's notes, as delegates "reprobated" and "animadverted" on policies they found "obnoxious." Feelings ran high not only because of clashing personalities—Hamilton had trouble controlling his temper—but also because the congressmen represented states with clashing interests. Absent the forced unity of fighting a war, which held the nation together tenuously anyhow, the Articles of Confederation provided little prospect of resolving differences between the states. Oliver Wolcott, a Connecticut delegate, summarized the mire for his son. "The Vehement Demands for Justice, the Variety of Interest, Opinion and partial Considerations, prevailing in different States and Classes of People," he wrote, "proves but too clearly that much is yet to be done before Such Establishments will be made or will effectually Unite, Secure and render the People of this Country happy."[9]

The officers were caught in the middle, and Wolcott's comment that "much is yet to be done" wasn't comforting. But he was right. The officers' goals—pensions, pay, not going home in humiliation—could not be addressed without a source of funding, and no source of funding could be found unless the quota system sprang to life (sometime after the 1784 due date for surveys) or unless the Articles were amended to allow new taxes, which would inevitably be tied down in debate.

The nationalists in Philadelphia knew the officers' dilemma—and they knew how resolving it could serve their larger goals of a stronger, more unified central government. Throughout February, they reached out to their army contacts and urged closer cooperation. Three paths emerged, and if the nationalists and the officers walked together, they might jolt Congress and the states to action.

Gouverneur Morris urged the first path: the army should unite with the nation's other creditors and send the clear message that they all stood together in seeking payment from Congress not the states. Writing to General Knox in early February, Morris stressed the dangers of seeking payment from the states. "Separate Provision and no Provision are tantamount in my Idea," he wrote. Any promises made by the states—even laws enacted by the states—"they will repeal as soon as they find it expedient." He also advised Knox to be on the *qui vive* against any scheme to separate classes of creditors, even though the army might be favored. The state that would jilt one creditor, however noble the reason, would surely jilt another. "After a Peace," Morris continued, "they will wish to get rid of you and then they will see you starve rather than pay a Six Penny Tax." The "only wise mode" left to the army was to stick together with the other creditors and use their influence, while they still had influence, to lobby the states and "unremittantly to urge the Grant of general Funds." Morris closed with a martial flourish. "After you have carried the Post the public Creditors will garrison it for you."[10]

A few days later, Morris wrote to General Greene, commander of the Southern Army, which, although not directly included in the officers' memorial, was implicated in any settlement Congress might reach. Morris again warned against the peril of seeking payment from the states. It was, he said, a step on the "Road to Ruin" that if taken "would have divided them into thirteen different Parts" and "made it easy to elude the force of their applications." Here Morris was slippery. To Greene, he presented the matter as largely settled, a position already adopted by the officers' delegation and destined to "soon become the general Sentiment." He made no mention of his letter to Knox.[11]

Morris continued with another appeal to unify with other national creditors, not only for the good of the army, but the good of the nation. With the army standing shoulder to shoulder with bondholders "there can be little Doubt that such Revenue will be obtained," and everyone would end up with "a solid Security." Morris concluded emphatically. The states would never agree to payment "unless the army be united and determined in the Pursuit of it" alongside the other creditors. The only alternative, he wrote, was to pray for a miracle.[12]

The officers, however, hesitated to accept Morris's invitation to engage in open political combat. General Greene, stationed in Charleston, South Carolina, did not reply until April, and then it was mostly to complain and worry and pronounce himself resigned to whatever the outcome might be. "I have done my duty," he wrote, "and wait events."[13]

Closer to the action, Alexander McDougall and Matthias Ogden, members of the officers' delegation, believed it was wise to hedge their bets rather than going all in with the other creditors. Writing to Knox a day after Morris, they reported feeling squeezed, on the one side, by "the Zeal of a great number of the members of Congress to get Continental Funds" and on the other by the determination of a smaller number of congressmen who wanted to send the army to the states for payment. The officers' delegation demurred joining one side or the other, lest they antagonize one side or the other and delay or imperil the settlement of their accounts. McDougall and Ogden preferred a measure that both converted their pensions into a lump sum and established sufficient continental revenue to pay for it. Still, they were prepared for half measures. If Congress would only approve a lump sum, they would take it as a win, since it would establish the principle that they were owed a certain, concrete amount, an amount that was technically no longer a pension, thereby removing one of the objections to a settlement. If they had to go to the states, they would go to the states.[14]

General Knox likewise doubted Morris's "wise mode." The officers relished their role as warriors for the nation and not for their own states only, he told Morris. In camp, their favorite toasts were "a hoop to the barrel" and "cement to the union." But though they might be hoops and cement they were not politicians, and their needs, though serious, required a political solution. Knox counseled addressing the problem at its root. "You great men," he told Morris, ought to convoke a convention to reform the Articles of Confederation and "form a better constitution." Knox was right—in the long term. At the moment, however, it was a thoroughly unhelpful suggestion and evidence that the general was certainly no politician.[15]

A second path, pursued by several members of Congress whose identities were never specified, emerged as February wore on. In order to prevent a showdown with the army, these congressmen planned to introduce a motion pledging not to disband the army until its accounts were settled. Such a motion promised a face-saving solution for everyone. The army could relax. They would not be dismissed and forgotten with peace. Congress could relax. They would have more time to find a new source of revenue acceptable to the states without fear of the army rising up against them. Best of all, the motion would preserve Congress's authority; the army would stay in the field following orders.[16]

Knox, for one, heartily approved. It would, he told McDougall, "preclude the necessity of any thing on the part of the Army." Staying out of politics was the proper course, he said, the honorable course. "I consider the reputation of the American Army as one of the most immaculate things on earth," he wrote. "We should even suffer wrongs to the almost verge of toleration rather than sully it in the last degree."[17]

A third path opened sometime after the reports of peace arrived and developed alongside the proposed motion for Congress not to disband the army. As reported to Knox by Baron Friedrich Wilhelm von Steuben, "an expedient was proposed" by "persons who have the honor & dignity of the nation at heart & who wish to see the army receive the justice to which they are entitled." The expedient called for the army to wait until the peace was confirmed. Then, the army should write Congress a carefully worded letter, one expressing "their great confidence in the justice of Congress & of the People," reassuring Congress that "neither officers nor soldiers have the least doubt that their services will be recompensed," conceding that Congress needed more time, reminding Congress that "the distress of the army would be intolerable if they are obliged to enter into the class of Citizens in their present situation," and, finally, after that long list of respect and assurance and loyal obedience, the letter would "supplicate Congress & the people to continue their subsistence & emoluments" until "the necessary arrangements are made." Even with its cautious tone, the letter would be inflammatory, dangerously close to threatening American liberties with a standing army. Von Steuben told Knox the letter could only come from one man, the commander in chief: General Washington.[18]

All three paths—uniting with other creditors, Congress pledging not to disband, Washington writing to Congress—promised to lead to the officers' destination, where they would meet their long-lost back pay and embrace their long-sought pensions (or the lump sum equivalent). All three paths, however, would eventually have to go through General Washington, and although he had encouraged the original officers' memorial, mostly by allowing it to go forward under the direction of General Knox, he would have to be involved more actively this time. Gifted with a sharp political mind, Washington assiduously avoided entangling the army in civilian affairs. What role, if any, would he be willing to play now?

—ᴍ—

Hamilton wrote Washington to find out. The task was emotionally fraught. Though Hamilton had spent most of the war by Washington's side as aide-de-camp, they had fallen out almost exactly two years earlier.

One day in February 1781 when headquartered in a New Windsor farmhouse, Hamilton passed Washington while heading downstairs to deliver some papers to another staff officer, and the general asked to see him when the errand was done. On his way back, another officer caught Hamilton's attention for a moment at the top of the stairs. It seemed to him that Washington was fuming. "Col Hamilton," said Washington, "you have kept me waiting at the head of the stairs these ten minutes." Washington stiffened. "I must tell you Sir you treat me with disrespect." Hamilton didn't back down. "I am not conscious of it Sir," he replied, "but since you have thought it necessary to tell me so we part."[19]

Less than an hour after the staircase incident, Washington, cooled off, invited Hamilton to reconcile. He also had a temper. Both men had been up late the previous night working on the army's never-ending correspondence. Hamilton swatted away the olive branch. His tender sense of honor wouldn't allow it. "I am importuned by such friends as are privy to the affair, to listen to a reconciliation," he wrote his father-in-law, but he wouldn't budge. "My resolution is unalterable."[20]

Hamilton's anger toward Washington had been simmering for years. Although he had risen to real importance as an aide—no one was as gifted at anticipating Washington's views and acting on his behalf as Hamilton was—no one ever distinguished himself as another man's clerk. Hamilton craved a return to the field, where he had begun the war as captain of an artillery company, but every time he asked, Washington said no. Hamilton resented it, and a small slight opened a much deeper wound. Thanks to continued pestering and Washington's refusal to nurse a grudge, Hamilton finally did get a command, at Yorktown, where he led a nighttime bayonet attack against a British redoubt. Since returning to civilian life and entering politics, however, Hamilton was mostly silent toward the general. Until he scrawled "Sir" on February 13.[21]

Hamilton began the letter obliquely, recalling their former relationship but without warmth. "Flattering myself that your knowlege of me will induce you to receive the observations I make as dictated by a regard to the public good," he wrote, "I take the liberty to suggest to you my ideas on some matters of delicacy and importance." The nation's finances were worse than ever, Hamilton continued, and Congress was not up to the challenge of providing a remedy. "Unfortunately for us we are a body not governed by reason or foresight but by circumstances." Time was running out. If Congress failed to act, "a few months may open an embarrassing scene," namely, abandoning the army once the war ended, just as the officers feared.[22]

None of what Hamilton wrote so far was entirely new. The army's condition was the same as it was six weeks earlier when the officers' delegation left camp for Philadelphia. It was the same as it had been two years earlier during the winter of 1781 to 1782 following Yorktown: the war was winding down with promises coming due but little evidence from Congress that the promises would be kept. The king's speech, however, showed the day of decision could not be delayed much longer. It was no coincidence that Hamilton wrote Washington the same day the speech arrived in Philadelphia.

Having outlined the situation, Hamilton turned to action, telling Washington that "the claims of the army urged with moderation, but with firmness, may operate on those weak minds which are influenced by their apprehensions more than their judgments." The officers had already sent one memorial to Congress urging their claims with moderation and firmness, as both men knew. Implicitly, then, Hamilton asked Washington for something new, a new message that, he said, "may add weight to the applications of Congress to the several states." Hamilton anticipated the problem. A new message from the officers would stir up bad feelings. It would signal that the first memorial had failed or, at least, that their weeks of waiting were wasted, adding new fuel to their already smoldering resentment. "The difficulty will be to keep a complaining and suffering army within the bounds of moderation," Hamilton warned. "This Your Excellency's influence must effect."[23]

Hamilton recommended an indirect approach. He advised the general to let the officers' complaints crescendo so that their voices could be heard in Philadelphia. Washington should remain offstage, neither applauding nor discouraging them, but trusting "the intervention of confidential and prudent persons," meaning someone like Knox, *"to take the direction of them."* Washington would preserve his reputation for disinterestedness in case the whole thing went sideways and the officers got out of hand. "This will enable you in case of extremity to guide the torrent, and bring order, perhaps even good, out of confusion."[24]

Hamilton had no single plan in mind for Washington to execute. He was convinced the army must speak again in order for Congress to listen, and he gamed out the different possible scenarios, sensitive to how events could get out of control and careful to head off Washington's objections to plunging the army more deeply into politics. Hamilton never came out and directly asked Washington to write the army's message to Congress as envisioned in the expedient described by von Steuben. But Hamilton clearly wanted something more than a reprise of Washington's silent role in the first officers' memorial.

Knowing Washington would likely demur, Hamilton dropped a bit of gossip to cut off a retreat. "An idea is propagated in the army that delicacy carried to an extreme prevents your espousing its interests with sufficient warmth," Hamilton confided. It wasn't true, Hamilton wrote, but it was dangerous nonetheless because any doubts about Washington's command would hurt his ability to respond, "should any commotions unhappily ensue." Inaction, Hamilton implied, cleverly trying to box Washington in, wasn't safe. It would anger the army, providing fresh oxygen for inflamed passions.[25]

Hamilton's letter is one of the most misunderstood documents of the supposed Newburgh Conspiracy. It's been interpreted as an invitation for Washington to lead a coup or to rally political resistance to Congress, or to coach the general on how to deploy his prestige to advance the nationalists' program, or, most bizarrely, to warn Washington that Hamilton and the Morrises were about to foment an officers' mutiny that Washington should put down, the idea being that the nationalists, including Hamilton, wanted Congress scared but not actually overthrown. Hamilton biographer Ron Chernow puts it succinctly. "The letter," he writes, "shows Hamilton at his most devious, playing with combustible forces."[26]

The letter looks like the closest thing to a smoking gun—or Brown Bess musket—of true conspiracy we'll likely ever get. But in this case, the smoke is an obstruction, not a revelation. Since Hamilton's style in this letter is so cryptic, his reputation for intrigue substitutes for direct evidence and it becomes another example of his machinations. Hamilton was a schemer, and he played the often-nasty game of early republic politics vigorously. But the commonly held opinion that he was uniquely Machiavellian is overstated, a distortion passed down to us from the pungent commentary of rivals such as John Adams—who later in life excoriated Hamilton as a "Creature" who "hated every Man young or old, who stood in his Way"—and Thomas Jefferson, who as secretary of state couldn't believe President Washington shared Hamilton's views unless advanced age made the president vulnerable to manipulation. Though no innocent, Hamilton tended to act impulsively, self-destructively, and to blurt out things at the wrong moment, unlike Jefferson who practiced the dark political arts while cultivating the image of a mountaintop sage.[27]

The existence of a plan to ask Washington to write Congress on the army's behalf, previously overlooked by scholars, shows Hamilton's letter in a different light. Hamilton was feeling out Washington ever so gingerly to discover how far the general would be willing to go in leading the officers' charge into politics. Hamilton style was cryptic, then, because it was tentative. He prodded Washington with information about the nation's dire finances and the prevailing opinion in Congress. He poked Washington with gossip. He plied Washington with advice so he would be prepared for the worst. Ultimately, Hamilton's letter implied a challenge to the general: Would he commit himself, as commander in chief, to a political position? Or would he stand by and risk a more dangerous outcome?

Hamilton had come to believe that appeals to reason were insufficient. If the nation's finances, credit, and very future were to be rescued, every interested party, civilian and soldier alike, would have to make every appeal possible, to both the head and the heart, to move as much opposition as possible in both Congress and the states. Hamilton didn't give up on persuasion. From the statehouse floor he argued, often "strenuously," as Madison observed. But he believed the army was an invaluable ally, alternately emphasizing the justice of their claims and the danger of failure. [28]

Like other 18th-century politicians, Hamilton supplemented his public arguments with weapons less hidden, but not less effective. For example, gossip was a standard part of any politician's arsenal. While gathered in taverns and coffeehouses, swanning about at receptions, or reclining at table after dinner, politicians recounted events, whispered about opponents, and speculated about the future. For those with ears to hear, gossip unmasked threats to the republic, condemned the actions and character of enemies, and strategized a common path forward. More than idly moaning or shamefully abusing others, gossipers usually offered proof to substantiate their claims and the act of secret sharing galvanized political unity in the face of a perceived danger to good government. [29]

At the end of February, Hamilton returned to the story that Washington's popularity was sinking dangerously low, this time passing it to a group of delegates gathered for dinner at the Society Hill home of Pennsylvania delegate Thomas FitzSimons. According to Madison, Hamilton teamed with Pennsylvania congressman Richard Peters, a former commissioner of the Board of War, to report on the mood of the army. "It was certain," the two men reported, "that the army had secretly determined not to lay down their arms" until they were paid. Worse, the army planned to make a "public declaration to this effect," and it was prepared to turn its back on Congress and begin "subsisting itself." Washington's grip was loosening, Hamilton and Peters continued. "The Commander was already become extremely unpopular among almost all ranks from his known dislike to every unlawful proceeding." And it was no accident. "This unpopularity," they said, "was daily increasing & industriously promoted by many leading characters." Supposedly, some officers even wanted Washington removed.[30]

Apparently, Hamilton and Peters identified the man contemplated as Washington's replacement, and at first Madison recorded his name before having second thoughts and crossing it out so thoroughly that it is illegible. The line now reads "in order to substitute Genl.   as the conductor of their efforts to obtain justice." It might have said "Genl. Gates' expert hand as the conductor of their efforts to obtain justice," but as the editors of Madison's papers admit, that is only a guess based on two or three still-visible letters. Whoever the would-be usurper might have been, the message was clear: the army was dangerously angry, and Washington was dangerously weak.[31]

Hamilton then pivoted. Proceeding alone, he doubled back on much of what he and Peters had just shared with the group. Announcing that "he knew Genl. Washington intimately & perfectly," Hamilton granted that the general's "extreme reserve, mixed sometimes with a degree of asperity of temper both of which were said to have increased of late, had contributed to the decline of his popularity." Curiously, Hamilton's description of Washington's faults—coldness, irritability, lower-than-expected popularity—echoed his own criticism of Washington following their staircase falling-out. On that occasion he had told his father-in-law that "for three years past I have felt no friendship for him and, professed none" and bragged to a friend that he would make Washington "for once at least repent his ill-humour."[32]

Whatever drama was playing out in Hamilton's psyche, his message to the congressmen at FitzSimons's house was clear: count on Washington to handle any trouble. "His virtue his patriotism & his firmness would it might be depended upon never yield to any dishonorable or disloyal plans into which he might be called," Hamilton assured his colleagues. Rather than allow such a travesty, Washington "would sooner suffer himself to be cut into pieces." Hamilton then mentioned his February 13 letter to Washington, and assured everyone that the general was ready for whatever challenge might come.[33]

The gossip that night at the FitzSimons' house was certainly frightening. It was unsettling to hear that the army was on the verge of rebellion and that a putsch against Washington was even a fleeting thought. Hamilton and Peters aimed to monger fears about the army in order to influence the debate in Congress.

At the same time, gossip about the army refusing to disband was commonplace by the end of February. Throughout the winter the idea grew from whispers to hints to rumors to stories to news to testimonies to the obvious, rock-solid conventional wisdom. Delegates talked about it freely, even casually, suggesting that they didn't take the threat literally. After all, to contemplate mutiny is tantamount to doing it, and if anyone believed the army really was on the verge of refusing orders, then the Revolution had already ended in a military despotism as all right-thinking republicans always feared. Instead, delegates wrote about the army's sour mood as if it were a bad storm or an ugly case of the gout. Painful. Worrisome. Something to remedy. But not an existential threat to liberty. The story about Washington's sinking reputation was new, but even there Hamilton provided reassurance. Thanks to his intervention, Washington could be relied on to save the day.

In the Revolutionary era, gossip had another function still: cementing bonds among the gossipers. Networks of information sharing formed so-called "gossip communities" that not only passed along intelligence about common enemies, but also reinforced members' in-group status. Together they puzzled out secrets, and unmasked plots, and in the process built a foundation of shared assumptions that was imaginary, but sturdy, and gave structure to how events were interpreted. [34]

In the end, Hamilton's gossip about Washington told a palatable tale. Yes, the army was dangerous—as all armies were in the republican mental universe—but because Washington was virtuous and alert, as good republicans must be when their liberties are at stake—he would suppress any trouble that might arise. As a result, Hamilton and other nationalists could push as hard as they needed to. They could argue as strenuously as possible and forge alliances with every interest group possible—including the army—and still not cross the line into despotism. Hamilton's message: full speed ahead and don't worry about the army.

Hamilton was certainly involved with all three paths laid out for the army's officers. It's hard to believe he didn't coordinate with Gouverneur Morris or that he wasn't one of Baron von Steuben's unnamed "persons who have the honor & dignity of the nation at heart." Hamilton, though, offered not so much a distinct plan as a method—pull every lever possible—and an attitude—aggressive, with a high tolerance for risk so that good might come out of an increasingly dire situation.

—m—

While Hamilton, Gouverneur Morris, and others expended enormous energy strategizing the army's role in the day's political debates, the officers still hadn't given up on Congress. Crafty expedients and clever political tactics wouldn't be necessary if Congress answered the officers' memorial with salutary measures. That path—the most direct path—remained open and on February 25, Congress resumed debate on the officers' pensions.

Straight off, bad news. John Taylor Gilman, from die-hard anti-pension New Hampshire, motioned to be done with the matter and send the officers to their states, with the amount each state paid to its officers credited toward its annual quota. Brought to a vote, the motion was defeated, for the moment.[35]

The next day, Congress reconsidered the proposal to convert the officers' half pay for life pensions to a single lump sum. Earlier in the month, it had been impossible to reach agreement on how many years of half pay should be lumped together, with six and six and one half considered too many. Hamilton moved for five-and-a-half years. Still too many. Congress voted no. Nathaniel Gorham, a no at five and a half, suggested five. That was the number. With Gorham's vote, Massachusetts approved, and the motion carried. The officers would receive the equivalent of five years' salary, if their state line approved the conversion.[36]

It was progress, but it still only settled the number of years used to calculate the amount due each officer. It said nothing about the source of the funds: the states or the central government. The Connecticut delegation brought back the motion to send the officers to their states. The debate wasn't any more congenial. Mercer sneered that national funding of debts would "establish & perpetuate a monied interest" that would outstrip the landed interest, virtuous men all, and "resort to places of luxury & splendor, and by their example & influence, become dangerous to our republican constitutions." Madison, frustrated, told his fellow Virginian to stop it with the talk of "administering poison to our republican constitutions"; a debt was a debt and it would have to be paid. When the motion came back to a vote the next day, February 28, it was defeated, with only Connecticut signaling assent and every other state apparently willing to risk poisoning the republic.[37]

Congress then voted on the commutation resolution as a whole. At last, good news for the officers: it passed! Seven states said, "aye!" But not so fast. A question arose about whether the commutation was a new appropriation, which, according the Articles of Confederation, required a supermajority of nine. After some discussion, Congress decided nine was probably the right answer. But that just raised another question: how many votes, seven or nine, were needed to determine how many votes, seven or nine, a particular measure needed to pass? The delegates argued for a while until they realized the point was moot. "Fortunately, on the case in question," Madison wrote, "there were 9 States of opinion that nine were requisite, so the difficulty was got over for the present." That may have resolved the head-throbbing question of how many votes were needed to decide how many votes were needed to decide something, but it meant the officers didn't have enough votes to approve the conversion of their pensions. [38]

The pension conversation stalling in Congress compounded failure on another front. The plan to have Congress direct the army not to disband until paid had been rejected without even coming to the floor. As McDougall reported to Knox on February 27, it was "declined, for fear the states would consider it as a design in Congress to Establish a Force to awe the states." Worse still, the suggestion fanned the ever-present suspicion of the authority of a national government and its army. "The fears of Congress are awake," McDougall lamented. He feared Congress would fend off a refusal to disband not by giving in and paying, but by hitting back and attempting "to split the Army into *detachments to prevent their being formidable.*" That would save Congress from the people's wrath, putting Congress on the people's side of liberty against the would-be army tyrants. At best, the officers would be sent to the states, which would force them "to commute for a trifle." [39]

Gouverneur Morris was similarly glum. He complained to Knox at the end of February that he had "three Months more of hopeless Slavery to encounter in this Office." Morris rejected Knox's suggestion of the "great men" calling a constitutional convention. "It is not in them to conceive great nor to pursue just Ideas," he wrote. "Nature sparing in good Gifts has been prodigal of Littleness to them." Morris had no plans to offer, no strategy to discuss, only gloom. "I almost despair of making them act with Desperation unless they should be plunged into a Situation which neither you nor I would wish for," he continued. "There is a Callosity of Soul about them which must be seen to be conceived of." [40]

McDougall and Morris sounded desperate, Morris said he was desperate, and conditions were desperate. In spite of his melancholia, McDougall soldiered on. He joined with others, possibly Gouverneur Morris, to work the delegates over one more time. McDougall had counted the votes and although a commutation of pensions was not promising, it was still close. If he could just find a couple of votes.

McDougall targeted Eliphalet Dyer of Connecticut, a sixty-one-year-old lawyer from north of New London who was exhausted by his service in Philadelphia, where, he confided to a friend, "our prospects are general Confusion, Clamour & tumult & intestine broils." Connecticut's other delegate, Oliver Wolcott, had come around to vote yes on commutation, leaving the state's vote divided. Meanwhile, Delaware's representatives had still not turned up (from all the way across the Delaware River). If McDougall could get Dyer to change his mind, and if Delaware's delegation voted yes, and if no other states defected—that's a lot of ifs but the officers still might get their money from Congress.[41]

In the event that the Congressional dominos didn't fall true, however, the army might have to send a new memorial to Philadelphia, but whether the message would come from the commander in chief's pen was still unknown as February turned to March. With no word from Washington, Hamilton grew anxious. A ship carrying news of an armistice was expected daily. In fact, the ship was the *George Washington* and it was then surging through the waves of the Atlantic for Philadelphia, sure to precipitate the final showdown on disbanding.

A final if: if General Washington declined, might the officers go ahead without him? And write a new letter on their own?

SIX

The Anonymous Letter

In mid-February Colonel Brooks handed General Washington his eagerly anticipated shipment from David Rittenhouse in Philadelphia. It didn't have anything to do with the officers' problems. Rather, it was to alleviate a health condition that had worsened during the war, a condition that, while easily treatable today, required the attention of a skilled specialist in the 18th century. The problem wasn't Washington's teeth. He'd asked Lund Washington to send those from Mount Vernon in December, when he told his cousin to rummage through the desk in his study where he swore he'd left them. No, General Washington's eyesight was going, the result of age, stress, and extensive close work reading and writing. The package contained a pair of glasses. Washington was pleased. "The Spectacles suit my Eyes extremely well," he told Rittenhouse.[1]

As Washington adjusted to his new reading glasses, he received a pressing letter from his friend and delegate to Congress, Joseph Jones. A fifty-six-year-old planter from Fredericksburg, Jones was a fixture in Virginia politics, a close associate of James Madison, and the uncle of James Monroe. Jones rehearsed the tedious business of establishing a national source of revenue and then asked Washington for patience. The apparent lethargy of Congress was not the result of hostility to the army. It was simply the way legislatures worked, especially this legislature governed by the Articles of Confederation.[2]

Well aware that delay might be seen as denial, Jones echoed Hamilton's prior warning about the temper of the army. "Reports are freely circulated here," Jones wrote, "that there are dangerous combinations in the Army, and within a few days past it has been said, they are about to declare, they will not disband untill their demands are complied with." Malignant forces worked their influence from inside the army; Washington was not exempted from their poison. "I have lately heard," Jones confided, "there are those who are abandoned enough to use their arts to lessen your reputation [for] popularity in the Army, in hopes ultimately the weight of your opposition will prove no obstacle to their ambitious designs." If such slander took effect and anyone other than Washington enjoyed supremacy, he could no longer support the army's cause. "I own it will prove a bad prognostic of the future & I shall be among the number of those who entertain fears of the Army." Over the tumultuous week that followed, Washington kept Jones's letter close by.[3]

Around the same time, Washington finally answered Hamilton's February 13 letter sounding out the general's willingness to take a new active part in obtaining justice for the army. Hamilton, anxious to hear back, wrote two additional letters to Washington, although they crossed with the general's response heading south. When Hamilton did at last see a sheet of paper with Washington's familiar script, he couldn't have been happy.[4]

"The predicament in which I stand as Citizen & Soldier, is as critical and delicate as can well be conceived," Washington wrote. "It has been the subject of many contemplative hours." He knew well the dilemma and the danger of the situation. "The sufferings of a complaining army on one hand, and the inability of Congress and tardiness of the States on the other, are the forebodings of evil." Yet, he rejected any change of course. Congress must act. Congress must convince the states. To communicate their just demands, the officers had used traditional channels that respected civilian leadership. Washington saw no reason to change now. He would not take on any new role.[5]

Washington rejected the talk deprecating his reputation. It was the spirit of backbiting and two-faced criticism of his leadership that he had frequently experienced during the war. "I shall," he told Hamilton, "pursue the same steady line of conduct which has governed me hitherto; fully convinced that the sensible, and discerning part of the army, cannot be unacquainted (although I never took pains to inform them) of the services I have rendered it, on more occasions than one." Trust the army, he concluded, and the army will trust Congress.[6]

Washington's letter was the work of a man exhausted from eight years of ruminating on the very questions implied by Hamilton's hints about joining the political fray: what was the proper relationship between the army and the people, between the citizen and the soldier? According to the story of power and liberty, only militia were true soldier-citizens; a regular army were mere hirelings, dependent on others, and therefore not full members of the community. The officers disagreed. As Americans fighting for their liberty, they saw themselves as citizens and professional soldiers. Any distinction was invidious. But civilians wouldn't budge. As the war ended and the men prepared to leave behind their identity as soldiers, Washington pondered how the officers could again become citizens if the country did not honor their service with tangible rewards. On the other hand, what would be left to honor if the army did not remember who they served?

The questions were urgent, but Washington restrained himself. The energetic Hamilton might have preferred a brilliant new strategy, a novel tactic, a clever political sleight of hand to spring a surprise victory at the war's last moments, but Washington saw the danger in doing something new and different. Joining the army to one side in a political debate would damage civil-military relations without a chance of success. Washington disputed the jaundiced view of a regular army's virtue, but he knew how widespread the sentiment was. Farmers might pursue their political interests unencumbered by the suspicions of power and liberty, but the army couldn't because pursuing its interests would simply confirm the danger they posed to the nation. Hamilton's strategy wouldn't work. "It would, in my opinion," he wrote, "be impolitic to introduce the Army on the Tapis [tablecloth], lest it should excite jealousy, and bring on its concomitants." In this case, doing nothing was better than doing something.[7]

Washington had a shrewd grasp of politics and given the status quo—the army unhappy but quiet, Congress and the states sluggish but still open to addressing the army's memorial—hanging back and allowing the political process to play out made sense. Until someone rode into camp and changed the status quo.

His name was Colonel Walter Stewart, inspector general of the army's Northern Department responsible for overseeing the drill and discipline of the troops in New York, and he rode into camp on Saturday, March 8, after a five-month absence in Philadelphia. He'd come down with a fever the previous October, which the doctor diagnosed as a liver problem. Oddly, a course of "severe Blisters" and "frequent Bleedings" failed to bring relief and the malady persisted.[8]

Stewart, in his mid-twenties, was a native of Ireland. Settling in the City of Brotherly Love, he enchanted the ladies, who called him the "Irish Beauty." A 1781 painting shows a slim figure in a dark blue uniform trimmed with red, his left foot stepping forward for action while his right hand covers his heart and his left hand rests on his hip holding a plumed hat. His left arm is bent in what looks like a model pose. A thin smile beckons, and atop his slightly cocked head sits a fine gray wig.[9]

As Stewart's convalescence dragged on, Washington suspected a malingerer, or, at least, a young officer with a young family (he'd wed the daughter of a Philadelphia merchant in 1781) more attached to the pleasures of hearth and home than duty to country. In mid-January, Washington ordered the Irish Beauty back to camp. Seven weeks later, Stewart finally turned up. Given the firestorm Stewart was about to touch off, Washington may have wished he had stayed in Philadelphia.[10]

Arriving in the Highlands, Stewart pointed his horse to Washington's headquarters in Newburgh, paid his respects to the commander in chief, and then rode back south to New Windsor. Stewart called on General Gates, whom he had served as an aide-de-camp early in the war, and circulated among the troops, part of his job as inspector. But Stewart was doing more than chatting up an old friend and observing how the men marched. Newly arrived from Philadelphia, he brought the latest news of politics in Philadelphia—and possibly more.

The next night, March 9, Stewart joined about a dozen other officers at the John Ellison House, the headquarters of General Gates. The assembled men were long-serving veterans, including Captain Christopher Richmond, Major William Barber, Major John Armstrong, Jr., and Doctor William Eustis. It is not clear if General Gates attended, but he did not deny knowing what transpired under his roof.[11]

The men huddled together in a first-floor room to discuss their predicament in light of Stewart's perception of the situation in Philadelphia. The December memorial hadn't been enough. The prospect of peace was rising and their days as gentlemen officers were declining. They were still unable to obtain the pay and pensions that would make their return home, if not a Roman triumph covered in laurels, then at least a respectable arrival with the security of some future income to compensate for their sacrifice. Rumors of refusing to disband flew through Philadelphia, and yet Congress plodded along, apparently unperturbed by what would happen to the army if it was disbanded before a settlement of their affairs.

Stewart likely knew of the political maneuvering with the Connecticut and Delaware delegations needed to bring the pension measure to fruition. It's possible he also knew of the idea to have Congress pledge not to disband the army until they could be paid. Depending on how politically connected he was, Stewart may also have had knowledge of the expedient mentioned by Baron von Steuben to General Knox—namely, having Washington write to Congress asking to keep the army intact pending a settlement of its financial affairs. Any of those options might have worked, but none were happening. In spite of the army delegation's prodding, in spite of the financier shuffling debts and credits and loans, in spite of nationalists like Hamilton scheming to find some way to compel the states to approve new money for creditors like the army, the officers' memorial was still under consideration, stuck in endless committees as if delay was the point, to make the army wait so long that the event of peace would make their denial a *fait accompli*.[12]

Stewart also had other financial interests on his mind beyond the officers' desire for pay and pensions. Along with his father-in-law, the Philadelphia merchant and privateer owner Blair McClenachan, Stewart owned significant amounts of loan office certificates: $47,700 for Stewart and $66,000 for McClenachan. Both men were furious when Robert Morris stopped interest payments on the certificates in the summer of 1782. Stewart accosted Morris at his office in late June; Morris directed Stewart to form a committee of "Sensible cool men" and take it up with Congress. Which is what Stewart did, enlisting McClenachan and other public creditors in Philadelphia to send Congress a memorial. Morris wanted the public creditors as an ally to organize support for his fiscal plan, but they couldn't stay cool. They just wanted their money, and Morris refused to reinstate interest payments unless Congress funded the nation's debt in its entirety.[13]

Informed by Stewart, the officers at the John Ellison House decided to act. They would lead the army and demand a new address to Congress. To unify themselves, they drafted a call for officers representing the various lines to meet at the Temple at 11:00 A.M.

on Tuesday, March 11, at which time they would prepare their message. To set the tone for the meeting, the John Ellison House officers decided to produce a letter that would circulate, unsigned, alongside the meeting invitation. Both would go out along with the daily general orders the next morning.

—⚬—

To write the letter, the officers chose twenty-four-year-old Major John Armstrong, Jr., Gates's aide-de-camp. Armstrong, from Carlisle, Pennsylvania, was a student at the College of New Jersey (Princeton) in 1776 when he joined the war. His father, who had served with General Washington in the French and Indian War, was already a general. Junior Armstrong saw action at the Battles of Trenton and Princeton, where his horse was shot out from under him, but he spent most of the war as a staff officer, first to General Hugh Mercer, and then, from 1777 on, to General Gates. The only portraits of Armstrong date to the 1800s, when he was middle-aged and bald. His head looks like an egg with gray tufts of hair on the sides. As a young major, Armstrong's hairline hadn't yet receded, but his reputation as a difficult person was already well advanced. He was imperious, high and mighty about his status, perhaps overcompensating for the anxiety he felt about outranking older men whose fathers weren't generals or friends of the commander in chief. Armstrong's writing style, which he credited to Princeton's legendary president John Witherspoon, was mean, slashing, disdainful of disagreement (probably to Witherspoon's chagrin). Armstrong was, in a word, obnoxious, though he was not completely antisocial and was capable of friendship with those he considered worthy of his attention. By choosing Armstrong, who probably wasn't shy about advertising his talents, the officers ensured the letter would be something spirited.[14]

Armstrong opened by establishing his authority to speak to his fellow officers. He was young, he admitted, and not of the highest rank.

But he claimed to know from experience how they must feel because he, too, had served throughout the long, hard war. Referring to himself in the third person to preserve his anonymity, Armstrong presented the story of his service as the story of America's contest with Britain throughout the Revolutionary period. Like the colonists, who once abhorred the thought of a separation, he entered the fray reluctantly, driven to fight by the "enemies of his Country, the slaves of pow'r and the hirelings of injustice." He suffered because of the war, but persisted, confident that his sacrifices, borne for the greater good, would be rewarded in the end. Yet, just at the moment of triumph, Armstrong continued, his confidence faltered. His interests and the interests of his fellow Americans diverged. Armstrong concluded the letter's first section with a confession of his fear—the civilians were not going to pay—accompanied by a challenge: if the officers allowed Congress to get away with not paying them, the fault would be theirs and their service would have been for nothing. "To be tame and unprovoked when injuries press hard upon you," Armstrong wrote, "is more than weakness, but to look up for Kinder usage, without one manly Effort of your own, would fix your character & shew the world how richly you deserve those Chains you broke."[15]

His bona fides established, Armstrong next turned to the officers' political dilemma. He peppered his prose with a series of rhetorical questions to reveal the chasm between the officers' expectations and reality. It was their "suffering Courage" that won independence, he said, and now "Peace returns again to bless—Whom?—a Country willing to redress your wrongs?" The answer, of course, was no. Armstrong pushed forward with more rhetorical questions, each probing a sore point among the officers, aiming to knife open their wounds. What would be their fate, he asked, but to languish in "infirmities & Tears," to "grow old in poverty, wretchedness, and Contempt," to "owe the miserable remnant" of their lives to "Charity" rather than honor?[16]

Asking rhetorical questions was clever. Armstrong invited his officer readers to silently answer for themselves, ideally according to his prompting, but still supplying their assent on their own. For such explosive material, a direct attack would have been too much. Armstrong also knew the letter would be read communally, with officers discussing and debating his analysis, arguments, and recommendations. Some officers would resist. Some would be hostile. Armstrong gave his supporters ammunition against the wary. The rhetorical questions put the doubters on the defensive, forcing them to refute his words.[17]

Armstrong brought the letter to a climax in the third and final section as he laid out what the officers should do. Write a new letter to Congress, he exhorted, "carry your appeal from the Justice to the fears of government—Change the Milk & Water stile of your last Memorial—assume a bolder Tone, decent, but lively, spirited and determined." No moderation this time, he warned. No more patience. He called for the officers to appoint a committee, "two or three Men, who can feel as well as write," to draft the new letter. Clearly, he had himself in mind, and as if to audition for the part, he outlined what the letter, which he now called a "Remonstrance" rather than the "sueing, soft unsuccessful Epithet of Memorial," should say.[18]

Armstrong recommended starting with the familiar complaints about promises made and broken, services heroically rendered and ignored, suffering borne and unrewarded. He then veered into making threats, at first veiled, then naked. Tell Congress, he wrote, that "the wound often irritated and never healed may at length become incurable—and that the slightest mark of indignity from Congress now, must operate like the Grave, and part you forever." According to Armstrong, the officers should emphasize their options. Come war or peace they would have their way, either refusing to disband or refusing to fight. The army could, he said, "retire to some unsettled Country, Smile in your Turn, and 'mock when their fear cometh on.'" Armstrong drew his last comment from the book of Proverbs (1:26), a reference to those who spurned the call of wisdom. To provide a way back to the course of wisdom, Armstrong finished by reiterating how easily Congress could appease them. Simply approve the measures recommended by the December memorial. When that happened, the officers "would withdraw into the shade of private Life—and give the World another subject of Wonder & applause—An Army victorious over its Enemies, Victorious over itself."[19]

Armstrong's composition was remarkable. In 1,200 words, balanced almost perfectly among the three sections, he voiced the fears, anxieties, and anger ripping through camp like a March wind. That he produced the letter in a few hours, though no doubt with editorial assistance, shows he was a man who could "feel as well as write."

Nevertheless, Armstrong's letter was problematic. It was underdeveloped, the whole amounting to less than the sum of its parts because Armstrong never quite said what he wanted, other than what the December memorial had already asked for, so that it was not clear what the purpose of a new letter would be, except to yell at Congress and vent the officers' spleen. Perhaps Armstrong expected to hash out the details at the meeting.

Whatever debate followed, however, would be colored by Armstrong's harsh words, adding friction. He advised the officers to issue threats they could never make good on. The army was not going to refuse orders to disband, much less move to some distant country because the army was mostly enlisted men who wanted to go home, not crusade for officers' pensions. Also, unlike the officers, who got Morris Notes for one month of current pay in February, the soldiers had received coin.[20]

The letter also divided the officers against each other. It appealed to the superior masculinity of those officers who thought as Armstrong did while ridiculing the manliness of anyone who disagreed. Restraint, forbearance, self-control were not virtues in Armstrong's account but signs of weakness, even cowardice. In one especially sharp passage, Armstrong contrasted the manly warriors they were with the meek civilians they would become if they did nothing but trust Congress. "If this then be your treatment while the swords you wear are necessary for the Defense of America," Armstrong warned, "what have you to expect from peace; when your voice shall sink, and your strength dissipate by division—when those very swords, the Instruments and Companions of your Glory, shall be taken from your sides, and no remaining mark of Military distinction left."[21]

Armstrong twice mentioned swords as the symbol of the officers' manhood, and although it might seem like cheap Freudianism to point out the phallic association, 18th-century soldiers used "sword" as a euphemism for "penis" (it's common in Shakespeare, too), and it was no accident that once losing their swords the officers' voice would "sink," as if rendered prepubescent or womanly. A young man like Armstrong had reason for anxiety about his masculine status. Over the past eight years, his cohort of officers grew to adulthood in the army. They were older and had achieved the chronological status of men. But without money to confirm their independence and gentility, would they be seen as true men of honor ready to raise families and take on roles of leadership? Or would their communities reject them as overgrown boys?[22]

The anxieties of young officers aside, Armstrong's letter also carried a dangerous message about civil-military relations. The letter dripped with contempt for Congress and the civilians they represented and pitted the officers against the people. He roused the officers to "oppose tyranny, under whatever Garb it may assume—whether it be the plain Coat of Republicanism—or the splendid Robe of Royalty." He encouraged the officers to "discriminate between a people and a Cause—between men & principles." Separated, even rhetorically, from the people they served, Armstrong stoked the officers' resentments and bid them to think of themselves as somehow superior to everyone on the outside.[23]

Armstrong finished the letter, read it over with his brother officers, and once they agreed on a final text, Captain Richmond scratched out copies. Major Barber carried the documents up to the Temple for distribution the next morning. No turning back now.[24]

—m—

As Monday, March 10, dawned in the Highlands the men of the Continental Army rose from their beds and stepped out from their huts to see the fruit of Armstrong's labor from the previous night, along with an invitation for the officers to send representatives to meet the next day at the Temple. "The Object of this Convention," the note explained, "is to consider the late Letter from our Representatives in Philadelphia; and what measures (if any) should be adopted, to obtain that redress of Grievances, which they seem to have solicited in vain." Some versions of the invitation ended with an extra bite, calling the officers to meet "and to hear the last dying Speech of the Army." Together, the documents swept through the cantonment, south to West Point, and north to Newburgh, where they arrived at headquarters.[25]

When General Washington read the anonymous letter and the invitation he was, according to one officer, "amazingly agitated"—and for good reason. The documents circumvented the chain of command, an implicit challenge to Washington's authority and derogatory to the good order of the army. Worse, Armstrong's letter, in all its angry glory and talk of desperate measures, confirmed the rumors of Hamilton and Jones, which Washington had dismissed as the overwrought intrigues of Philadelphia politicians who didn't know the true mood or character of the American army. But here was evidence that there really were men "determined to blow the coals of discord." Still, even after reading Armstrong's letter, Washington could not bring himself to believe it originated with his men. He thought it was written by someone in Philadelphia and couriered to camp by Stewart for release. Washington was wrong, and his failure to grasp the origins of the letter revealed that he did not understand his army the way he thought he did.[26]

Washington, however, understood that he faced a threat, and he countered it on several fronts. Publicly, to the army, he was the calm commander in chief, master of men, and rock of routine. He waited until Tuesday's general orders to notice the documents publicly. Washington could have issued supplemental orders Monday night, but he didn't. There was no emergency, he implied. When Washington did address the letters, he issued a direct order not to meet on Tuesday. Yet, he avoided the appearance of an ultimatum. He was confident "the good sense of the officers would induce them to pay very little attention to such an irregular invitation." The meeting was a temptation, but not a crisis. Washington then permitted the officers to hold their meeting anyway—on his authority, at a time of his choosing (noon, Saturday, March 15), and with his agenda: "mature deliberation" on how "to attain the just and important object in view." Then the general orders moved on to announce the promotion of a Massachusetts captain to major and to direct the Third Massachusetts regiment to prepare to relieve the Second New York the next week. The anonymous letter was wrong, he signaled. The army would still exist a week later.[27]

In the following days, Washington used his general orders to maintain the air of camp life as usual. On Wednesday, March 12, for example, Washington's orders covered the logistics and paperwork of supply, the regulation of contractors, repairs to the officers' guard house, the formation of a court-martial, and a lengthy, detailed, urgent exhortation to cleanliness of persons, uniforms, barracks, floors, beds, and eating utensils. "Too much attention cannot be paid" to such matters, the general decreed.[28]

An exception was the orders of Thursday, March 13. First the orders reported a court-martial's sentence for a New Hampshire sergeant convicted of stealing shoes and boots (100 lashes on his naked back). Then Washington published the text of Congress's late January resolutions addressing the problems of current pay, back pay, depreciation, and pensions. Though presented as "lately received by the Commander in Chief," Washington had known about the resolutions since the return of Colonel Brooks to camp in mid-February. Washington released the resolutions now to begin laying the groundwork for the argument he would soon make to the officers: Congress has not abandoned you.[29]

Outside the army's view, Washington confessed his doubts in a less-guarded way. On March 12, he wrote to Elias Boudinot, president of Congress, and to Jones and Hamilton. Because the letter to Boudinot would be shown to Congress, Washington was cautious. He confessed his "inexpressible concern," but assured Boudinot everything was under control. He transmitted copies of the documents circulating in camp, as well as his general orders postponing the officers' meeting, and he asked Congress to approve his decisions. Washington closed by urging Congress, indirectly, to resolve the army's problems. He had "the most lively Expectation, that Congress have the best Intentions of doing ample Justice to the Army, as soon as Circumstances will possibly admit." Translation: *Hurry up!*[30]

Washington was freer in his letters to Jones and Hamilton. In nearly identical wording to each man, he dilated on his message to Boudinot. The army had been content to wait for Congress, Washington wrote, though perhaps they were a bit peevish or perhaps even "very irritable on acct of their long protracted sufferings." Then Stewart arrived and "a storm very suddenly arose with unfavourable prognostics." Washington laid out what he knew of "a scheme [that] was not only planned but also digested and matured in Philadelphia." False rumors were spread in the City of Brotherly Love that the army was determined not to disband; government creditors promised to align themselves with the army and seek payment together; some congressmen hoped the combined force of all creditors, soldier and civilian alike, would "compel the public, particularly the delinquent states, to do justice." It was as if some cabal hoped to manufacture a crisis where none existed. Although Washington did not mention him by name, he blamed Stewart for spreading discontent in camp just in time for the anonymous letter to break everything open. Washington feared for his men. With their emotions at the reins, there was no telling what they might do. He intervened, he told Hamilton, to rescue "the foot that stood wavering on a tremendous precipice."[31]

By postponing the officers' meeting, Washington was sure he had bought time. The men could be diverted from disaster. But that didn't solve the underlying problem of no action from Congress. A new crisis might flare up at any time.

Washington closed both letters with a blunt message. Lean into Congress, he told Jones and Hamilton. Get the army a firm commitment. Now. If anyone refused or balked or temporized, tell them it would be their fault if something terrible happened. "Push this matter to an issue," he wrote Jones, "and if there are Delegates among you, who are really opposed to doing justice to the Army, scruple not to tell them—if matters do come to extremity—that they must be answerable for all the ineffable horrors which may be occasioned thereby." To Hamilton he was even more emphatic. "If any disastrous consequences should follow, by reason of their delinquency," he wrote, "they must be answerable to God & their Country for the ineffable horrors which may be occasioned thereby."[32]

—◊—

While Washington was writing to Boudinot, Jones, and Hamilton, he received more unpleasant news. A new anonymous publication had appeared in camp, demonstrating that Monday's letter could not have come from Philadelphia. However much it might disturb Washington, an officer was the author, there was no doubt about it now.[33]

The new anonymous letter also issued from the pen of John Armstrong, Jr. It was a response to criticism of the first letter and a response to Washington's general orders. Armstrong proclaimed himself proud of his earlier work. He said aloud what other, more timid officers only thought or grumbled about under their breath. Armstrong praised distrust of Congress as a virtue. "*Suspicion*," he wrote, "is the loveliest trait of political Characters." General Washington's suppression of the meeting was not what it seemed, Armstrong continued. In fact, the general postponing the meeting showed that he approved the idea of the officers gathering to write a stern letter to Congress. If not, why didn't he simply cancel the meeting outright? Finally, Armstrong swatted away criticism of his anonymity. Putting his name to the letter wouldn't change the argument, or alter the officers' situation, or recommend against gathering as proposed.[34]

Armstrong's testiness suggests the officers greeted his first letter with something less than the universal applause he desired. The only extended record of the officers' reaction to the March 10 letter corroborates that impression. Written by Lieutenant Colonel Benjamin Walker, an aide to Washington, the account excoriated Armstrong. Though the anonymous letter was "extremely well written," Walker said, it was pernicious, "perfectly calculated to inflame the passions & prepare the Minds of the Officers for any Violent measures which might be recommended to them." Walker zeroed in on one aspect of Armstrong's plea: the threat to refuse to disband in peace or abandon their post if war continued. He had no ears to hear Armstrong's more moderate request for a new, strongly worded letter to Congress. [35]

According to Walker, only a minority shared Armstrong's view; the most respected officers deplored it. Like Washington, Walker suspected someone in Philadelphia wrote the letter and sent it to the Highlands as part of a scheme for the officers to come out in league with the public creditors. Walker scorned collaboration. "The army will not be their tools nor will they Join with any body of Men however numerous." They would not sacrifice their reputations. Although some officers doubted Congress, Walker admitted, they trusted their states to make them whole. Everyone rejected threats. Only after a peace and only after exhausting both Congressional and the state remedies would the officers consider retiring "like a band of Brothers into the Wilderness." All would end well, Walker finished. "A few whose feelings actuate them more than their Reason—would sacrifice everything to their Resentment but it is a small party who think thus." Come noon on March 15, he predicted, the majority would prevail. [36]

Other officers weren't so sure.

General Knox feared what the army might do. "Officers expectations are at an end," he moaned to McDougall. "What will be the consequences God knows." Like Washington, Knox placed a heavy stone of blame on Congress's side of the scale. "The men who by their illiberality and injustice drive the Army to the very brink of destruction, ought to be punished with severity," he fumed. But though Congress's slow-moving stinginess was to blame, Knox knew only one solution. Congress must act. Or, as he told Benjamin Lincoln in a similar letter, "Press the matter instantly my dear Sire, with all your might and main."[37]

Other officers planned a direct attack on the ideas convulsing the army. Late in the week, Brigadier General Rufus Putnam, a military engineer, commander of the Massachusetts regiment, and part of his line's 1782 delegation to Boston, drafted an answer to Armstrong. No doubt drafted with the assistance of others, Putnam designed the letter to help retake the framing of the meeting from Armstrong.[38]

Addressed to "the Officers of the Army," it opened fire on Armstrong, the "anonymous writer who stiles himself your *fellow soldier*," though this letter, too, was unsigned. Putnam, like Walker, homed in on Armstrong's offensive alternatives: refusal to disband in peace or abandonment of the country in war. Putnam also dismissed Armstrong's more moderate call for a new petition to Congress. It was a "high toned remonstrance" calculated to "frighten Congress into our measures." Putnam, however, borrowed Armstrong's penchant for rhetorical questions. Even if the officers succeed in frightening Congress and extracted a promise for pay and pensions, how could they believe Congress would follow through once the alarm of the moment passed? An agreement under duress bound no one, Putnam argued. Worse, the officers might find themselves punished, even hanged, as traitors. Divide the civilian from the military, Congress from the army, Putnam warned, and "you have *then* passed the *Rubicon*."[39]

Putnam heaped ridicule on Armstrong's arguments with more rhetorical questions. Could the officers really fight the whole civilian nation? Would the enlisted men support them? Really? If by some miracle the soldiers did join the officers, how would they survive? Armstrong had the army living happily ever after in a distant country. More likely, said Putnam, they would have no shelter, no clothing, no food, no supplies, and no way to obtain any except by despoiling civilians. Using force against Congress would certainly fail. *"Despised and insulted,* by an *enraged* populace, *exposed* to the *revenging* hand of *justice,"* Putnam concluded, "You will then flee to *Caves* & *Dens* to hide yourselves from the *face* of *day,* and of Man."[40]

Putnam then turned from attacking Armstrong to defending Congress. The January resolutions published in the March 13 general orders showed Congress's good will. Robert Morris sent all the money he could. But no one could do the impossible. Funding the officers' demands required action from the states. Putnam finished with a simple action plan for the upcoming meeting: trust Washington—"our *Illustrious Chief"*—to speak to Congress on their behalf. In other words, Putnam asked for the expedient Baron von Steuben had mentioned to General Knox. The officers should offer Washington "a warm & affectionate address" asking him to write to Congress and "Beseeching his Excellcy. that he would use his influence to have the business set about immediately." Unlike von Steuben's expedient, however, Putnam did not call on the commander in chief to request any particular measure, such as Congress keeping the army in the field.[41]

Despite its close refutation of the ideas roiling camp, Putnam's letter never circulated—fortunately for Putnam's larger cause. Though well intentioned, it struck the wrong notes by lending Armstrong legitimacy as someone worthy of a close refutation. Dueling anonymous letters implied there were equally meritorious positions—pro- and anti-Congress, pro- and antithreats, pro- and antirefusing to disband—and implicitly invited officers to take sides before the meeting. If Putnam's letter had passed among the officers, Armstrong might have gotten the discussion of alternatives he wanted on March 15.

Instead, General Washington, the commander in chief and "Illustrious Leader," planned a more cunning response.

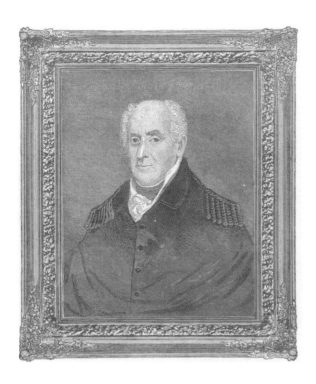

ABOVE: John Armstrong, Jr., engraving, unknown date. *Courtesy of the New York Public Library Digital Collections.* BELOW: Horatio Gates, portrait by Gilbert Stuart, ca. 1793–1794. *Courtesy of the Metropolitan Museum of Art.*

Alexander Hamilton, portrait
by John Trumbull, ca. 1792.
*Courtesy of the National
Gallery of Art.*

David Howell, etching by
Marx Rosenthal, 1885.
*Courtesy of the New York Public
Library Digital Collections.*

James Madison, portrait by Charles Willson Peale, 1783. *Courtesy of the Library of Congress*

Alexander McDougall, engraving by H. B. Hall and Sons, ca. 1870. *Courtesy of the New York Public Library Digital Collections.*

Henry Knox, portrait by Charles Willson Peale, 1778. *Courtesy of the Metropolitan Museum of Art.*

Gouverneur Morris, engraving by Pierre Eugène Du Simitière, 1783. *Courtesy of the Library of Congress.*

Robert Morris, portrait by Charles Willson Peale, 1782. *Courtesy of the Library of Congress.*

Timothy Pickering, engraving by J. B. Longacre, 1834. *Courtesy of the New York Public Library Digital Collections.*

ABOVE: Baron Friedrich Wilhelm von Steuben, engraving by Pierre Eugène Du Simitière, 1783. *Courtesy of the Library of Congress.* BELOW: Walter Stewart, portrait by Charles Willson Peale, 1781. *Courtesy Yale University Art Gallery.*

George Washington, portrait by Joseph Wright, 1783. *Courtesy of the Mount Vernon Ladies'
Association.*

ABOVE: Pennsylvania State House, exterior, engraving by William Russell, 1800. *Courtesy Library of Congress.* BELOW: Pennsylvania State House, assembly room, engraving by Edward Savage, unknown date. *Courtesy Library of Congress.*

ABOVE: Washington's headquarters at Newburgh, New York, painting by George Gunther Hartwick, c. 1850. *Courtesy Mount Vernon Ladies' Association.* BELOW: Horatio Gates's headquarters, New Windsor, New York. *Picture by the author.*

New Windsor Cantonment hut. *Picture by the author.*

ABOVE: Temple of Virtue, exterior. *Picture by the author.* BELOW: Temple of Virtue, interior. *Picture by the author.*

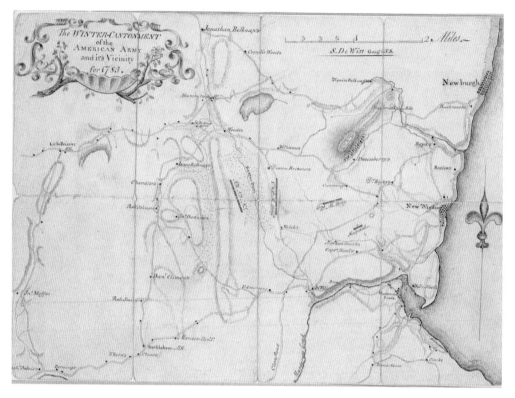

ABOVE: The Winter-Cantonment of the American army and its vicinity for 1783, map by Simeon De Witt, 1783. *Courtesy of the Boston Public Library.* OPPOSITE: Disbanding the Continental Army, at New Windsor, New York, November 3, 1783, engraving by H. A. Ogden for *Harper's Weekly*, 1883. *Courtesy of the Library of Congress.* BELOW: Panoramic view of West Point, painting by Pierre L'Enfant, 1782. *Courtesy of the Library of Congress.*

Surrender of Lord Cornwallis, painting by John Trumbull, 1820. *Courtesy of the Architect of the Capitol.*

ABOVE: *Washington's Entry into New York, on the Evacuation of the City by the British, Nov. 25th 1783.* Lithograph by Currier & Ives, 1857. *Courtesy of the Library of Congress.* BELOW: Glasses owned by Washington similar to what he wore at Newburgh. *Courtesy of Mount Vernon Ladies' Association.*

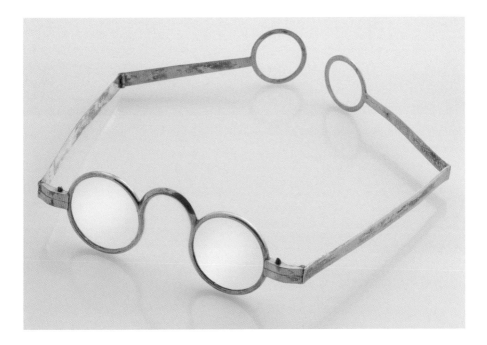

General George Washington Resigning His Commission, painting by John Trumbull, 1824. *Courtesy of the Architect of the Capitol.*

SEVEN

General Washington in the Temple of Virtue

As the week ended, General Washington finalized his strategy. He would overawe the officers with a heartfelt address denouncing the anonymous letter. Their passions cooled, he intended to offer himself as a pledge of Congress's fidelity. His words would restore unity between the officers and the civilians they served.

The general's plan depended on surprise, a favorite tactic. The officers would not expect him to appear and speak at the Temple of Virtue. Although he never expressly declined to attend, the March 11 general order indicated that the senior officer would preside and send him a report of the proceedings—both unnecessary to mention if he would be on the scene. Addressing a large group was also rare for Washington. He regularly held councils of war, of course, and occasionally spoke inspiring words to the army. But at this late day in the war the commander in chief had never spoken to his officers gathered en masse.[1]

Washington lacked the gifts of a natural orator. He possessed a commanding physical presence, but his voice was often raspy and a bit shaky, the result of a bout of pleurisy as a youth. Washington seldom spoke for long, both from preference (he cultivated silence as a strength) and from necessity (his poor teeth, supplemented by dentures, needed a closed mouth to stay in place).[2]

Washington prized action above talk, but in these circumstances his options for action weren't promising. He could have suppressed the meeting, rooted out the author of the address, and arrested anyone involved in its composition and distribution for fomenting mutiny. Crushing the opposition would cause more problems than it solved, however. The army would be humiliated, revealed as dysfunctional and disloyal. A mass of rebellious officers would disfigure the reputation of all officers. Once word of an officers' revolt reached Philadelphia, they could all bid farewell to their pensions. Who could support taxes to raise money for officers who sullied their honor with mutiny? They might as well vote for a pension for Benedict Arnold.[3]

Washington might also have composed a message and sent it to the officers gathered on the fifteenth, addressing them while staying aloof. On this occasion, words on a page wouldn't suffice. Washington could offer reasons for the officers to endure longer, to wait a bit more for Congress. But reason alone would not quiet the officers' not unreasonable fears that Congress had abandoned them. The officers needed a person to vouchsafe Congress's intentions. Washington needed to deliver his speech in his men's presence to offer himself and his honor as the ultimate guarantee of their cause and their honor. Washington's words, performed as only he could, would be his action.[4]

Washington likely received help planning the operation. The commander in chief favored a collaborative approach to making decisions. When he held councils of war he would speak succinctly, defining the challenge as he saw it, and then invite input from all present, including junior officers and occasional civilians. Early in the war Washington put decisions to a vote, but he later abandoned the practice. He learned he could better formulate a plan by promoting open discussion and respectful disagreement and then making the decision himself.[5]

Washington sent for Knox early in the week, but bad weather prevailed through at least Thursday. It's possible Knox was not able to leave West Point before riding to New Windsor on Saturday. At the same time, Knox would play a crucial role directing the meeting after Washington's speech, which suggests prior coordination.[6]

Washington had other trustworthy officers close by, including Rufus Putnam, the author of the counteranonymous letter that never circulated. Some accounts, though written after the events of March 1783, asserted that Washington held more extensive, more formal consultations. Colonel Philip Van Cortlandt of New York recalled Washington visiting the cantonment to meet with brigade-level officers. Everyone present, he said, "agreed with Genl Washington to Suppress Every attempt at disorderly conduct." Similarly, the son of Colonel Samuel Webb, aide-de-camp to Washington early in the war, recounted a family legend that Colonel Webb personally delivered the anonymous letter to Washington, who then requested that every loyal officer should attend the meeting and counterbalance any effort to sway the officers off the path of rectitude. According to the biographer of David Humphreys, Washington's aide, the commander in chief spoke individually with officers and dissuaded them from supporting the sentiments of the anonymous letter. William Gordon, a Congregationalist minister from Massachusetts, wrote an early history of the war based on interviews with participants, and in his account of the events at Newburgh he also said Washington met personally with the officers. The general sent "for one officer after another and talked to them privately," Gordon wrote, to set "before them the ill consequences of violent measures, and the loss of character that would follow; and brought several to their tears." Gordon's version is a bit much, but combined with the others a grain of truth emerges: Washington met with at least some officers to plan their attack.[7]

As the sun went down on Friday, the uncertainty of the next day hung heavy in camp. Timothy Pickering, for one, felt conflicted. Sitting in his Newburgh quarters, he wrote his wife, Rebecca, that the meeting could easily go sideways. "Should rashness govern the proceedings, the consequences may be such as are dreadful even in idea," he confided. "God forbid the event should be so calamitous!"[8]

In the Hasbrouck House, Washington made his final preparations. He wrote out the address himself in a large, elegant script covering nine thirteen-by-eight-inch pages. He noted where to pause. He underlined words to emphasize. He peppered the text with large, robust exclamation marks for added punch. Washington must have proofread the document and practiced its performance. The manuscript shows he crossed out and corrected a few errors, added a few missed words, and on one page, he jotted down a thought along the margin.[9]

If Washington followed his routine—and the general loved routine—he ended the night of March 14 by retiring to the private room he shared with Martha on the first floor of the widow Hasbrouck's house, poised to rise early and save the Revolution once more. He was so anxious, he hardly slept.[10]

—⟜⟞—

March 15 dawned in the Highlands. No one recorded that it was the Ides of March, but gentlemen officers knew their classics and their Shakespeare, and it must have crossed someone's mind that it was an inauspicious date for rejecting political violence and preserving a republic. The commander in chief's orders went out, perfunctory and terse, with no word of the approaching meeting.[11]

Also out early and oblivious to the day's impending events was Benjamin Gilbert, the Massachusetts lieutenant hiding in the army to avoid a shotgun wedding at home. He was sneaking back into camp after an evening at Wyoma, his favorite cat house. It was his second visit that week.[12]

As noon approached, some 100 officers crunched through the New Windsor snow to the Temple of Virtue. When they were assembled, General Gates, the highest-ranking member present, called the meeting to order. Suddenly, hoofbeats—the sound of a late arrival—were heard from outside. The door opened. The commander in chief stepped inside.[13]

Washington strode to the building's south end, his footsteps pounding on the wood floor as the officers looked on in silence, awe-struck. He ascended the stairs to the dais and took his place at the lectern. Washington hardly needed the extra few feet to capture every eye in the building, but there he stood, his presence unexpected but magnetic and larger-than-life.[14]

The general began not with thunder, but courtesy. He apologized for interrupting their meeting and explained that he had not intended to speak to them when he issued the general orders for March 11, but the prevalence of the anonymous letter around camp convinced him not to lose the chance to share his thoughts on the present moment. Washington begged the officers' indulgence as he read his address.[15]

Then he brought the heat. "By an anonymous summons, an attempt has been made to convene you together," he said, "how inconsistent with the rules of propriety! how unmilitary! and how subversive of all order and discipline—let the good sense of the Army decide."[16]

Washington's reliance on the officers' good sense previewed his argument in the speech's first section: emotions had overcome reason and the officers who gave in to their feelings risked a tragedy they would regret.

He hammered at the anonymous author's pernicious intentions. Although Washington conceded the author was "entitled to much credit for the goodness of his Pen," he did not deserve "much credit for the rectitude of his Heart." The letter lacked charity in its abuse of the man who recommended moderation. According to Major J. A. Wright, Washington was "sensibly agitated" by the anonymous letter's lines about the man of moderation, which everyone believed was a reference to the commander in chief. Washington turned from personal rancor, however, and focused back on the larger problem. The anonymous author was trying to alienate the officers' affections for their country, for their cause, for their honor. He had in mind a plan "in which candor and liberality of Sentiment, regard to justice, and love of Country, have no part."[17]

Washington continued, attacking the same object from a different angle. The anonymous address was part of a dark plot that could not survive the pure light of day. It aimed to arouse the officers' resentment against Congress and "intended to take advantage of the passions, while they were warmed by the recollection of past distresses, without giving time for cool, deliberative thinking."[18]

Throughout the opening section, Washington pursued his argument through a series of paired opposites. The anonymous summons versus his personal appearance. Unmilitary conduct versus the good sense of the army. The artful pen versus the honest heart. Severity versus moderation. Detraction versus candor and liberality of sentiment. Selfishness versus justice and patriotism. Corruption versus honor. Warm passions versus cool, deliberative thinking.[19]

The gathered officers fell into four broad groups, and the paired opposites allowed Washington to communicate a vital message to each one simultaneously. Contrasting positive values against the negative ones attributed to the anonymous address helped Washington isolate the first group, the hardline advocates of the letter's sentiments such as Armstrong and his cronies. The more negative associations he could tie to them, the less influence they would have in whatever discussion followed the speech. For a second group—those officers who were angry and tempted to follow Armstrong's lead—the paired opposites opened distance between them and the hardliners. As much as they might have liked the anonymous letter, did they really agree with its implications? Did they really want to risk their honor in its defense? A third group leaned the other way. They were unhappy with Congress but inclined to stick with Washington. The commander in chief's rhetoric bucked them up. They were on the right side. Take heart. No wavering. Finally, Washington had his own die-hards, men of unassailable loyalty he counted on to steer the meeting after he left. The paired opposites gave them ammunition in a fight. Whose side were you on, they could charge: Deception or honesty? Self-interest or love of country?

After stigmatizing the anonymous letter and the ugly emotions it aroused, Washington attempted to divert the officers' feelings to a new object. The gratitude, patriotism, and pride in service that should be theirs to enjoy. Washington first described his own feelings. He was hurt that they might suppose he wanted to deny them every opportunity to express themselves and remedy their grievances. Their reputation was his reputation. Their successes were his successes. What insulted them insulted him. He had shared their sufferings. In this passage Washington dwelled on himself at length, using thirteen first-person pronouns in three sentences. The tactic was not egotism, however, but rather a way to redirect the officers' emotions to a nobler purpose. Washington reminded his audience of what he fought for, and in doing so reminded them of what they fought for. They shared a common purpose and common values. They should join him in rejecting the anonymous letter. [20]

Emotions bridled, Washington developed a long, less effective section on what was to be done. He started by ridiculing the anonymous letter's notorious alternatives: abandoning the country to its fate if the war continued or refusing to disband if peace arrived. Washington mocked the idea of heading west if the war continued. Were they really supposed to pack up their wives and children and walk away from their homes to live in some miserable wilderness?

The argument fell flat here. Many of the younger officers didn't have wives or children or property of their own because they'd given up those things to serve in the army, and now they might never have wives or children or property because of the parsimony of civilians. General Washington could go home to lovely Mount Vernon. They couldn't. [21]

Washington followed up with a new series of rhetorical questions, this time punctuated by condemning the anonymous author as treasonous. "Can he be a friend to the Army? Can he be a friend to this Country?" Washington asked. "Rather, is he not an insidious Foe? Some Emissary, perhaps, from [the British in] New York, plotting the ruin of both [the army and the country], by sowing the seeds of discord & seperation between the Civil & Military powers of the Continent?" These lines didn't land any better. Some officers, such as Pickering, approved the anonymous letter's general goals without endorsing all its methods. Branding the author a traitor didn't sit well. [22]

With those rhetorical questions hanging, Washington's address meandered through two paragraphs that rehashed previous material. He hit again on emotion versus reason, the foolishness of the anonymous letter's alternatives, and the mischief of casting suspicion on the moderate man—the second time he referenced that passage of the anonymous letter. The line pierced Washington's feelings.

Washington then regained his footing for the final push. He defended Congress and invited the officers to trust its good intentions. Yes, that was asking a lot, he admitted, given the way that Congress had treated the army throughout the war. But he still trusted Congress. Any other course would compromise their honor and lose the reputation they'd earned. And would any other course bring a redress of their grievances closer? "No!" Washington answered. "Most certainly, in my opinion, it will cast it at a greater distance." [23]

Knowing the officers would want some kind of proof of Congress's good intentions, Washington offered himself and his honor. The officers could trust Congress because he trusted Congress. He would do whatever he could to intervene on their behalf. "So far as may be done consistently with the great duty I owe my Country," he promised, "you may freely command my services to the utmost of my abilities." Left unsaid was the likely shape his service would take: a letter to Congress on the officers' behalf, the expedient mentioned by Baron von Steuben. [24]

Washington then challenged his men to turn back to the way of duty, back to the patriotism of the war's early days. "Let me conjure you, in the name of our common Country—as you value your own sacred honor—as you respect the rights of humanity, & as you regard the Military & national character of America, to express your utmost horror & detestation of the Man who wishes, under any specious pretences, to overturn the liberties of our Country, & who wickedly attempts to open the flood Gates of Civil discord, & deluge our rising Empire in Blood." Invoking their "sacred honor" echoed the Declaration of Independence's closing lines and reminded the men of the day seven years earlier when they first heard the Declaration's words. [25]

One obstacle remained. Even if the officers turned back now, there was still the embarrassing fact that a crisis had broken out. Surely the world would soon know their failure, however brief it might have been. Throughout the address Washington avoided blaming anyone except the author of the anonymous address. He pointed to excess emotion, not deliberate insubordination, for bringing along the rest. By doing so, Washington gave the officers an easy out; they could walk away blameless if they just said no to the anonymous letter. Now Washington went even further. The crisis—safely averted—was proof of the American Army's greatness. "You will," he promised, "afford occasion for Posterity to say, when speaking of the glorious example you have exhibited to man kind, 'had this day been wanting, the World had never seen the last stage of perfection to which human nature is capable of attaining.'" The line was Washington's own, but in its invocation of future glory conferred by present shared suffering, the words echoed Shakespeare's St. Crispin's Day speech from *Henry V*, because that's what Washington held out to the men: the promise that they were a band of brothers who deserved immortal glory. [26]

Washington spoke his inspiring last words, but the men remained silent, the tension suffocating the room as a fire crackled at the Temple's north end. He knew he had many friends present, men who revered him and would fight any foe with him to the end. But he also feared

other officers, weary of waiting for Congress and vulnerable to temptation, mistrusted his words. He couldn't know how large the second
group was—or how desperate they might be without more proof of
Congress's good will.

The general, well prepared, had brought several documents to lay
before the officers to consider during the deliberations that would
follow his speech. Among them was the recent letter from Joseph
Jones. It was evidence of Congress's true intentions. Washington began
to read. He stumbled over the first lines. Written in a small hand, he
couldn't make out the words clearly.[27]

Washington paused and removed his new glasses from his waistcoat.
"Gentlemen," he said, apologizing, "you will permit me to put on my
Spectacles, for I have not only grown gray but almost blind, in the
service of my country."[28]

Hearts melted. Tears flowed. Washington returned to Jones's letter
and continued over the sobs.

When he finished speaking, Washington tucked his spectacles
back into his waistcoat and prepared to depart. He left behind the text
of his speech and Jones's letter, which joined several other documents
regarding pensions on a table for the officers' perusal. The general
then strode out of the Temple, mounted his horse, and rode back to
Newburgh, the fate of the army in the officers' hands.

Washington's gesture with his glasses was so dramatic it's almost
too good to be true. Did he bring them along as a prop for a bit of
theatricality? Did he plan to read Jones's letter all along? Or was it truly
a spontaneous moment, with Washington's uncharacteristic vulnerability moving the men to tears? Only Washington could say for sure,
but several clues suggest the climactic moment was part planned and
part improvised.

Two sources include copies of Jones's letter: an orderly book kept
by a Massachusetts captain named Ebenezer Smith and the papers of
Timothy Pickering. Both men made copies of Washington's speech, the
anonymous letters, and other documents associated with the affair,

such as the Jones letter. Orderly books recorded official materials for general dissemination in a unit and Pickering wanted his friends outside camp to have an account of what transpired so they could spread the news. Importantly, the Smith and Pickering copies match each other, but they do not include the full text of Jones's letter because, it seems, Washington didn't read all of it that day. For good reason: the letter was nearly 1,800 words long (Washington's speech was 1,600) and not all of it was relevant to the officers (a long paragraph reported on affairs in Vermont and its disputed independence from New Hampshire and New York). The copies also left out two shorter passages. In the first, Jones opined that Washington was best positioned to decide "whether to temporise, or oppose with steady unremitting firmness, what is supposed to be in agitation of dangerous tendency." In the second, Jones predicted that peace "is almost reduced to a certainty" and confessed his disquiet that "it will not be attended with those blessings generally expected" because so many domestic questions remained unsettled. Neither piece would have sat well with apprehensive officers. Instead, the copies moved directly from material on the rumors challenging Washington to an optimistic view of the prospects for commutation once more states were represented in Congress. The Smith-Pickering version of Jones's letter was tighter, more focused on the officers' problems and the likelihood of Congress addressing their needs in the near future.[29]

If the Smith and Pickering copies accurately reflect what Washington read, then it suggests significant preparation by the general. The Jones letter itself provides more evidence of preparation. Now held by the Library of Congress, the document contains several marks that correspond to the material edited from the two copies. A thick vertical line appears where the copies first break from Jones's original. Parentheses bracket the paragraph on Vermont. More marks accompany other starting and stopping points. Unfortunately, there's no way to tell when the marks were made: by Jones, by Washington, or by an officer who copied the documents later on. Nevertheless, when combined with the Smith and Pickering copies—which edited out the exact same passages—the marks indicate Washington came ready to read the letter.[30]

Why, then, didn't Washington bring a fresh copy with writing large enough for him to see clearly what it said? Washington might not have planned to use it for certain. He might have brought the letter along as a plan B in case extra evidence was needed, depending on how the speech went. If he only intended to offer it to the officers to read on their own along with the other documents on hand as evidence of Congress's good will, having it in Jones's script enhanced its authenticity.

As for the glasses, they were reading glasses, which indicates Washington was ready to read something. But his famous line about growing gray and blind was certainly ad-libbed. Even if Washington were prepared to don his spectacles, the emotion of the moment was overwhelming. The long war. The sacrifices borne together. The danger of the anonymous letter. The insulting remarks about the "man of moderation." And then, after speaking for twenty minutes, he stopped to put on his glasses, which he'd been wearing for only a month (and which weren't nearly so easy to slip on as a modern pair). Standing in front of a hundred men, it was only polite to ask pardon for the delay.

The men's reaction was equally unscripted. Officers remembered Washington's words a touch differently from each other. David Cobb, who was not present at the meeting, recalled the standard version around camp in the days following was "Gentlemen, you will permit me to put on my Spectacles, for I have not only grown gray but almost blind, in the service of my country." Samuel Shaw recounted Washington saying, "he had grown gray in their service, and now found himself growing blind." Pickering rendered it as "I have grown gray in the service, and am now growing blind." Each man perceived a slightly different object of Washington's devotion, reflecting what he felt was most important: serving the country or serving the officers. But no one doubted the impact of Washington's speech or the importance of reading the letter from Jones. Shaw called the letter "exceedingly sensible." Pickering, who was skeptical of Congress, felt reassured by Jones's "great good sense." General Edward Hand was laconic. "A letter from the South read by His Excy, turned all right about." General Philip Schuyler, stunned by the whole performance, was effusive. "Never, through all the war did his Excellency achieve a greater victory than on this occasion," he wrote, still in disbelief after two days. "The whole assembly were in tears at the conclusion of his address." Jones's letter along with Washington's words, glasses, and vulnerability carried the day. [31]

—∭—

As General Gates resumed the chair, generals Knox and Putnam seized the initiative. Knox made a motion to thank Washington for his speech, Putnam seconded, and without objection, the assembly announced their gratitude for the "excellent address," and affirmed that they "reciprocate his affectionate expressions with the greatest Sincerity of which the human heart is capable." No need to worry about rashness, now sentimentality ruled. [32]

Then, a reading commenced of the officers' December memorial to Congress, the delegation's official February 8 report to Knox, and Congress's January 25 resolution on the army's grievances, which Washington had recently published in his March 13 general orders. [33]

The officers next turned to adopting resolutions, the ostensible purpose of the meeting. By now, Washington and his allies had built up such a bulwark around their message—the old documents, plus Washington's speech, plus Jones's letter, plus the glasses, plus the crying—that Armstrong's argument didn't have a chance. They would not be calling for someone who could feel as well as write to draft a letter to Congress. [34]

Putnam offered a motion, seconded by General Hand, to appoint a drafting committee. Led by Knox, the committee stepped into one of the small offices at either end of the Temple, prepared resolutions, and returned to the main hall a half hour later. [35]

First, the officers declared themselves "engaged in the service of their Country" from motives of "the purest love and attachment to the rights and liberties of human nature." Such motives impelled them in 1775; such motives moved their hearts in 1783. Nothing could change their feelings. [36]

Second, the officers proclaimed their "unshaken confidence in the justice of Congress and their Country." Congress, they believed, would not disband the army before settling their accounts. The resolution also expressed confidence that funds would be established to actually produce the money for payment. Still, the resolution was not phrased as conditional, even though everyone knew the contingencies involved in securing a permanent source of revenue for debt payments. The army placed itself fully under Congress's care, which soothed the present crisis. They would later regret it. [37]

Third, the officers asked General Washington to write Congress on their behalf to ask for "the most speedy decision" on the December memorial. Here was a version of the expedient reported by Baron von Steuben, hinted at by Hamilton, and recently rejected by Washington. The resolution did not call for Washington to ask Congress to keep the army in the field as the original expedient envisioned. The second resolution already covered that ground in a way that assumed Congress would do the right thing. Washington's letter could then have a softer edge—asking for the same substance as the December memorial, only faster—while still implying the urgency of settling accounts before a showdown over disbanding might finally come about. The resolution, then, did not ask anything from Congress, other than a quick decision. [38]

The resolution continued by offering a benefit, without demanding action from Congress first—a quo that quietly implied the quid. "In the alternative of Peace of War," the resolution stated in a clever inversion of Armstrong's most notorious passage, a positive answer to the December memorial "would be highly satisfying" and the army would enjoy "immediate tranquility." With the officers' minds at ease, there would be no more "machinations of designing men to sow discord between the civil and Military powers of the United States." Peace and harmony would reign across the land for civilian and soldier alike. If only Congress would approve the memorial's requests.[39]

The full body of officers added two more resolutions to the three drawn up by Knox, Brooks, and Howard. One thanked the army delegation to Congress (which included Brooks) for its service and asked McDougall to continue his mission in Philadelphia. The other resolution condemned Armstrong's anonymous letter. The resolution announced, "infamous propositions" that the officers "view with abhorrence and reject with disdain."[40]

All five resolutions passed unanimously, although Pickering abstained from voting in favor of calling the anonymous letters "infamous." He could not raise his hand when the vote was called, he said, because the resolution was gratuitous. The author (Pickering didn't know it was Armstrong) was well intentioned and brave enough to speak harsh truths. He didn't deserve to be "damned with infamy."[41]

With no dissent voiced, the official resolutions were drawn up and put in the care of Gates to transmit to Washington. The meeting ended, and the men returned to their quarters. The crisis was defused, but the impact of the day's events lingered.

As Knox rode back to West Point with General Schuyler, not a word passed between them. "I have no doubts," Schuyler wrote two days later, still overcome by what had transpired, "that posterity will repeat the closing words of his Excellency's address—'Had this day been wanting, the world had never seen the last stage of perfection to which human nature is capable of attaining.'"[42]

—◊—

Washington accomplished his mission. The officers no longer stood on a precipice but on the firm soil of commitment to duty. The temptation to disorder aroused by the anonymous letter lay smothered in infamy. Even waiting patiently for Congress, once a torture, now felt like sublime virtue. [43]

But with the immediate crisis allayed, questions remained: What, exactly, had Washington prevented? Did his command really hang in the balance with a usurper, General Gates, nearby? Were the officers who issued the anonymous letter executing a plan drawn up in Philadelphia by nationalist leaders so anxious to secure new taxes and a more powerful central government that they would risk a coup? In short, was there really a Newburgh Conspiracy?

The key to unlocking the mystery lies with Walter Stewart, the beautiful Irish colonel who clip-clopped into camp and set the officers on fire with whatever information he brought from Philadelphia. Unfortunately, we don't know what Stewart said as he circulated through camp on March 8, and we also don't know what was said at the March 9 gathering at Gates's headquarters. In both cases, the officers conversed face to face, and they didn't leave the kind of written evidence that would have been captured by sending letters to someone outside camp.

Though what Stewart said to set off the crisis is mysterious, four sources have left clues.

Benjamin Walker described Stewart buzzing around camp putting a most unwelcome bug in the officers' ears. "His Sentiments on the State of Army Affairs at Philadelphia were so unfavorable and spoken so freely in all Companies that the minds of many began to be uneasy," Walker wrote. Stewart's sentiments are not hard to guess. The people were set against the army. Congress intended to disband them as soon as possible. Delay was a chosen strategy to run out the clock. They weren't getting their pensions. Stewart was also upset because he was highly leveraged in loan office certificates, and along with his father-in-law, he was angry about Robert Morris's refusal to pay interest. If the army joined the public creditors, however, both groups could obtain together what neither could achieve on its own: payment of debts.[44]

A second glimpse at Stewart's activities comes from a somewhat garbled account recorded in 1788 by Rufus King, a former delegate to the Confederation Congress from Massachusetts and a future United States senator from New York, following a conversation with William Duer, who was as an army contractor during the war and visited camp following the climactic week. In this version, Stewart ventured from Philadelphia to find a leader for a plot. He approached Washington, but finding the commander in chief unmovable, he turned to Gates, for whom "the conspiracy was too inviting to be rejected."[45]

In addition to appearing several years after the fact and deriving from a secondhand source, King mangled the sequence of events. For example, he had Stewart arrive in the Highlands, secure Gates, then recruit Robert Morris (in Philadelphia), all within a day. Still, some useful information can be extracted from King's account.[46]

Stewart did see Washington on arriving at camp. Assuming he didn't try to recruit his commanding officer into a conspiracy, he might have hinted at the need for von Steuben's expedient: a new letter from Washington to Congress. Stewart wouldn't have known about Washington's letter to Hamilton refusing to do so. It's possible that Hamilton, who was anxious to hear from Washington, had asked Stewart to check in with the general and give him a (careful) push. Unsuccessful, Stewart kicked up a fuss in New Windsor, eventually finding sympathetic ears in Gates's military family.

A third angle on what Stewart was up to comes from John Armstrong writing many years later. In an 1820 letter to Timothy Pickering, Armstrong, adopting the alias John Montgars, tried to enlist the old quartermaster's aid in refighting by then ancient battles from their army days. Armstrong described the whole business with the anonymous letter as an innocent attempt to assist the nationalists in raising new funds for the government in light of the impost's failure. Stewart, he wrote, undertook a "mission to the army" and spread "the prevailing sentiment of Congress and of the Department of Finance, on the necessity of the army's *speaking* a more decisive language."[47]

Three years later, Armstrong, still in a fighting mood, published an anonymous review of a recent biography of Nathanael Greene that said things about the Newburgh affair that Armstrong found unflattering, such as denying Armstrong's authorship of the anonymous letter. Armstrong again portrayed the Irish Beauty as carrying out a mission, though this time he didn't specify who sent him. Stewart "saw all grades [of officers], and communicated freely with *all*," spreading the message that they should demand payment from Congress, not the states, and that they should unite with the civil creditors.[48]

Stewart's communications, according to Armstrong, were like the anonymous letter the two helped produce: honest, praiseworthy, and likely to bring success. Their efforts only went awry, Armstrong said, because at the very same time that they were calling the officers to meet, Washington happened to receive a letter warning against machinations by Philadelphia officials and Washington overreacted.[49]

A fourth account of Stewart's would-be mission to the cantonment comes from General Gates. Written in June 1783, it has advantages over the others. Gates was present at the drafting of the anonymous letter, unlike King's source Duer. He was sympathetic to the anonymous letter's argument, unlike Walker, who was hostile. Gates's account also hit a sweet spot in timing: he wrote close enough to the events of March to lessen the problems of memory that affect King's and Armstrong's versions, but also long enough after the event that the immediate issue of commutation was over and there was no cost for candor, while at the same time his remarks came before Washington's speech was immortalized with any opposition branded heresy.

Unfortunately, Gates's account is brief. Writing to Armstrong, the general mentioned he had exchanged letters with Reverend Gordon, who was collecting material for his book. "Gordon has been very importunate to know," Gates wrote, "what he calls the secret history of the anonymous letters." Gates told Armstrong he replied directly:

"Stewart was a kind of agent from our friends in congress and in the administration, with no object, however, beyond that of getting the army to co-operate with the civil creditors, as the way most likely for both to obtain justice." Stewart's message, the meeting at his house, and the anonymous letter were political but aimed at nothing more than joining the political debate more directly, more openly than before.

Gates's statement has two parts: a disclosure that Stewart acted as a go-between for political figures in Philadelphia and the officers and a claim that Stewart's actions were innocuous. Traditional accounts of a conspiracy at Newburgh accept the first as an admission of a plotting connection between the nationalists and the officers, while rejecting the second as an after-the-fact whitewash of an ugly plan.

It's hard to dispute Gates's incentive to downplay his involvement in anything underhanded if he were plotting to supplant Washington, as the strong version of Gates's role in a Newburgh Conspiracy holds. However, little evidence supports the notion that Gates had eyes on Washington's command in March 1783. By that time, General Gates was a broken man. He'd enjoyed one triumphant moment in the war—and suffered one unforgettable defeat. Though he rendered the cause of independence valuable service as an administrator, he made enemies of other officers, such as Washington, and of congressmen, who blocked his advance. Gates and Washington were no longer rivals because Washington was the victor, and Gates knew it. He accepted his role in the Highlands and maintained a correct, civil tone with the commander in chief. [50]

Throughout the winter Gates had more urgent personal matters on his mind. His wife of thirty years, Elizabeth, was gravely ill. On March 5, Gates wrote Elizabeth. He was "truly unhappy," he said, because of her precarious health. "I would set out immediately for home were I my own Master." The roads were too poor for travel. Gates was in no mood to lead a charge against Washington and Congress and the states. He wanted to go home and see his dying wife. [51]

In his letter to Gordon, then, Gates was not trying to deflect attention from his own ambitions for power. Yet, he was still involved in whatever Stewart, Armstrong, and the other officers at his house were planning. He knew, as he said, that "Stewart was a kind of agent from our friends in congress and in the administration." Though a bit mysterious, Gates's statement offers clues about who in Philadelphia might have used Stewart to contact the general and his officers and what they all might have been planning.

To understand Gates's letter, two key words—"agent" and "friends"—need definition.

In the 18th century, "agent" had many meanings, drawn from the worlds of science and medicine, law, diplomacy, grammar, commerce, and philosophy. All shared the notion of a person (or thing) that acted upon someone (or something) else. "Agent" in a covert sense—as in "secret agent"—developed later, in the 19th century.[52]

The meaning Gates intended came from the commercial and diplomatic realms: the idea of an agent as someone who acts on behalf of another. That definition suggests Stewart was in fact carrying out orders given to him in Philadelphia to be transacted in the cantonment. Significantly, though, Gates described Stewart as "a kind of agent," indicating that the ordinary definition didn't quite fit. Gates's modifier muddies the relationship among Stewart, the Philadelphians, and the officers.[53]

Like "agent," "friend" also had many shades of meaning in the 18th century. Lexicographer Samuel Johnson defined a friend as "one joined to another in mutual benevolence and intimacy; opposed to foe or enemy." Meanings of "friend" also included a relationship somewhat closer than an acquaintance; a trusted companion; a business associate (or patron); a kinsman; a Quaker; a sex partner; and a political ally. Gates no doubt had the last definition in mind.[54]

In the 18th century, friend-as-political-ally implied more of a personal relationship than it does today. When political parties did not yet exist in any structured way—remember: even "nationalist" is a shorthand term of convenience, not an actual party—politics was carried out among those who shared a sense of personal honor and commitment to what they perceived as the common good. Personal relationships made politics possible. Political friends shared information, gamed out strategies, gossiped about enemies, negotiated policies, protected each other's reputations, protected each other's financial interests, looked after each other's families when absent, and, if need be, managed affairs of honor and stood beside each other in a duel. For a politician or a politically engaged officer, "friend" was not a euphemism, as it might be today, for someone a politician will profess to like only as long as it is expedient.[55]

Gates specified that the "friends" were in Congress and the administration. By "administration" he meant the departments of War, Finance, Marine Affairs, and Foreign Affairs. "Congress," of course, meant Congress. Who, then, were Gates's friends in Congress and the administration, the men for whom Stewart was acting as agent?

Traditional accounts of a Newburgh Conspiracy point to the leading nationalists: Robert and Gouverneur Morris in the Finance Department and Hamilton in Congress. Of the three, however, only Robert Morris could be called a friend of Gates—a friend in the 18th-century sense of a political ally united by a shared sense of honor.

Gates and Morris enjoyed a cordial relationship. In the face of Congressional opposition, Morris supported Gates's campaign to clear his name from the debacle at Camden, so he could rejoin the army without the stigma of a pending inquiry. Once Gates regained his position in the fall of 1782 the two corresponded periodically. They mostly wrote about Elizabeth Gates, her health, and making travel arrangements for her to join her husband (which never happened). Like many other officers, Gates was indebted to Morris, but it had little effect on their relationship. Morris provided financial services for Gates and his wife and wrote that he welcomed the general's letters, though he protested that he was often too busy to respond. Their notes betray no hint of conspiracy. Just the opposite. Morris, like Gates, wanted the war over and the burden of service lifted from his shoulders. "I am heartily tired of Financeering," Morris confessed in late January. "God Send Peace and Soon."[56]

Gates was much less cordial with the financier's assistant, Gouverneur Morris. The precise status of their relationship in 1783 isn't clear (they didn't write each other), but Morris was a friend and ally of General Schuyler, who was a rival of Gates's. The two generals clashed in 1777 over command of the Northern Army. Schuyler had the command. Gates wanted it. Morris thought Gates a bungler who unfairly benefitted from political favoritism and New Englanders' prejudice against New Yorkers like Schuyler. The icy feeling was probably mutual, if the way Gates tolerated others talking about Gouverneur is any indication. In February 1783, Reverend Gordon called Morris "a person of no principle, a downright Machiavelian Politician."[57]

No ambiguity clouded Gates's relationship with Hamilton. The two hated each other. "I am his enemy personally," Hamilton wrote in 1780 while bursting with *schadenfreude* over Gates's humiliation at Camden. Hamilton was Philip Schuyler's son-in-law, but the feud transcended family politics. It originated in a 1777 mission Hamilton carried out on behalf of General Washington, who wanted Gates to send three brigades south from his victorious army at Saratoga to the main army's position near the British in Philadelphia. Gates, perfumed by triumph, recoiled from having to listen to an aide-de-camp barely able to shave give what sounded awfully close to orders. Hamilton didn't back down. Gates eventually relented and detached a pair of regiments.[58]

Later, during the so-called Conway Cabal, Gates outraged Hamilton's honor when he accused the younger man of stealing a look at his private letter to Thomas Conway, the letter in which Gates maligned Washington, which was the crux of the supposed intrigue. Blaming Hamilton for the letter's discovery, Gates called him a "thief" and angled to "disgrace" both Hamilton and Washington.[59]

If none of the big three launched Stewart's mission to the Highlands, then who else did Gates have in mind when he mentioned friends in the administration and Congress? Throughout the winter of 1782 to 1783, Gates was in contact with several men who fit that bill.

General Benjamin Lincoln, the secretary at war, was a friend of Gates's. Lincoln served happily under Gates at Saratoga, where Gates gave Lincoln command of the Northern Army's right wing. When it came time to name the first secretary at war in 1781 Gates was a candidate, but he still labored under the cloud of Camden and accepted Lincoln winning the post. When he finally returned to service, Lincoln delivered the news to his old commander with professions of his affection. Lincoln, then, might make a good candidate to link the nationalists to Gates through Stewart. [60]

However, the secretary at war dissented from the nationalist program on pensions. A Massachusetts man, Lincoln looked askance at half pay pensions because an officer who received one would be notorious in his neighborhood as a pensioner. Commutation was an improvement, but Lincoln thought the states should pay their own officers, not Congress. Lincoln also dissented from the nationalists' strategy for the army to join the civil creditors in demanding payment together. He didn't even want Congress to treat both classes of creditors equally. The army deserved priority, he argued. Their sacrifice was greater. More broadly, Lincoln disagreed with the larger nationalist program. After the war, he said, Congress should divvy up the debt for the states to pay on their own not arrogate to itself the responsibility for paying the debt with new funds secured from new taxes. [61]

Pennsylvania delegate Richard Peters, by contrast, was both sympathetic to the nationalist program and a friend of Gates's. A Philadelphia lawyer before the war, Peters knew Gates from their service together on the Board of War, on which Peters had been both secretary and a member. Peters was a jovial fellow with a waggish sense of humor, and, gifted with a fine singing voice, he delighted in regaling dinner companions with original songs both bawdy and clean. Well connected to both nationalist politics and the army, his correspondence with Gates was casual in February and March 1783. They shared news about peace, swapped gossip, traded sarcastic barbs, and teased each other. Gates asked for updates on his wife; Peters passed along what he knew (sadly not good).[62]

As spring approached, Peters was upbeat about the officers' prospects for a settlement. Obstacles remained, and the course wouldn't be easy, he wrote on March 5, but they were only one state short of approving a commutation of pensions. Referencing the *Aeneid*, Peters compared the officers' memorial to an arduous sea voyage full of twists and turns before a safe arrival on shore.[63]

Lower down in the administrative hierarchy was another friend of Gates's: Joseph Nourse, register of the Treasury. Serving under Robert Morris, Nourse tallied receipts and expenditures, tracked the debt, adjusted accounts, and prepared reports for the financier and for Congress. Like Gates, Nourse was an Englishman, born in London, who had planted himself in the same Virginia soil—the two were neighbors in Berkeley County. Upright, sober (he left army service disgusted by all the swearing, gambling, and drinking), precise, and moderately ambitious, he was a career bureaucrat who found his calling in government accounting. Nourse was not in a position to originate action himself. Although potentially a conduit of political information, Nourse most often wrote the general about the health of Elizabeth Gates.[64]

Finally, though neither an administrator nor a congressman, Alexander McDougall, the leader of the army delegation, was in Philadelphia and in the middle of anything involving the officers' memorial. He also would have been a logical person to send a message through Stewart to Gates, if the two were friends. They weren't. The two men had clashed over command of the Highlands, with Congress displacing McDougall for Gates in 1778. McDougall's judgement of Gates's leadership leaned closer to the judgement of Hamilton, Gouverneur Morris, and Schuyler: he was just lucky at Saratoga.[65]

Looking at the lineup Gates indicated by "friends in congress and in the administration" casts doubt on a core argument that there was a conspiracy in Newburgh: the existence of a tightly knit group of nationalists in Philadelphia sending a clear message through Stewart to a tightly knit group of officers centered around Gates in the Highlands. The men involved didn't relate to each other that way. Men who might have wanted to send a nationalist message, such as Hamilton, Gouverneur Morris, and McDougall, didn't trust Gates. Others who did trust Gates weren't nationalists on pensions (Lincoln), sounded optimistic about the officers' chances in Congress (Peters), appeared ambivalent about public service and reluctant to launch a bitter new fight (Robert Morris), or were more concerned with personal matters than politics (Nourse). The nature of Stewart's mission, then, was far more diffuse than might be suspected. He was "a kind of agent," not a direct messenger.

The various accounts of Stewart's role in the Newburgh affair bring together four pieces: Stewart's indiscriminate complaining to the officers (Walker); being rebuffed in his attempt to push Washington to write to Congress (King); expressing the standard nationalist strategy for the officers to seek payment from Congress and declare their unity with the civil creditors (Armstrong), and the lack of a tight connection between Philadelphia nationalists and a Gates group (Gates).

Putting those pieces together shows that when Stewart rode into camp and set off the stormy week in March—the central event of a supposed conspiracy—he did not bring orders from anyone in Philadelphia. Rather, he brought a mixture of news, rumor, and political analysis about the status of the officers' memorial, the proximity of peace, the prospect of the army refusing to disband, and the best strategy for getting the officers what they wanted—all gleaned from the different players in Philadelphia and filtered through his own sense of what was most likely, who was most reliable, and what course of action was most promising, all of it overshadowed by the specter of his and his family's exposure to loan office certificates.

Stewart was not simply a courier. He was a participant. He was not simply a conduit of commands from more powerful men. He was an active shaper of information, which he transmitted to the officers, who then decided what to do. The decision to call a meeting, draft the anonymous letter, and, presumably, write a new letter to Congress all came from the officers. They expected support from their allies in Congress and in the administration, since their purpose was the nationalist purpose. But the officers who met at Gates's house on the night of March 9 were not carrying out anyone else's orders. They wanted to make a statement they thought would unite them with the civilian creditors and press Congress with a common front. They failed. The anonymous letter was too hot. Its inflammatory passages about abandoning the country to its fate blinded readers to its call for a muscular but respectful letter to Congress.

Quiet for the moment, the officers went back to waiting, their trust placed in the commander in chief, wearied by another responsibility: to persuade Congress to approve the officers' pensions.

EIGHT

Peace and Pensions

In the days after the thrilling meeting at the Temple, Washington was all praise for his men. He proclaimed himself "highly satisfied" with the proceedings after he departed, and he admitted finding himself "unable to communicate an adequate idea of the pleasing feelings which have been excited in his breast by the affectionate sentiments expressed towards him on that occasion." Well, the commander in chief was mostly praise. In general orders he followed the expression of heartfelt thanks overflowing from his bosom by scolding the Massachusetts regiments for the excrement piled around their huts. Washington's work was never done.[1]

Once the meeting concluded Washington dispatched a note to Elias Boudinot, president of Congress, to let him know the army was at peace. The officers' assembly, he revealed, "terminated in a manner, which I had reason to expect, from a knowledge of that good Sense & steady Patriotism of the Gentlemen of the Army." On March 18, Washington sat down to the more difficult task of addressing Congress on the officers' behalf. His letter needed to demonstrate the army's loyalty while simultaneously communicating how angry the men were, though without implying they were angry enough to refuse disbanding.[2]

Sitting in his Hasbrouck House office, Washington began with a bold recasting of the crisis not as a precipice on which the officers stood wavering but as a conquest over temptation. The meeting, Washington wrote, was "the last glorious proof of Patriotism which will have been given by Men who aspired to the distinction of a patriot Army." Following the usual obeisance about devotion to country and respect for the dignity of Congress and its "Sovereign Power," Washington made his argument: the officers deserved everything they asked for, including pensions, because Congress had promised it to them. But Washington's status as the commander in chief meant he couldn't be so blunt when making a political argument in favor of one group's interests. As a result, he deployed the rhetorical technique of apophasis, a method of indirection in which the speaker raises a subject by denying the necessity of discussing it.[3]

"I humbly conceive it is altogether unnecessary," Washington wrote, "to expatiate on their Claims to the most ample compensation for their meritorious Services—because they are perfectly known to the whole World—and because, (altho' the topics are inexhaustible) enough has already been said on the subject." Then he imparted 600 more words on the subject and attached two prior letters to Congress supporting officers' pensions.[4]

Washington laid into the opposition. "If this Country should not in the event perform every thing which has been requested in the late Memorial to Congress," he warned, "then will my belief become vain, and the hope that has been excited void of foundation." After building tension over what Congress—and the army—might do, Washington resolved it. Of course, Congress wouldn't let the army down. "I am under no such apprehensions, [that] a Country rescued by their Arms from impending ruin, will never leave unpaid the debt of gratitude," he soothed.[5]

Washington entered the debate over the officers' memorial and produced the expedient whispered about by von Steuben and hinted at by Hamilton. Three weeks earlier, Washington refused. But now he put his reputation on the line for his officers to rescue their reputation for virtue. The crisis of the previous week and its successful resolution gave Washington a new way into the pension debate. Previously, he wasn't shy about addressing Congress on army affairs with political implications. Earlier in the war, he advocated pensions as a way to stem the loss of officers. But in the spring of 1783, the political calculation had changed. With the war's pressures relaxed, Washington could not make a nonpartisan argument that pensions were a necessary war measure. The war was almost won, and civilians schooled in the story of power and liberty reasserted their suspicions of the military without fear that republican purity might cost them independence. In February and early March, Washington's advocacy would have been interpreted as yet more evidence of corruption: Behold! The allure of pensions ensnared even the vaunted commander in chief! He's looking out for his officer buddies, not the good of the country!

But once facing the anonymous letter's danger, Washington turned the officers' passions into evidence of their patriotism. Their rage against civilians, once rejected, became proof they warranted the praise of civilians and could receive pensions without fear of corruption. Washington's letter echoed the final line of his March 15 speech— "had this day been wanting, the World had never seen the last stage of perfection to which human nature is capable of attaining"—and challenged Congress: *We are patriots who keep our promises. Are you?*[6]

—◊—

As a courier whisked Washington's letter south to an uncertain reception in Philadelphia, Congress continued wrestling over national finances and the officers' memorial, with the usual recriminations now shaded by a new drama with Robert Morris. On February 26,

Morris asked Congress's permission to make public his desire to leave office at the end of May. He offered two reasons: to allow for a smooth transition to a new superintendent of finance and to give the men he'd done business with as financier time to adjust their affairs. Morris's deeper motivations are hard to determine. On the one hand, his original January resignation appeared conditional. If Congress approved adequate funding, he implied he might remain in office and implement the program. If not, there was no point in staying. A month passed and still nothing from Congress. Even worse, the Pennsylvania legislature was discussing the state assumption of Congressional debts owed to Pennsylvanians, which would disrupt Morris's plans for Congress to build credit by paying its own debts. He might have wanted no more than he said: to wrap up Finance Office business and go home. On the other hand, Morris might have been playing his last card to finally give Congress and the states a true ultimatum: approve a fiscal program or he'd really leave.[7]

Congress granted Morris's request, and on March 1 his resignation letter appeared in the local papers. If Morris hoped to bring Congress to heel, he badly miscalculated. From the floor of the Assembly Room, Virginians Arthur Lee and Theodorick Bland tag teamed a beat down, "disparaging the administration of Mr. Morris, and throwing oblique censure on his character," as Madison recorded. Bland followed up with a motion to reorganize the Finance Department and neuter Morris's influence. Hamilton and James Wilson repulsed the attack, but outside the statehouse, it was open season on Morris. An anonymous author, "Lucius," after Lucius Junius Brutus, the founder of the Roman Republic who toppled the last Roman king, launched a series of essays hacking away at the financier with all the bloodlust of Caligula at a gladiator fight. "I Have done the deed! . . . I have murdered public credit as she slept," Lucius had Morris say in one hit piece.[8]

When the articles appeared, people thought Lucius must have been Arthur Lee, and though no evidence unmasks Lucius as Lee (or anyone else), the Virginian and other Morris enemies exalted in his misfortune. Rhode Island delegate Jonathan Arnold shared the good news with David Howell, back in Providence. The superintendent of finance "seems greatly on the decline in the estimation of many," he crowed. Arnold was right. Confidence in Morris was sinking fast. The way he put leaving off until May suggested he was playing games and publishing his letters embarrassed Congress, tilting even sympathetic members against him. Morris's enemies, then and later, feasted on his error, implicating the financier in wrongdoing every way they could.[9]

While Morris defended his actions, Congress forged ahead with its own financial program. Cobbled together by a committee led by Madison, the plan called for a new impost, a mix of tariffs, and a modification of the Articles of Confederation's tax quota system to use population rather than land value as the means of divvying up each state's share. To get buy in, Madison's proposal also offered abatements for states occupied by the British, held out generous credits for war expenses already paid by states, encouraged states to cede their western lands to Congress for sale, empowered states to appoint tax collectors, and limited the impost's duration to twenty-five years. Congress accepted the report, ordered it to be printed for debate, and sent a copy to Mr. Morris for his consideration[10]

Morris was not happy with it. He flayed the proposal as an insult to the creditors and a surrender of Congress's power. "*Justice requires that the Debts be paid*," he thundered. Congress must stand up to the states and flex the muscle implied by the Articles of Confederation when it gave the body responsibility to discharge national debts. "*The Right of Congress is perfect and the Duty* [of the states] *to pay absolute*," Morris wrote, breathing uncharacteristic fire.[11]

Morris wouldn't budge on two issues dear to skeptics of national power. The duration of taxes must not be limited, he argued. The taxes must be guaranteed to last as long as it took to pay creditors. "No Man in his Senses, Morris lectured, "will lend Money on any other Terms." Also, Congress must appoint the tax collectors. Morris offered seven reasons why, concluding with the frustrated observation that "it is a

Kind of Absurdity in itself that Congress should have a Right to the Tax and yet no Right to send their Servants to receive it."[12]

Morris capped his response to Congress's tax plan with a breath-taking assertion of centralized authority. He turned the request that the states receive generous credit for payments already made to defray war expenses into a call for the total assumption of state war debts by Congress, the same measure with which Hamilton would later roil the new nation as treasury secretary in 1790.[13]

As audacious as Hamilton's plan would be under the new Consti-tution in the Washington administration, it was beyond the pale in 1783. Congress rebuffed Morris's assumption bid without a vote, "its impropriety being generally proclaimed," Madison recorded. Congress was no more impressed with the rest of Morris's report. The body reaf-firmed that revenue should be raised solely from taxes on imports and an excise on spirituous liquor. Then, Morris's proposals were sent back to committee for more study. Congress had grown deaf to warnings from the Finance Office.[14]

While Congress pushed forward with its financial reforms, the del-egates also appeared to make progress addressing the officers' memo-rial. When debate began, commutation was two states short, and since the new representatives from Delaware (expected any day) were said to favor commutation, General McDougall appealed to Connecticut delegate Eliphalet Dyer. With the state's other delegate supporting commutation, Dyer made McDougall a promise: if Delaware assented, he would not be the last holdout. He would say yes, and with both Delaware and Connecticut, the officers would have the nine states for commutation.[15]

On March 10, the Delaware delegates presented their credentials (they'd been appointed February 1, no rush in traveling). Dyer, a pre-vious no, brought commutation back to the floor, as was allowed by Congressional rules. So far, so good. The roll call began.

New Hampshire: everyone "no"—as expected.

Massachusetts: all "aye"—a positive sign from New England.

Rhode Island: both "no"—of course.

Connecticut: Mr. Wolcott, "aye," and Mr. Dyer. . . "no!"

Dyer voted "no!" At the last minute! On his own motion! McDougall was dumbfounded. "To the astonishment of Congress," he related to Knox, Dyer "*voted against it* and lost us the question." Supposedly, McDougall said, Dyer decided out of nowhere that commutation was only fair if it were approved by each individual officer, universally, with not one dissent or missed vote. McDougall vowed to get to the bottom of things with the gentleman from Connecticut and "tell him in plain terms, in what light the Army, and all honest Men, must consider this Conduct."[16]

Contrary to McDougall's information, Dyer had no new conditions in mind. He was simply torn, unable to make a decision that was sure to anger either the civilians in Connecticut, who deprecated pensions, or the Connecticut officers, who demanded pensions. Mortified that he was the critical vote, Dyer was overwhelmed, self-pitying, and praying for some miraculous way out that didn't require him to do anything. In the end, Dyer followed his antipension heart and made McDougall furious.[17]

On March 12, Dyer received an unexpected reprieve from the spotlight, and for once it was for a positive reason: the long-awaited preliminary peace treaty with Britain was confirmed. The ship *George Washington* arrived from Lorient, France, with the official dispatches from the American peace commissioners. The hints from the king's speech were true. The United States and Britain made a treaty on November 30 that recognized American independence. There was more. The *George Washington* carried 600,000 livres ($111,000 US) the first installment of a 6-million-livres loan ($1.1 million US) promised by the king of France. Britain still needed to reconcile with the other belligerents, France, Spain, and the Netherlands, but since the dispatches were dated in December, it was reasonable to conclude that a general peace was already signed and the announcement on its way across the Atlantic.[18]

The treaty bumped commutation from the spotlight in the following week and deciding what to tell the French minister—whose king had just approved a loan for an ally that cut him out of negotiations—took precedence over debating financial plans. Although commutation depended on the gentleman from Connecticut, a new financial program became more likely as a result of peace because the war was ending and even the most difficult members thought it was time to settle affairs. The arrival of a new French loan also emboldened Morris's enemies to move forward with Congress's plan, ignoring the financier. Here was a new loan. Why the rush for liberty-depriving taxes?[19]

On March 17, more news from outside Philadelphia resurrected commutation and brought the officers' memorial demands to a head. Congress learned about the crisis in the Highlands. Washington's March 12 letter to Boudinot was read to Congress along with the enclosed anonymous letters and Washington's general orders postponing the proposed meeting.

"This alarming intelligence from the army" staggered Congress, Madison recorded, and added to concerns about treaty negotiations, debts and finances, unity among the states, and the financier's resignation. The news, Madison lamented, "gave peculiar awe & solemnity to the present moment, & oppressed the minds of Congs. with an anxiety & distress which had been scarcely felt in any period of the revolution."[20]

Not only depressed, Congress felt threatened. In the surviving reactions, no one picked up on Major Armstrong's reasonable requests for timely redress of the officers' grievances. Instead, his outrageous lines about the army's alternatives caught the ears of the delegates, who were taken aback by the anonymous letter's insinuation of justified violence. Madison deplored the "inflammatory exhortations to the army to assemble for the purpose of seeking by other means, that justice which their country shewed no disposition to afford them." Dyer condemned the "many Indecent threats" aimed at obtaining justice "at the Point of the Bayonet."[21]

Less dangerous but no less hurtful were the officers' suspicions of their motives. "We have been for five or Six weeks past, most faithfully & honestly engaged in laying a Foundation for their future security," Boudinot assured Washington about the officers' pensions. Being a delegate was hard, thankless work, he emphasized, and the officers should stop pretending they were the only ones who suffered. "There is not a Man among them," Boudinot concluded, "who would envy our Station, was he to be one week in Congress."[22]

The one ray of light for Congress in the storm of the officers' discontent was General Washington: his constancy, his wisdom, his loyalty to civilian rule, his skill in dissipating the emergency. "The conduct of Washington does equal honor to his prudence and to his virtue," Madison confirmed to Edmund Randolph in Virginia. For fellow Virginian John Francis Mercer, Washington was all that stood between the army and catastrophe—but Washington was enough. "The Army are in a Situation truly alarming & highly critical," he revealed to a friend. "But for the pru[dence] & discretion of the Commander in chief, the [con]sequences would perhaps prove a reiteration of those Calamities which have already desolated this Country."[23]

Anxious, some congressmen were also vindictive. After the dispatch from Newburgh was read, Congress designated a committee to prepare a response, choosing Dyer and other members blamed for obstructing commutation and general revenue in an attempt to "saddle" the recalcitrant members with "embarrassment."[24]

With the officers' crisis in full view inside the statehouse, attention returned to Dyer. McDougall and Lincoln, who'd received Knox's letters urging them to action, no doubt knocked on the door of the gentleman from Connecticut. Squeezed by the army, Dyer complained that he "found the whole Weight of all their resentments" pressing down on him as his vote, his assent, his change of heart, was "what alone would quiet & pacifye the Army."[25]

On March 20, Dyer relented. He resurrected commutation for a fresh vote. With the measure referred to a committee, Dyer insisted on adding an explanatory preamble of his own composition trying to thread the needle between his civilian and officer constituents and make everyone happy (or at least avoid making everyone angry with him). Other congressmen found the preamble tedious, but they indulged Dyer's attempt to cover himself. [26]

On March 22, Congress was ready to vote. But first, a new letter from Washington. The general's March 18 appeal on behalf of the officers alighted in Philadelphia and was read to the body. The reaction was surprisingly muted. "A letter was recd. from Genl Washington inclosing his address to the convention of Officers with result of their consultation," Madison recorded, with understatement. "This dissipation of the cloud which seemed to have been gathering afforded great pleasure on the whole to Congress." Theodorick Bland, writing to von Steuben, was more exuberant. He "cordially felicitate[d]" the baron "on the happy termination of a late meeting of the army." But that was it. Congress sent Washington's letter to yet another committee and proceeded to vote on commutation. [27]

Dyer was now onboard and too afraid to change his mind again, but his enemies weren't gracious winners. They prolonged debate over the preamble and "he was kept for an hour as pale as a sheet under the apprehension that his preamble would be rejected," Madison remembered. In the end, the same states that voted yes on March 10 voted yes again and with Dyer joining Wolcott, Connecticut became an "aye." The officers won commutation of their pensions. [28]

That Washington's letter on behalf of the officers' quest for pensions fell flat on the day of decision reveals the true persuasive power of Washington's leadership—and its limits. Though the cause of so much anguish for the officers, the general, and the advocates of commutation, Washington's letter made little difference because he had already made his strongest impression with his actions in confronting the crisis. By delaying the meeting, "in very gentle terms," as the Maryland delegates pointed out, Washington showed he had everything under control.

The words that mattered most for Congress came in the March 12 letter that Washington had written to Boudinot in reaction to the appearance of Armstrong's address. The delegates heard the general reaffirm his subservience to civilian authority and his unshakeable loyalty to Congress. "In every vicissitude of Circumstances, [and] still activated with the greatest Zeal in their Service," Washington had written, "I shall continue my utmost Exertions to promote the welfare of my Country under the most lively Expectation, that Congress have the best Intentions of doing ample Justice to the Army, as soon as Circumstances will possibly admit." Washington's confidence calmed. Washington's reputation sufficed.[29]

Before Congress restarted debate on national finance, another bulletin hit Philadelphia, and it was more good news: a general peace was agreed to in Europe. On March 23, the French corvette *Triomphe* dropped anchor in the Delaware River, and its captain, sent by Admiral d'Estaing and the Marquis de Lafayette, stepped onto the dock with a proclamation of the cessation of hostilities. Accompanying letters confirmed it was true. The fighting was over, and an armistice was declared pending final approval of the treaty by all sides.[30]

Elias Boudinot sent word to Washington right away. "It is with the most unfeigned Joy," he trumpeted, "that I congratulate your Excellency and the whole army on the confirmation of the signing of the definitive Treaty of peace by all the belligerent powers." As president of Congress, it was Boudinot's responsibility to broadcast the news, which he did, scrawling letter after letter by hand until he was "so weary of writing, that I am almost sick of a Pen & Ink." But it was a happy chore. "My Head is perfectly wild," he told a friend.[31]

—⁂—

In the Highlands and in the dark, Washington awaited the result of his plea to Congress. He was anxious, and learning about the preliminary treaty with Britain on March 19 did nothing to calm his nerves. He expected the war to continue. "I have my fears," he told Boudinot, "that we shall be obliged to worry thro' another Campaign." He couldn't shake his obsession with an attack on New York City and ruminated over battle plans.[32]

The general's greatest uneasiness concerned the officers. Despite the confidence voiced in his message to Congress, Washington worried that passions might flare anew at any moment. "Do not, my dear Sir, suffer this appearance of tranquility to relax your endeavours to bring the requests of the Army to a conclusion," he told Jones, in answer to the Virginia delegate's now well-known letter. "Believe me, the Officers are too much pressed by their present wants, & are rendered too sore by the recollection of their past sufferings to be touched much longer upon the string of forbearance." And don't expect another timely intervention from the commander in chief. "Nor would I have further reliance placed on any influence of mine to dispel other clouds if more should arise from the causes of the last." Washington confided the same fears to his cousin Lund. If the states continued obstructing pensions, "well may another anonymous addresser step forward, & with more effect than the last did, say with him [to the officers], 'You have Arms in your hands, do justice to yourselves, & never sheath the sword, 'till you have obtained it.'"[33]

Washington fumed about the anonymous letter as March turned to April. He believed it was part of a conspiracy to inflame the passions of the officers and to "sow the seeds of discord between the Civil & military powers of the continent." To Robert Livingston, Washington damned the letter as "insidious"; to Lund Washington, "most insidious." The general was so worked up he didn't even give Lund orders about Mount Vernon.[34]

For Washington, the timing of events was all too adroit to be an accident. The arrival of Walter Stewart from Philadelphia . . . the appearance of the anonymous letter . . . the summons for the officers to meet . . . it must have resulted from some malign influence. The expert composition of the letter was another piece of evidence to Washington. It was nearly perfect. "In elegance and force of expression [it] has rarely been equaled in the English language," Washington marveled. Though the appearance of the second letter confirmed the author was in camp, Washington still couldn't believe an officer had written it alone or timed its release so deftly to take advantage of Congress's delayed response to the officers' memorial. [35]

Like other people of his time, Washington was a conspiracy theorist, just as susceptible to the paranoia of no coincidences as anybody else. Though Washington suspected he knew the identity of the anonymous author, he refused to name him. The way he described the threat, however, as an attempt to sow discord between the civilian and military powers suggests Washington still blamed one or several people outside of the army.

In Philadelphia, Madison speculated that the holders of loan office certificates were the culprits, informing Edmund Randolph "there seems to be reason to suspect that the intrigues of the civil creditors fan the discontents of the army." Independently, Washington reached a similar conclusion. When the first anonymous letter appeared, Washington disclosed to Hamilton a rumor passing around camp "that the public creditors looked up to them for Redress of their own grievances, w[oul]d afford them every aid, and even join them in the Field if necessary." Washington also floated the possible involvement of "some members of Congress" who hoped "to compel the public, particularly the delinquent States, to do justice." [36]

Though Washington reserved judgment on any particular person until ascertaining the facts more fully, he had several men in mind. Immediately after the appearance of the first anonymous letter, rumor around headquarters had it that Gouverneur Morris was the author, an excellent guess in light of his strong pen, avid support of uniting the army with the civil creditors, and reputation as an intriguer. The second anonymous letter dispelled the notion that a Philadelphian was the author, but Morris did not escape scrutiny. In an April letter to

Hamilton, Washington charged Gouverneur as responsible for laying "in a great degree, the ground work of the superstructure which was intended to be raised in the Army by the Anonymous Addresser."[37]

Morris certainly wanted the army to declare itself united with the public creditors as a way to spike the pressure on Congress and the states. He had said so directly in February letters to Knox and to Nathanael Greene. But Gouverneur was simply pushing the well-known policy of Robert Morris that all creditors—wealthy merchants, supply contractors, farmers who had a cow impressed by the army, wizened old widows, as well as soldiers and officers—should harmonize their political voices and call for general funds together. The army was one piece among many in the financier's solution to the puzzle of national debt.[38]

When Gouverneur learned that Knox refused to endorse his plan, he was disappointed but accepted the answer. "I agree with you most perfectly in Opinion," Morris replied, that the officers should "not be obliged to employ yourselves." Morris was frustrated, without a doubt, and he gave Knox an earful about the "slavery" of his office, the "Littleness" of congressmen, and the "Folly" into which they were headed, but he offered no further plan, other than to trust in "the Guardian Genius of America." Written on February 28, right before Stewart departed Philadelphia for the north (Stewart probably carried it himself), the letter reveals Morris's forlorn state of mind. In it, he spoke the language of resignation, not cabal.[39]

In attempting to penetrate the conspiracy, the commander in chief's gaze also focused on Gouverneur's boss, Robert Morris. In early May, Washington wrote Morris about his role in the affair and asked the financier . . . we don't know what exactly: the letter, so vital, is lost. Morris's reply later that month gives some hints, however. Washington must have demanded (in his polite, indirect way) to know how much of the whispers about Philadelphia politicians and the public debtors riling up the army was true. Morris blamed a misinterpretation of his resignation as the source of the calumny against him. "By some designing

Men my resignation of Office . . . was misconstrued," he protested. "It was represented as a factious Desire to raise civil Commotions." Morris deplored how much traction the attacks on his resignation had gotten. They were driven, he said, by jealousy, and a belief he was motivated by a "sinister Respect to my own private Emolument"—the old charge that he enriched himself at public expense. Morris was emphatic. "It shall not again be supposed that I am the Leader of Sedition."[40]

The financier's strategy of uniting creditors was well known by the spring of 1783. The previous year he had encouraged holders of loan officer certificates, such as Stewart and his father-in-law, Blair McClenachan, to organize themselves and complain to Congress and to their states. Their demands to approve funding would allow Morris to resume interest payments on the bonds. In that episode, however, Morris explicitly warned against the "language of Threats," including to McClenachan. Assuming Morris still wanted to pressure Congress, he didn't need to gin up army tensions because he had his own weapon to wield: his resignation, which he made public as March began. With the impact unknown when Stewart left for camp, there was no reason for Morris to also foment a crisis in the army.[41]

General Washington, though squinting hard for culprits, did not suspect several of the other key actors traditionally ascribed roles in a Newburgh Conspiracy.

He never thought Armstrong was the "anonymous addresser." No one around the Hasbrouck House did, and there's no reason Washington would have been acquainted with the young major's literary skill. Aside from being the son of a friend, there was no reason for Washington to have noticed Armstrong at all.[42]

Horatio Gates appears nowhere in Washington's postcrisis correspondence, and he received permission in late March to leave the Highlands to attend to his wife, Elizabeth. Gates arrived home to Berkeley County, Virginia, in time to see her pass in June. Though some historians play up Washington's suspicions of his one-time rival, the only evidence that Washington perceived a threat from Gates comes from an inadequate interpretation of Washington's reaction to rumors that he was losing the officers' confidence. Supposedly, Washington identified Gates as the source of such rumors, when, in his March 4 letter to Hamilton, he attributed the gossip to "the old leven," which "is again beginning to work, under the mask of the most perfect dissimulation & apparent cordiallity." According to Washington biographer Douglass Southall Freeman, "old leven" meant Gates because "the context scarcely affords ground for doubt of his meaning." The interpretation persists. [43]

However, unmentioned is the critical context of what "old leven" (really "old leaven") meant in the 18th century. It was a colloquialism drawn from a Bible verse (1 Corinthians 5:7) warning against old prejudices irrationally retained. The King James Version offers "Purge out therefore the old leaven, that ye may be a new lump, as ye are unleavened." Given that Washington was responding to the charge that his popularity was sinking because of a lukewarm advocacy for his officers, the "old leven" was more likely the old slander of indecision and not a specific person. [44]

Washington also failed to doubt the supposed arch manipulator, Alexander Hamilton. In traditional accounts of a Newburgh Conspiracy, Hamilton welcomed news of the crisis on the Hudson, pleased that his scheme to weaponize the army against Congress and the states came to fruition. Washington, however, didn't see it that way. He found Hamilton's explanation of his conduct in the affair persuasive.

Hamilton wrote Washington as soon as he learned about the crisis in camp. His letter was a torrent of incongruous tones. He was smug, disdainful, defensive, depressed, provocative, doubtful, confident (or affecting confidence), impractical, and rash all at the same time. The former aide-de-camp began like a know-it-all. "Your Excellency has in my opinion acted wisely," he said. "The best way is ever not to attempt to stem a torrent but to divert it." Hamilton then heaped more praise on the general for meeting his expectations. "I am happy to find You coincide in opinion with me on the conduct proper to be observed by yourself." A man less polite than Washington might have noted he didn't need his former aide's approval or advice.[45]

Hamilton then turned to the status of peace negotiations and suggested, bizarrely, that Washington use the precarious state of foreign affairs to help diffuse tensions with the army because such information might "operate upon the patriotism of the officers against hazarding any domestic commotions." Luckily, Washington's speech at the Temple of Virtue was already delivered, sans input from Hamilton.[46]

Hamilton stiffened against criticism of his willingness to use the army's discontent for political advantage. The states and their "dangerous prejudices" were the problem and "necessity alone can work a reform." But just as Hamilton puffed himself up, he sunk into despair. "I fear we have been contending for a shadow."[47]

Switching mood again, the letter ended with a sunny review of the progress of the officers' pension commutation (heading in the right direction), the prospects of securing new funding (good, in Congress at least), and the likelihood that British troops would soon evacuate New York City (strong, unless the officers did anything foolish, which "will be a pity").[48]

Hamilton had said nothing about Washington's charge that the crisis in the Highlands originated in Philadelphia, and uneasy about leaving the matter alone, Hamilton appended a lengthy postscript defending his conduct.

The charge was "partly true," Hamilton admitted. "I have myself urged in Congress the propriety of uniting the influence of the public creditors, & the army as a part of them, to prevail upon the states to enter into their views." It was no secret. "I have expressed the same sentiments out of doors," meaning publicly. Other congressmen, he revealed, had done the same, inside and out of the Pennsylvania Statehouse. Hamilton explained the strategy he had followed throughout the year. He wanted to enlist as many allies as possible to pressure as many of the opponents of reform as possible with as many arguments as possible. He aimed to unite all the national creditors, including the army, so "that Congress should adopt such a plan as would embrace the relief of all the public creditors including the army; in order that the personal influence of some, the connections of others, and a sense of justice to the army as well as the apprehension of ill consequences might form a mass of influence in each state in favour of the measures of Congress." Hamilton offered no apology. The officers' complaints were an opportunity, and the latest turn of events had not changed his mind. "I am still of opinion that their earnest, but respectful applications for redress will have a good effect." Concerned that he might appear too brazen, Hamilton clarified his meaning and disavowed violence. "As to any combination of *Force*," he wrote, meaning violence, "it would only be productive of the horrors of a civil war, might end in the ruin of the Country & would certainly end in the ruin of the army."[49]

Looking at Hamilton's extraordinary letter now it's easy to isolate his more extreme statements as evidence of a well-crafted conspiracy. But taken as a whole—with its abrupt changes in tone, its strange moodiness, its indecision—the letter calls for a subtler reading. In this case, Hamilton, though a man of many words, did not quite know what to say. In part, he couldn't have been sure how to respond to Washington, who was agitated and keen to blame Philadelphia politicians. Hamilton escaped the general's censure, but he was implicated in the criticism Washington lobbed southward. From their many years together, Hamilton thought he knew Washington—and he'd recently bragged that he knew the general "intimately & perfectly"—but they had not spoken in over a year. What's more, Hamilton lacked Washington's insight into conditions in camp and for all he knew, the March 15 meeting was a disaster.[50]

At the same time, Hamilton wanted to project certainty, as if events were unfolding according to his expectations, as if he could ensure the outcome. In truth, he feared that there was no solution for the nation's problems then within reach. The debt was the debt, overwhelming. The states were the states, suspicious of power. Congress was the Congress, limited to recommendations. The army was the army, unpaid and unhappy. But Hamilton charged ahead. Throughout the winter and early spring of 1783, his strategy was to attack on all fronts—to unite civilian creditors with the army, to laud the benefits of new revenue, to demand justice for the officers and soldiers, and to frighten the recalcitrant with the consequences of failure. He wanted men of wealth, the creditors who loaned money to the war effort, and the officers, the men who won independence, to work over everyone else, appealing to every selfish hope for payment, calling in every favor to vote for new taxes, and intimidating everyone attached to irrational state-first prejudices into believing that Continental policy alone could deliver them from impending domestic and foreign evils. Hamilton, then, did not try to create a crisis in the army. He tried to reveal the reality of crisis surrounding the army and the nation.

But he couldn't quite pull it off. Though a schemer, Hamilton was also a big mouth. Throughout his life, he acted impulsively, often at the worst possible times. His passions carried him away, especially when speaking. In a later letter to Washington, Hamilton admitted his emotions got the best of him in the pension and funding debate. "I often feel a mortification," he confided, "which it would be impolitic to express, that sets my passions at variance with my reason." Coupled with Hamilton's prior admission that he openly advocated influencing the states by uniting the army with the other creditors, it becomes clear what Hamilton did: he spoke loudly, incautiously, passionately and beyond the bounds of reason, about the supposed benefits of using the army for political effect. Rashness, not Machiavellianism, was Hamilton's true character flaw.[51]

To the extent Hamilton participated in a Newburgh Conspiracy, then, it was not the result of a calculated plan but because of a lack of one. Hamilton failed to restrain himself and let the ordinary political process unfold. The recklessness of Hamilton and others led Walter Stewart, under pressure from his father-in-law and the public creditors, to the conclusion that a new statement was urgently needed. And Armstrong, incautious and inflammatory, took it from there.

The conspiracy mindset common to everyone involved—politicians, administrator, officers, and even Washington himself—made it impossible for anyone to consider anything other than a plot, and their letters teem with the belief that some mysterious mastermind pulled the strings behind the scenes. But there wasn't any mastermind. The alleged prime movers—Gouverneur Morris, Robert Morris, Gates, and Hamilton—all contributed to the crisis without a grand design, more accidentally than by intention.

Armstrong himself gradually came to understand why his plan collapsed. In the immediate aftermath, he pounced on gossip from Matthias Ogden about fellow memorial committee member John Brooks to explain the failure. Brooks was a "timid Wretch" who scuttled the scheme in February when he returned to camp from Philadelphia. Rather than spreading among the officers "sentiments like those contained in the anonymous address . . . to prepare their minds for some manly, vigorous Association with the other public Creditors," Brooks divulged the secret to Washington, who then had a month's warning to thwart him. In 1803, as he was dogged by charges of disloyalty Armstrong published a pamphlet, anonymously, in which he tried to set the record straight. He pointed to his letter's moderate demands. All he wanted was a committee formed to write Congress. The talk of force, he said, was misconstrued by his enemies. Finally, as an old man in the 1820s Armstrong offered a new explanation. He and Stewart were simply trying to get a new letter to Congress and build support for uniting with the public creditors, when out of nowhere Washington received a note from a member of Congress alerting him to a conspiracy against his command, which he associated with the anonymous letter. Armstrong was still self-serving, but he'd come a long way in forty years from the classic conspiracy theorizing—Brooks intentionally ruined everything—to a more mature acceptance of the role of accident and bad timing.[52]

Though they weren't conspirators, the central figures weren't blameless, either. Gates allowed Armstrong, Stewart, and others to meet at his house. Robert Morris printed his resignation in the newspaper. Hamilton and Gouverneur Morris carelessly advocated unity among the creditors and irresponsibly spread rumors that the army had decided not to disband. Other congressmen could be faulted for accepting the rumors uncritically, although spreading and believing rumors is what 18th-century politicians did, especially when the rumors confirmed their prior ideological beliefs. Add all the mistakes together with a fondness for conspiracy theories; stir in the stress of eight years of war, an empty treasury, uncertainty about peace, and anxiety for the future; season everything with ideological antagonisms to central power, hostility to standing armies, and fondness for conspiracy thinking; and an army crisis was the result.

—◊—

Washington wasn't done hashing out conspiracy theories with Hamilton, but in the meantime he discovered one of his fears was unfounded. On March 26, Washington started hearing rumblings about a general peace. "God grant that the news may be true," he sighed to Knox. It was. The next night a rider dashed to headquarters with the dispatches received in Philadelphia, and in the following day's general orders, Washington, unable to "resist the pleasure of communicating the happiness he experiences from a certainty of that event," shared the intelligence with the army—while also reminding them not to go lax.[53]

Too late! The celebrations were already underway, and the warning went unheeded. Benjamin Gilbert and some of his friends were dining at their commanding officer's house when they heard, "on which we kept it up Dancing & drinking all Night." After seeing the general orders, "the Joy of the soldiers," Gilbert recalled, "was so great they caroused all Night" and into the next, which they spent "marching, Huzzaing, & drinking all day."[54]

The officers had even more reason to party. On March 29, they learned of Congress's resolution on commutation. "We were now for some time in high Spirits," Bernardus Swartwout remembered. "The news of Peace and the Resolutions of Congress passed in favor of the Continental Army together with the strongest assurances from the Commander in Chief that he would exert himself to obtain releif for the troops, all this had the desired Effect, and the Army felt Easy & Composed with all these fair promises." Peace and pensions in the same banner week. Gilbert and his buddies made merry with another visit to Wyoma. [55]

For Washington, the peace meant a flurry of sending and receiving congratulations, which he sent and received with his usual impeccable manners. The commutation of half pay and Congress's positive reaction to the officers' March 15 meeting were also encouraging. Washington relaxed for a moment and contemplated a happy future for the country. "The Army here, universally participate in the general Joy which this Event has diffused, and, from this consideration, together with the late Resolutions of Congress, for the Commutation of the Half pay, and for a Liquidation of all their Accounts, their Minds are filled with the highest Satisfaction," he told General Greene in South Carolina. One challenge remained, namely, "for the States to be wise" and to bind together the union. "May Heaven give them Wisdom to adopt the measures still necessary for this important purpose." [56]

It was a hard prayer to answer, and Washington knew it. The exuberance of peace brought a new dimension to the old problems of national finance, state authority, and army discontent: how to get everybody paid, discharged, and sent home, when there was still no money. The answer, as always, would depend on Robert Morris's credit, Congress's backbone, the states' willingness to tax, and General Washington's leadership.

NINE

The Army Disbands

In early April, Benjamin Gilbert basked in the warming days of spring. Out and about almost every day after the armistice, he dined and danced and drank, went shopping in New Windsor with friends (on credit), attended concerts at the Temple, and made three visits to the brothel with Ensign Wing and Dr. Finley (also on credit).[1]

Gilbert's roistering covered his anxiety about the peace. He didn't want to be a soldier all his life, and he assumed he'd have a career and a family, but after eight years, the army was what he knew best. An officer's rank gave him status and provided an honorable way to avoid dealing with Patience Converse, the girl he'd left pregnant back home in Brookfield, Massachusetts, and her increasingly impatient father. The young lieutenant palmed off the aggrieved *paterfamilias* with "a letter filled with surprise and evasion and smoothed over in such a manner that I presume he will let the matter rest for the present." But that wouldn't work much longer. The British were preparing to evacuate New York, Gilbert heard in March, and he expected to be discharged soon.[2]

Another young Massachusetts man, Captain Ebenezer Smith, revealed similar anxieties in the orderly book he kept for the Second Regiment. Interspersed among general orders and extracts of important documents, Smith wrote out dreamy poems with titles such as "Patriot and Patriotism," "Female Patriotism," "Essay on Women," and "Song, By a Young Lady Seeing a Freemasons' Procession, Wherein Her Love was Joined." Any guess what was on his mind?[3]

Smith's verses weren't original compositions—he copied and adapted them from others—but they suggest his worries about impending civilian life. In each poem, a woman pines for her warrior lover temporarily wrested from her arms by the nation's call to service. For example, in "Female Patriotism," Smith's name for an 18th-century ditty called "The Stipulation," a woman voices her passion for her husband-to-be, who leaves her side to defend his country. Its final stanza surely stirred the loins of any young officer:

> Then buckle on thy trusty sword;
>> And when our vanquish'd foes are fled,
> I plight to thee now my faithful word,
>> To take thee to my *virgin bed*.

As if anyone could miss the significance of the last two words, Smith wrote them large and underlined them vigorously.[4]

The anxieties of Gilbert and Smith were rife among the officers in the Highlands as April dawned. The armistice promised a discharge, but with their affairs unsettled, the final outcome of their service was still in doubt. The officers had pledged their faith in Congress and trusted Washington to represent their needs, and so their fate was in the hands of others. They could do nothing but wait and worry, the great question of the war's waning days hanging heavy: Would they actually be paid before going home?[5]

—⚏—

Working in his Hasbrouck House study, General Washington read the latest updates from Congress, and according to what he saw from Hamilton and Theodorick Bland, the army might not like their answer. "Our doubt arises solely from this Consideration," Bland informed Washington, "viz. that the Enormous Expence of keeping the whole Army in the field . . . would be productive of the most Ruinous Consequences to the United States." There would be "Clamors among the Citizens" and Congress's financial plans would be derailed as a result, making "it impossible to comply with what the Army most desire viz. a punctual discharge of the debt due to them, on settlement."[6]

That was the horns of the dilemma. Congress could neither subsist the army until a full settlement was ready nor pay the army prior to a discharge. Richard Peters noted the irony for the Baron von Steuben, inspecting the army in the cantonment. "The Difficulty which heretofore oppress'd us was how to raise an Army," he wrote. "The one which now embarrasses is how to dissolve it," and the stumbling block, as always, was that "an empty Purse is a Bar to the Execution of the best Intentions."[7]

Washington brought Bland's letter to a group of trusted officers, and they adjusted their expectations accordingly. When they asked Congress to keep them together until paid, the officers told Washington, they didn't expect to stay in the field solely to await payment, which would only intimidate Congress, something the officers abjured. The officers wanted their accounts adjusted to produce a firm amount owed. They just wanted the number; they didn't expect the full amount prior to discharge. The officers did, however, expect some kind of money in hand. Three months' pay, Washington informed Bland, was "absolutely indispensable." But the officers were flexible on how to receive it. One month's pay in hand would be satisfactory if they had "an absolute assurance of hav[in]g the other two Months in a short time." And if Congress couldn't produce the cash, they would accept their two month's pay directly from state tax receivers, taking off part of each state's requisition quota before it reached Philadelphia. But they had to have something. They couldn't go home empty-handed. They just couldn't. They weren't yet ready to admit that they might. [8]

As the officers once more waited on Congress, they confronted the reality that the war was ending too quickly. "We are now awaiting the arrival of the definitive treaty," Samuel Shaw told a friend. "What will become of a very large portion of the poor fellows who are about quitting a line of life that has rendered them almost unfit for any other, Heaven alone knows." For their plight, Shaw blamed civilians, who "think the distinction of a uniform coat and the splendor of a military character a sufficient compensation for the hardships and dangers it is obliged to encounter." [9]

Other officers suspected the Morrises and allied congressmen were up to no good again, stalling payment in some labyrinthine plot. The armistice brought joy, Bernardus Swartwout recalled, "but oh: Alas in a few days after, the Financier complains very much . . . news is circulating in the Cantonment that the Army is to be disbanded without a settlement." The result: "We are all thrown into the greatest & most painful Consternation." Pennsylvania officers, meanwhile, charged Morris with fraud. "Never was a more malignant and false Slander invented," Morris replied. It didn't make much difference. [10]

Washington never doubted Morris's integrity, but he hesitated to dismiss the army's suspicions of political machinations. In a confidential letter to Hamilton, the general revealed the bad vibes palpable in camp. "Some men (& leading ones too) in this Army," Washington wrote, "are beginning to entertain suspicions that Congress, or some members of it," planned to use them "as mere Puppits to establish Continental funds." The phrase "some members of Congress" included Hamilton, of course, though indirectly and without lodging the allegation personally. Washington did, however, specifically name "the Financier" as the man "suspected to be at the bottom of this scheme." The general concluded with a warning for his former aide, whom he trusted to decide whether to tell Morris: "the Army (considering the irritable state it is in, its sufferings & composition) is a dangerous instrument to play with."[11]

Hamilton replied with a long, detailed defense of himself and Morris. Recounting the ins and outs of Congress's debates that spring, Hamilton turned the allegation of playing politics with the army against the other side. It was the opponents of continental funds, he charged, who tried to destroy the impost (and therefore pensions) by tying its revenue exclusively to the army as justification for its limitations, as if debts owed to a part could be funded without establishing the credit of the whole. As for Morris, Hamilton asserted, he was a victim of Arthur Lee's venom, the true source of the animosity toward Morris among even moderate members. "Mr. Morris certainly deserves a great deal from his country," Hamilton concluded. "I believe no man in this country but himself could have kept the money-machine a going."[12]

Hamilton made it clear he considered the rumors about him a matter of honor. "I assure you on my honor Sir I have given you a candid state of facts to the best of my judgment," Hamilton pledged. As a gentleman, honor was Hamilton's most cherished possession, and he didn't invoke it lightly. He went further. Knowing that Washington might choose to share the letter with others to counter the gossip in camp, Hamilton called on respected third parties to vouch for his conduct, namely, the officers' delegation, McDougall, Ogden, and Brooks. "The Gentlemen who were here from the army; [and] General McDougall who is still here will be able to give a true account of those who have supported the just claims of the army," Hamilton promised.[13]

Washington's highly quotable line about the army being a "dangerous instrument to play with" is often cited by historians who believe in a Newburgh Conspiracy since it appears to confirm that Washington knew Hamilton and Morris were manipulating the officers for their own ends. Not well appreciated is the context in which Washington wrote, namely, following the armistice when the issue of receiving pay before discharge preoccupied the army. No one had forgotten about the events of mid-March, of course, but foremost in Washington's mind as he wrote in April was the army's desire for three-months' pay, not the earlier concern about rousing the army to pressure Congress and the states.

Also not well appreciated is the apology Washington wrote Hamilton. "My last letter to you was written in a hurry, when I was fatigued," Washington admitted. "Possibly," he continued, "I did not on that occasion express myself (in what I intended as a hint) with so much perspicuity as I ought—possibly too, what I then dropped, might have conveyed more than I intended; for I do not, at this time, recollect the force of my expression." What he really meant when he said the "Army is a dangerous instrument to play with" was that enlisting the army in the present debate was bad politics. The army was as divided as Congress on whether they should be paid by the nation or by their states, Washington explained. If anyone assumed they could line up the army in unanimous support of continental funds, they were mistaken. Washington supported continental funds. He thought like Morris and Hamilton. He wanted the nation to pay its debts, above all to the army, and establish its credit abroad. But he also wanted a strategy to obtain continental funds to work. In the end, Washington's objection to involving the army in politics was not ideological. He believed soldiers were citizens and should participate in politics like any civilian. Washington's objection was pragmatic. "For these reasons I said, or meant to say, the Army was a dangerous Engine to work with," Washington concluded. "Considering the Sufferings of it," the army "would, more than probably, throw its weight into that Scale which seemed most likely to preponderate towards its immediate relief, without looking forward (under the pressure of present wants) to future consequences with the eyes of Politicians." [14]

Washington backed off the accusations against Hamilton and the financier. It was Gouverneur Morris, not Robert, who the army eyed warily, Washington now said. Difficult though it might be to keep them straight, Washington's admission suggests more evidence of his exhaustion than a factual basis for suspecting Gouverneur. Whatever the case with the Morrises, Washington exonerated Hamilton. "The opinion of the Army," Washington promised, is "that they consider you as a friend, Zealous to serve them, and one who has espoused their interests in Congress upon every proper occasion." Washington didn't say it, but that was his opinion, too. Their relationship repaired, they corresponded regularly in the war's remaining days, forging a partnership that would build the new nation.[15]

—m—

While Hamilton and Washington grew closer, the officers as a whole felt increasingly isolated as their final separation from the army approached and each day brought them closer to the unwelcome status of civilian. Fearing the loss of comrades, General Knox spearheaded the creation of a fraternal order of officers to be called the Society of the Cincinnati, after the Roman general Lucius Quinctius Cincinnatus, a legend of civic virtue who gave up a dictator's power and returned to his farm. Knox consulted with Baron von Steuben and Jedediah Huntington, a Connecticut general also at West Point, and on April 15, he circulated his blueprint for the society among the troops in the Highlands.[16]

Knox had been thinking about a way to honor officers since early in the war, and by this time, Dr. William Eustis and Christopher Richmond, both associates of John Armstrong, Jr., had discussed holding reunions for officers, since it was "unhappy that such a band of friends and brothers should be separated perhaps never to meet again."[17]

For Knox, the society would provide fellowship for officers as well as charity for infirmed or indigent members and their families. The general also grasped the political utility of such a group. Building on the officers' organizing, drafting, and presenting their memorial of the previous fall, the society would help the officers lobby Congress and the states to fund their pensions. Of course, Knox's proposal avoided crass politicking for a grander vision that pledged members to "promote by all legal means That Union and harmony between the respective States so essentially necessary to their happiness and the future dignity of the American Empire." The society would have county and state chapters with delegates attending a general national meeting every three years. As a result, the Cincinnati were well positioned to wield influence at every level of government. [18]

All officers were eligible for membership, including those unceremoniously deranged by Congress's reorganization schemes, which was still a sore spot. French and other foreign officers, too, were invited to join. Fond of ribbons, Knox planned a medal for members to wear, with his design featuring two images of Cincinnatus, front and back, along with multiple Latin mottos and assorted symbols of liberty, virtue, farming, commerce, patriotism, friendship, family, and everlasting fame. Finally—and most controversially—Knox made the society hereditary, with membership passing from father to eldest son. [19]

The Society of the Cincinnati formally launched on May 13, the final charter, or "institution," agreed to at the headquarters of Baron von Steuben in Fishkill-on-Hudson, across the river from Newburgh. The original signers of the institution were a who's who of officers involved in the so-called Newburgh Conspiracy, though they were mostly men who opposed the anonymous letter, such as Knox, Rufus Putnam, and, of course, Washington. But Walter Stewart also signed. So did John Brooks and Alexander McDougall, who returned from Philadelphia in May, his mission at last complete. Not all original members were happy to be aboard. Timothy Pickering, a terrible joiner, sniffed at the society as typical of Knox's self-importance. Still he signed on to avoid the suspicion that he done something dishonorable to preclude membership. [20]

Pickering's scheme to avoid censure backfired. When the public learned about a society of officers with hereditary membership, critics shrieked the doom of the republic. Aristocracy! Monarchy! Foreign influence! Even the charitable fund was suspect because it proved pensions weren't needed. The officers could take care of each other, if they weren't so lazy, greedy, or hungry for power. South Carolina judge Aedanus Burke scorched the society's pretensions. If the officers were really citizen-soldiers, then "why in the name of God not be contented 'to return to citizenship,' without usurping an hereditary order?" Though eccentric, Burke was not a lone crank. John Adams, John Jay, Benjamin Franklin, and Thomas Jefferson all agreed that the Cincinnati were an aristocratic menace. The society's problems lay in the future, however. In the spring of 1783, Knox's creation served its purpose as a group that bonded brother officers and calmed anxieties about reentering civilian life.[21]

—◊—

With the officers finding support among themselves, the danger in camp now came from the enlisted men. They suffered no misgivings about leaving the army as soon as possible. They wanted out. Immediately. The difference between an armistice and a final definitive treaty ratified by Congress eluded them. No more hostilities meant no more service. Restlessness in camp led to drunken rowdiness. Fighting. Disobeying orders. Annoying civilians. One Pennsylvania soldier was charged with mutiny for "speaking disrespectfully of His Excellency Genl Washington & Congress" and, crime of crimes, "drinking a health to King George." He was sentenced to 100 lashes and drumming "out of the Army with a halter around his Neck."[22]

Washington's greatest dilemma was what to do with the men enlisted for the war, who not unreasonably considered the war over and their service complete. Congress, however, had never decided what "for the war" really meant, and the dragged-out ordeal of the war's desultory end left Washington without an answer. At the same time, the noncommissioned officers, the first line of defense against a mutiny, were getting uppity. Seeing the officers receive pensions made them wonder why they shouldn't get pensions, too. The corporals and sergeants from the New Jersey and Connecticut lines wanted half pay or commutation just like the lowliest ensign enjoyed. They were organizing themselves and preparing a memorial.[23]

Hierarchal from head to toe, Washington had no patience for the noncommissioned officers' claims to the emoluments of gentlemen officers. Still, he did what he could for his men, officers and enlisted alike. He pushed the states for a quick settlement of accounts and leaned on Robert Morris to scare up three months' pay prior to discharge. Aware of the mountain of paperwork to scale, Washington encouraged the paymaster to spare no expense assembling a team of strong-wristed penmen for the ascent.[24]

The commander in chief exhorted and prepared, but he needed Congress to act. In the first weeks of April, Congress's slowness was an asset—Washington could put off the soldiers' demands with the excuse that the armistice was not official until Congress made it official. But the excuse didn't work for long. Midway through the month, the proclamation of a cessation of hostilities arrived. Maddeningly—though typically—Congress failed to send Washington instructions on discharges.[25]

Left to fend for himself, on April 17 the commander in chief asked his generals to assemble at the Temple and advise him. Should they keep the proclamation secret from the men? If so, for how long? What should they do about the for-the-war men? Or discharging the army generally? To a man, the generals advised Washington not to conceal the proclamation. Withholding the news would be "impracticable as well as impolitic," and would only irritate the soldiers while kindling their suspicions.[26]

On the morning of April 18, the general orders went out with the armistice proclamation, prefaced by a long statement from the commander in chief flattering the men's courage, endurance, and patriotism and warning them—sometimes begging them—to behave themselves even though the war was over in every sense except for the one sense they now cared about most: a discharge from service.[27]

The next day, April 19, the eighth anniversary of the war's first shots at Lexington Green, was unseasonably cold. At noon, a group convened at the Temple to hear Congress's proclamation read aloud. "Huzza! Huzza! Huzza!" the crowd shouted. A chaplain prayed and an orchestra struck up the tune "Independence" by Bostonian songster William Billings, an expressly religious piece that was, oddly for the occasion, emphatic in its imagery of a kingly deity:

> May Rome, France and Spain and all the World proclaim
> The Glory and the Fame of our Royal King.
> Loud, Loudly sing that God is the King:
> May His reign be Glorious, America victorious
> And may the earth acknowledge God is the King.

The assembly belted out the words anyway. Then Washington capped the ceremony with a simple republican toast: "Happy & lasting Peace."[28]

Surrounded by surly soldiers and sullen officers, General Washington's toast was as much about imploring his men to control themselves as it was giving voice to the nation's aspirations.

While the army stood by unhappily, in Philadelphia Congress worked on getting them home. In late March, once the heady glow of the armistice faded, Congress took up national finances, the prerequisite for making good on its money promises. Over the following weeks the body slowly circled in on a final compromise. On April 7, Congress agreed to the target they needed to reach for debt service: $2.5 million yearly, with $1.5 million to come from requisitions on the states and $1 million to come from duties on imports. On April 18, Congress approved the final version of the plan. It called for a 5 percent impost on imports and a series of tariffs on alcohol, tea, sugar, molasses, cocoa, and coffee. Both taxes were limited to twenty-five years with revenues to accrue to Congress for no other purpose than retiring the war debt. The states would appoint collectors; Congress could fire them. The final resolution rejected abatements for states harmed by the war and ignored Morris's recommendation for Congress to assume state war debts. However, the states were exhorted to enact their own taxes to meet their quotas and to be generous in ceding western lands to Congress. Finally, the resolution embraced population as the new method for determining requisition quotas, with James Madison, as "a proof of the sincerity of his professions of liberality" offering to count three-fifths of enslaved persons toward a state's total population.[29]

As a printer cranked out copies for distribution to the states, Madison led a committee to draft a statement championing approval. The Virginian disagreed with several of the provisions; nevertheless, he prepared a 2,900-word address along with numerous attachments demonstrating each point. The army stood foremost in Madison's argument. They were "that illustrious & patriotic band of fellow Citizens, whose blood and whose bravery have defended the liberties of their Country" and who wanted only "such a portion of their dues as will enable them to retire from the field of victory & glory into the bosom of peace & private citizenship." Madison attached the December memorial and the key March documents, including the anonymous letters, Washington's speech, and the officers' resolutions, as proof of the army's "superiority to every species of seduction from the paths of virtue & of honor."[30]

Two stalwarts of restoring public credit and compensating the army couldn't join Madison in supporting the compromise resolution. Hamilton voted against it, dividing New York's delegation, although approval already had its necessary nine votes, so his defection didn't matter. According to Hamilton, no plan was better than a bad plan, and the resolution was a bad plan. It would not extinguish the debt, certainly not in twenty-five years; state-appointed collectors would drag their feet; state requisitions might not service the interest, harming every creditor who depended on interest payments for income. "Individuals have been already too long sacrificed to public convenience," he told New York's governor. "It will be shocking and indeed an eternal reproach to this country, if we begin the peaceable enjoyment of our independence by a violation of all the principles of honesty & true policy." As shocking as the delegates conduct might be, Hamilton saw the tide running against Congress becoming the stout ship he wanted it to be. Cast adrift among his colleagues, Hamilton's time in Philadelphia was nearly at an end. [31]

Robert Morris was just as dubious about the fiscal plan. Too much depended on the states. Too little revenue would be produced to secure the nation's credit. "There is indeed a Plan adopted by Congress," he informed a friend, "and if agreed to by the States it may procure to public Creditors some temporary Prospect of Releif but in my poor Opinion it is not well calculated to obtain a general Adoption nor to give (when adopted) a perfect Security." Morris, though, kept his misgivings private. He expected to leave office at the end of May. The time for battling Congress was over. [32]

But just when Morris thought he was out, Congress and the army pulled him back in—and not only to continue as financier but also to risk once more his personal fortune for public benefit. In early April, Bland and a committee visited Morris to share Washington's letter on the desperate necessity of three months' pay for the army prior to discharge. Morris must have groaned inside because he grasped immediately what was asked of him. Congress could not count on the states for the money, and he was still having trouble delivering the balance of the one month's pay promised to the army by Congress in January. Three months' pay would amount to some $750,000, and the only way to produce that amount rapidly was a "paper anticipation," meaning Morris Notes issued on the financier's own credit. A few days after their interview, Morris told the committee he wouldn't do it. He would have to either remain in office, which he had promised to resign, or trust the management of the notes to his successor, which would be an enormous risk. "But tho I would sacrifice much of my Property," Morris answered, "I cannot risk my Reputation as a Man of Integrity nor expose myself to absolute Ruin."[33]

At the end of the month, Bland and his committee, which included Hamilton and Madison, stepped up the pressure. On April 22, they waited on Morris at the Finance Office. He put them off, protesting "the difficulty of fulfilling Engagements and the danger of taking new Ones." The committee reported back to Congress and got approval to officially ask Morris to stay. On April 24, they walked back to the Finance Office. Morris begged to be left alone about paying the army. "I dread the Consequence of sending them into civil Life with Murmurs and Complaints in their Mouths," Morris conceded, but he had to think of himself. "My own Affairs call loudly for my Care and Attention." Still, Morris started to crack. "Being already engaged in this Business and willing to Oblige Congress if they think my Assistance essential," he told the committee, "I will Consent to remain in Office for the Purpose of Compleating such Payment to the Army as may be agreed on as necessary to disband them with their own Consent."[34]

Morris wanted to salvage some control over his engagements, however. On May 1 he wrote Congress asking for assurance that they would support him and that they expected no new commitments from him beyond overseeing the three months' pay and the other affairs he was already entangled in. When Morris took office he made demands on Congress, full of brashness and ambitious for wide-ranging power; now he pled for a narrow remit.[35]

Finally, on Saturday, May 3, Morris received another visit, this time from Hamilton, James Wilson, and Thomas FitzSimons. He relented. Finding "all my Friends so extremely anxious on this Subject," Morris agreed to "continue so much longer as may be necessary to disband the Army." With private life possibly months away, Morris dispensed with the day's usual "Sundry Applications" and got out of town for the weekend and "into the Country for fresh Air and Exercise." The following Tuesday, Morris ordered 15,000 sheets of paper on which to print the $750,000 worth of notes for the army. Issued in denominations ranging from $5 to $100, Morris would sign every one, each scribble plunging him deeper into debt but, perhaps, staving off the final collapse of the army. [36]

With Morris taking responsibility for paying the army, Congress addressed the other aspects of demobilization, such as deciding how much longer the men enlisted for the war had to serve now that the war was effectively over. Among the delegates, the answer depended on the practical effects of what definition of "duration of the war" they adopted. Some congressmen decried the expense of subsisting so many soldiers unnecessarily. Send them home immediately! Other congressmen denounced the folly of weakening the army while the British lingered in New York City. Watch the British with full force! On April 23, Congress split the difference with a compromise sure to confuse—and possibly enrage—the army. Congress ruled that the for-the-war-men's service "does not expire until the ratification of the definitive treaty of peace." Something that was likely months away. At the same time, Congress empowered General Washington to furlough men as needed and even issue discharges in individual cases. Furloughs allowed men to go home, while technically keeping them in the army subject to recall. [37]

Aware they needed to soothe military feelings, Congress also approved an idea proposed by Washington: soldiers and noncommissioned officers could keep their arms, marching home with pride and passing them down to their descendants as sacred objects of liberty. Some delegates, their antistanding army Spidey-senses tingling, objected to the prospect of armed soldiers roaming the countryside in peacetime. But in the end, Congress offered the weapons as "an extra reward for their long and faithful service." [38]

Individual furloughs and promises of guns, however, didn't do much to reduce the expense of maintaining an army. On May 15, Morris tried to make Congress see reality. "If your Army is kept together they will consume as much in one Month as the Taxes will produce in two and Probably much more," he informed a committee. The math just didn't work. The next week, Congress revisited its instructions to Washington. Security hawks still screeched about the danger of British occupation of New York City, now exacerbated by reports that Loyalists, in violation of the preliminary treaty, were helping slaves escape their American owners. But on May 26, economy won out. Congress directed that all men enlisted for the war and a proportional number of officers were furloughed, with discharges to follow "as soon as a definitive treaty of peace is concluded." The men were now going home. There was one tiny hiccup, however: the printer had not produced any Morris Notes. Actually, there were two tiny hiccups: the 15,000 sheets of paper needed to be made first (they weren't sitting around in a warehouse) and then sent to the printer. The army was running out of time.[39]

Secretary at War Benjamin Lincoln rode to Newburgh to present Congress's order to furlough the war men. When he arrived at headquarters without any Morris Notes, Washington sank. Discipline and supplies were deteriorating along with morale. At West Point, measles was rampant, and a riot broke out among the enlisted men. "The behaviour of most or all of the regiments was totally repugnant to discipline, and in many instances highly mutinous," Knox reported. The men were going stir-crazy, with "no particular objects in view; but huzzaring and uttering indecent expressions," Knox wrote, his Boston accent reproduced in his spelling.[40]

The only thing that might reverse the army's disintegration in disgust was money. Washington dispatched an express rider to fetch whatever notes Morris had ready. The courier made it to Philadelphia in two days, but he came back empty-handed. "Nothing would please me better than to comply instantly with your wishes," Morris replied, but the notes still weren't ready. Once printed, he promised to "devote

my whole Time to the expeditious accomplishment of this Business"—
meaning a marathon signing session followed by rapid delivery to the
Highlands.[41]

Washington didn't wait for Morris. In spite of his apprehensions,
Washington, ever obedient to his civilian masters, lost no time in carrying out the furloughs, and in the June 2 general orders, he announced
Congress's policy. All men enlisted for the war and an appropriate
number of officers were told to get ready to leave camp. Washington
said nothing about pay, except to ask the regimental paymasters to stay
behind to help settle accounts. The general's silence communicated
everything the army needed to know. They weren't getting paid.[42]

The end came swiftly. On June 5, the Marylanders left camp first.
Major Thomas Lansdale, the officer that Washington had upbraided
in February for allowing filth around his soldiers' huts, led the way out
of New Windsor. To ease concerns about marauding soldiers, Lansdale
marched his men home together via a carefully prescribed route, as
if they were traversing a neutral country between the battlefield and
their native place—because that's how the states still saw each other.
Once in Maryland, the men received their furlough papers and went
their separate ways.[43]

Other state lines followed. On June 6, the New York and New
Jersey lines departed. June 7 was New Hampshire's turn. Massachusetts, the largest contingent, was the most complicated. Beginning
June 8, men formed up each morning on the parade ground outside
the Temple. Standing in formation with their muskets and their
personal effects, they received provisions for the journey, and then an
officer ordered them up and marching, headed home to the Common-
wealth. When the last duration-of-the-war men left New Windsor on
June 13, a force of some 10,000 men was reduced to 2,700.[44]

The first delivery of Morris Notes arrived in the Highlands the
next day. A batch of $50,000 was ready June 7, but the notes, for no
apparent reason, stayed in Philadelphia with the deputy paymaster.
With the notes inexplicably and cruelly late, the men enlisted for the

war and the officers who accompanied them left without a single day's worth of the three months' pay they claimed was indispensable. The men lucky enough to be in camp when the notes arrived didn't fare much better. Even before the order to disband arrived, sutlers flush with goods descended on New Windsor eager to make deals, and all the soldiers had to do was accept a steep discount on the value of their notes. Speculators swarmed, too, sometimes abetted by officers willing to despoil their own men. They offered forty to fifty cents on the dollar for Morris Notes. Soldiers could get money now or wait and maybe get something later from Morris, if he could be trusted, which many soldiers no longer did. They thought he purposely delayed payment to cheat them. Even men who hung on to their notes had to take 20 percent cuts when the time came for redemption. Washington warned against the "foolish practice" of soldiers "disposing of their Notes and securities of pay, at a very great discount," but few listened when the sutlers had gallons of smooth whiskey on hand. [45]

Seeing the chaos, some officers protested their rapid demobilization. Through General William Heath, Gates's replacement as senior officer, they called on Washington to intervene with Congress and prevent their discharge before their affairs were settled. "It is with a mixture of astonishment and chagrin that we view the late resolve of Congress," the officers informed the commander in chief. In spite of all the promises, the long-feared "scene of woe" was at hand: families impoverished, credit to start new businesses unattainable, the sheriff on the prowl to arrest them for debt. The officers begged Washington "that no officer or soldier be obliged to receive a furlough" until Congress "can be apprised of the wretched situation into which the army must be plunged." [46]

Washington forwarded the officers' letter to Congress, but first he took the initiative and granted the officers' request. He made the furloughs voluntary, and Congress, careful to avoid a fight with the army and trusting Washington's judgment, ratified his decision. A duration-of-the-war man who wanted to stay was allowed to exchange his spot with a three-year man who wanted to leave. Nevertheless, few soldiers took up the offer. Besides a handful of men from areas still occupied by the British, most soldiers took their furloughs. Officers, meanwhile, decided among themselves who would accompany the men out of camp.[47]

Despite their reluctance to become civilians, staying in camp was losing its charm. The officers found themselves in "pretty much the same doleful predicament," Swartwout remembered. "All this agonizing & lamentable transaction produces universal & heart rending lamentations & dejection throughout the whole Cantonment." Even Gilbert couldn't take much more. "It is impossible for me to paint to you the disagreeable feelings which I have undergone for four or five days past," he confided to his brother-in-law. "I am at some times almost tempted to wish I had not lived to se[e] the day when those brave heroes the deliverers of my Country should be drove from the field of Glory without one farthing of reward for their services." It got worse. In August, Gilbert received "a disagreeable letter" from Wyoma: a bill telling him to pay up for all the sex.[48]

Among all the dark days of a long, ugly war, the first weeks of June 1783 ranked among the darkest and ugliest. It wasn't as cold and famishing as Valley Forge, or as dangerous as a rout like Camden, but it crushed the army to be let go without the civilians fulfilling their promises. In a war sustained by the ideology of liberty, the army's expectations of appreciation from civilians mattered. They were citizen-soldiers, not mercenaries; men risking their lives for a cause, not a professional standing army. The army and especially the officers had long felt alienated from the people they served, and no officer really expected a young woman to pull him into her virgin bed (well, probably not). But for the officers to go home empty-handed felt like one more kick in the gut, all the more painful because it was so unnecessary.[49]

—◊—

In Philadelphia, Robert Morris signed the remaining notes for the now-dispersed army, and then he returned to the business of settling accounts, chasing away people clamoring for money, wrestling with Congress, managing contractors, bargaining to sell surplus army hats, and fighting against slanders of corruption lobbed by Arthur Lee.[50]

Congress, receiving Washington's letter about the officers' desire to slow down the furloughs, asked Morris to explain what the holdup was. The obstacles, Morris retorted, were two: Congress and the states. Congress never gave him authority to settle certain kinds of accounts, such as for undelivered rations and clothing, for which soldiers were entitled to receive an equivalent sum. The states never provided figures for advances made to their own regiments, so Morris still didn't know how much was owed. Morris asked, sensibly, that the paymaster general have authority to adjust all accounts without further need to wait for permission.[51]

Before Congress could approve, however, a new army crisis exploded, the crisis long feared and frequently threatened in rhetoric: furious, mutinous soldiers were marching on the city, and Congress was their target.

The trouble started on June 12 when Major Lansdale's regiment stopped in Philadelphia on its way to Maryland. The men picked up their Morris Notes and bunked overnight in the city barracks. Chatting with the Pennsylvania troops stationed there, some curious tidbits emerged. The Marylanders had received the one month's pay promised in January; the Pennsylvanians hadn't. The Maryland legislature had voted to give their troops five months' pay; Pennsylvania hadn't approved a cent. The Maryland men also had the option of taking furloughs; the Pennsylvania men didn't, because they served in a different department and Washington's deal didn't apply to them. Same army. Same risks. Same sacrifices. But one line was compensated better than another.[52]

The Maryland regiment left town without incident, but the Pennsylvanians erupted. A group of noncoms sent a blistering protest to

Congress—sadly the document no longer exists—which "excited much indignation" among the delegates. Still, the delegates relented, made furloughs optional, and promised to scare up the one month's pay promised in January. It would take some time, since by coincidence Robert Morris was out of town in Bethlehem.[53]

A few days later, the mutiny metastasized. Some eighty to a hundred troops stationed in Lancaster, Pennsylvania, about 80 miles west of Philadelphia, started marching on the city, reportedly, "in order to obtain *justice*," even by violence against the Bank of North America, if the rumors were true. Alarmed, Congress demanded protection. Call out the militia! The Supreme Executive Council of Pennsylvania refused. The militia couldn't be trusted to turn out, Council President John Dickinson explained, absent "some outrages on persons or property." Not waiting around to suffer "outrages," Congress made plans to flee. "If the City would not support Congress," some members said, "it was high time to remove to some other place."[54]

For some bitter officers, Congress was getting the humiliation it deserved. John Armstrong, Jr., watched the mutiny firsthand in Philadelphia, where he moved after separating from the army to work as secretary to the executive council. He applauded the mutineers' audacity. "They feel like Men," Armstrong informed General Gates, "and could they be brought to think like politicians, weak as they are, they might do some good." Positioned in the thick of the tumult at the statehouse, it's possible Armstrong egged the mutineers on, but the evidence that he did anything more than sympathize is tenuous. The conspiratorial fixations of the time led people to believe the soldiers were manipulated by others, even if the rising was led from the bottom up. Armstrong spewed his poison everywhere, making it hard to tell where talk ended and action began.[55]

On June 20, the Lancaster mutineers entered Philadelphia. The following days were tense—and surreal. Mutineers surrounded the Pennsylvania Statehouse, the scene of the adoption of the Declaration of Independence, while Congress holed up inside, desperate to make the soldiers go away. The delegates were not hostages, however, and they came and went freely, though not without intimidation from the armed and increasingly inebriated soldiers ringed outside. One day a bunch followed President Boudinot home, menacingly, until their sergeant told them to stop.

While Congress negotiated with the mutineers, Boudinot sped word to Washington to rescue them. Denouncing the "infamous and outrageous Mutiny of a part of the Pennsylvania Troops," the commander in chief dispatched 1,500 men, the bulk of his remaining force in the Highlands, to restore order. By the time they arrived, Congress had already skedaddled across the river, setting up in Princeton, New Jersey. With reinforcements on the way, the mutiny collapsed, and the ringleaders were arrested, though they were later pardoned. The damage was already done. On the eve of Independence Day, the Revolution was unravelling just as its leaders had always feared.[56]

—⁓—

When Washington learned of the mutiny, he was finishing work on a 4,000-word circular to the states arguing for a strong union and an adequate peacetime army. The rebellion in the ranks undercut the general's message, but he deftly controlled the damage by painting the mutineers as a handful of raw recruits, "contemptable in numbers, and equally so in point of service" who did not deserve the title of soldiers. Washington salvaged a silver lining. "I feel an inexpressible satisfaction," he assured Boudinot, "that even this behaviour cannot stain the name of the American Soldiery." Like the anonymous letter, a great crisis proved the loyal soldiers' superior virtue.[57]

With the ranks thinned by furloughs and the regiments consolidated, the men from the outer huts moved into the cantonment's core. In July a long-awaited day came for the officers. They received a lump sum payment for the commuted pensions, back pay, and undelivered rations. Once the paymaster general, John Pierce, received authority to settle all classes of accounts, he knocked out $11 million worth of final settlement certificates for the army. Lieutenants received some $1,500; generals almost $10,000. Few officers realized the full value of their notes, however. Like their soldiers, they sold them directly, and in the years following the war the so-called "Pierce Notes" circulated as a medium of exchange, though at a deep discount. Congress delivered at last, but the dire economic conditions prevented the officers from enjoying the full fruit of their labors. [58]

With payments distributed, boredom returned to camp. Washington found himself in a "distressing Tedium," with "little else to do, than to be teased with troublesome applications & demands." Still awaiting the British evacuation, in July Washington decided to explore Upstate New York. He rode north to Albany, Saratoga, and Ticonderoga before swinging around to Schenectady, Fort Schuyler, and back to Albany. Always eagle-eyed for rich land, Washington invested in New York real estate with Governor George Clinton, nabbing 6,000 acres along the Mohawk River. [59]

Washington returned to Newburgh in August to disagreeable news. Martha was laid low with a fever, and Congress wanted him in Princeton. Washington didn't want to pack up and leave Newburgh unless he was leaving for Mount Vernon, but once Lady Washington recovered later in the month, the couple traveled south and braved the usual rounds of huzzahs, speeches, songs, and dinners. [60]

In New Jersey, the Washingtons lived more comfortably than at Newburgh, occupying a 320-acre farm south of Princeton called Rocky Hill. But despite the lovely accommodations, there still wasn't much for the general to do. Congress didn't have much work either. The flight from Philadelphia left the body enervated. "Our Affairs here, go on rather indifferently," Boudinot reported. "Members [are] grumbling & dissatisfied at our remaining at this Place—no great appetite for Business." Robert Morris snuck out of Philadelphia with Gouverneur on the night of June 24, but finding that not enough delegates had followed to make a quorum, they waited a couple of days and turned around. When Congress did meet, it assembled at the college in Nassau Hall, but life on campus was less than dignified. Congress's secretary, Charles Thomson, complained about having to pass the dorm rooms and experience the "warm steams from the beds, foul linen & dirty lodgings of the boys."[61]

Always in demand for honors, Washington attended dinners, had speeches read at him, and endured a commencement at the college (thankfully with no "warm steams" wafting nearby). As the stress of command—the cause of his graying and going blind—lessened, the general relaxed and appreciated seeing the sites of former battles, the outcome of the war no longer in doubt. Washington regained his wit and charm. At a garden party held to honor Congress in early September, David Howell, again a delegate, noticed the change in Washington's appearance. He was "uncommonly open & pleasant—the contracted, pensive Air betokening deep thought & much care . . . is done away," Howell recorded. "A pleasant smile sparkling vivacity of wit & humor succeeds."[62]

—※—

In mid-October Sir Guy Carleton sent word from New York City that he expected to evacuate by the end of November, and Congress and Washington began preparing the final disbandment of the army. On October 18, Congress approved discharges for all furloughed men, and on October 24, all troops were discharged, aside from garrisons at Fort Pitt in Western Pennsylvania, and at West Point in New York.[63]

Before Washington could join the men in going home, he had four duties left: one entrance and three farewells. Highly theatrical, Washington excelled at both entrances and exits, but his departures were especially influential. Washington won fame by giving up power, not attaining it, and public goodbyes signaled that the United States was something different, not an old-world monarchy inhabited by old-world aristocrats hungry for military glory to feed their ambition for power.[64]

Washington's first farewell was said through an address to the army written in late October and sent from Princeton. The message was part sentimental reminiscence of hardships endured and part lecture on observing proper conduct as civilians, since much "will depend upon the wise and manly conduct" exhibited "when they are mingled with the great body of the Community." The political message was unmistakable. The army departed with far less than they'd been promised, far less than they deserved. But Washington could do no more to mitigate their suffering. They could only persevere and work to strengthen the union of states.[65]

News of the definitive treaty arrived in the country's major ports on November 1, confirming the end was at hand, even as the official dispatches with the treaty text took another three weeks to reach Congress. To prepare for the transfer of New York City, Washington left Princeton the next week for West Point. Back with his men, Washington received a formal reply to his address. Drafted by Pickering on a committee with McDougall and Knox, it was the last official statement from the officers to their commander in chief. Pickering said he kept the text "moderato" and avoided "stuffing it with fulsome adulation," but it, too, was political, filled with lamentations about the "disingenuousness" of some states, and it lavished praise on Washington, who deserved "from the *Unerring Judge* the rewards of valor exerted to save the oppressed, of patriotism and disinterested virtue."[66]

A few days later Washington set aside farewells to make his entrance into New York City, the object of his dreams of conquest. Receiving word from Carleton that he was ready to leave the city for good, Washington rendezvoused with Governor Clinton, and rode south along the Hudson, retracing the 1776 retreat when he was almost trapped on Manhattan and lost the war. Stopped at the Harlem River on November 24, Washington got the confirmation from Carleton. The British would be out by noon the next day.[67]

Washington and his retinue were ready early. General Knox rode ahead to make sure good order prevailed. The waning days of British rule had been chaotic. Drunken sailors rampaged. Loyalists and patriots brawled. Fires blazed. But finding all quiet, Knox returned in the company of numerous civilians who wanted to join the triumphant entry. Their presence was appropriate, since although the military presence was unmistakable, civil authority, led by Governor Clinton, was the star of the show.[68]

With everything in place, Washington urged his gray horse forward alongside Clinton, with a New York militia unit providing the escort and the various soldiers and civilians marching and riding behind, in a column eight men across. Cheered along by the crowds, the parade snaked its way through the city and stopped on Broadway at Cape's Tavern for brief remarks by Clinton. Then, the parade continued to the battery to take down the British flag and unfurl the stars and stripes, which proved more difficult than anticipated when it was discovered the British had left their flag nailed to the pole. At last the flag was raised and a thirteen-gun salute fired. New York City belonged to America.[69]

A few British units lingered on Long Island and Staten Island, however, and so Washington lingered for a week of dinners, speeches, fireworks, and plenty of salutes and toasts delivered in thirteens. On December 4, the British were leaving, and so was Washington. That afternoon he said his second farewell, to the officers who came with him to New York City.

Only a handful of officers met Washington on the second floor of Fraunces Tavern on Queen Street (now Pearl Street), where he had lodged in the city. There simply weren't that many officers left. Knox attended, as did von Steuben, McDougall, and others. Benjamin Walker, David Cobb, and David Humphreys were present too. Colonel Benjamin Tallmadge, New York dragoon and spymaster, witnessed the reception and left the best firsthand account. When Washington arrived promptly at noon, a cold collation was laid out as the officers waited. The finality of the moment hung heavily. In a time of difficult travel, poor communications, and precarious mortality, everyone knew it might be the last time they saw Washington and heard his voice.[70]

The general's steely self-control faltered. Unsure of what to say or do after entering, Washington first thought to start the meal, but he then decided a toast would be better. Washington raised his glass. "With a heart full of love and gratitude, I now take my leave of you," he rasped. "I most devoutly wish that your latter days may be as prosperous and happy as your former ones have been glorious and honorable." He then invited each man to share a personal farewell. "I cannot come to each of you, but shall feel obliged if each of you will come and take me by the hand." General Knox approached first, and a handshake turned to a hug. Washington's taciturn nature helped him conceal strong emotions, and his famous detachment helped keep social relations in proper order. Both habits broke down in the moment. Washington embraced each man in turn as tears flowed all around.[71]

After leaving the reception in silence, Washington stepped onto the street to take a barge out of the city. Washington had one more farewell, the most politically important of all. He needed to return his commission to Congress. Washington departed New York and headed for Annapolis, Maryland, where Congress had moved in November. Princeton was too small, and the delegates, still angry about the mutiny, refused to go back to Philadelphia. To appease sectional interests, Congress resolved to split time in Annapolis and Trenton, New Jersey. Washington arrived on December 20, his journey prolonged by a stop in Philadelphia and more celebrations, dinners, and fireworks. Out to meet Washington as he arrived was Horatio Gates, coincidentally in town on business. Nothing remarkable passed between them.[72]

In Annapolis more dinners ensued. The stateliest was a reception on December 22 held by Thomas Mifflin, the new president of Congress. More than 200 people turned out for a joyful celebration. "Every man seemed to be in heaven," one reveler remembered. Washington, however, did not lose the opportunity to make a political point with his toast. After the traditional thirteen, he added one more: "competent powers to congress for general purposes." A ball followed at the

Maryland Statehouse. Washington danced through the night, taking a turn with every young woman, so that, as the quip went, they might all "*get a touch of him.*"[73]

Washington's appearance before Congress the next day had been choreographed by a committee that included Thomas Jefferson, a new delegate trading international diplomacy for the glamor of congressional service. Washington entered the statehouse chamber at noon flanked by aides Benjamin Walker and David Humphries and was greeted by Secretary Thomson, who escorted them to President Mifflin. The room was full, including numerous women on the gallery above the main floor, though not because of a full complement of delegates. Only seven states were represented, and a bare quorum was in town to make the ceremony official.[74]

General Washington delivered a short speech from a prepared text. Fighting back his emotions, Washington's hand tremored, visibly shaking his paper as he spoke. As he came to the last lines, his voice breaking, Washington paused to steady himself. "Having now finished the work assigned me," he at last managed, "I retire from the great theatre of Action—and bidding an Affectionate farewell to this August body under whose orders I have so long acted, I here offer my Commission, and take my leave of all the employments of public life." Washington reached into his waistcoat, retrieved his commission, and presented it to Mifflin, who read remarks prepared by Jefferson in response. Washington left Annapolis and rode west for Mount Vernon, intent, one delegate reported, "upon eating his christmas dinner at home." Now a Virginia planter, Washington made it in time, reaching his mansion on the Potomac River on Christmas Eve.[75]

Since he last saw Mount Vernon in the fall of 1781 following Yorktown, Washington had led no more victories, engaged in no more battles. His military record amounted to two years of waiting and worrying as he maintained the army, enforced discipline, and pressured Congress and the states to support the men who made the nation's freedom possible.

Still, for all the lack of action, Washington's leadership during the war's last two years was as essential as during any campaign. He kept the army together, reminded the officers of their duty, defused the explosiveness of the anonymous letter, and managed the rapid demobilization of the army. Washington wasn't flawless. He misjudged the impetus for the anonymous letter and suspected malign influence too easily. He succeeded only partially in representing the army's interests with Congress and the states.

But Washington understood his men and his country. In an hour of grave danger when the foot stood on a tremendous precipice, Washington knew how to inspire his officers' perseverance by asking for their trust. He was their commander and they followed. As the country lurched from crisis to crisis toward peace, Washington intervened and preserved the Revolution with his character.

Conclusion

Washington's homecoming marked the end of the war and the beginning of a decade-and-a-half fight to secure the blessings of independence. Washington watched from Mount Vernon as the nation limped along, its debts unpaid and the states antagonizing each other. Then he joined a group of nationalist-minded men who aimed to reform the Articles of Confederation. When reform wouldn't do, Washington returned to Philadelphia and along with old hands like Robert Morris, Gouverneur Morris, James Madison, and Alexander Hamilton, he helped frame a new form of government. Acclaimed the first president under the Constitution, Washington presided over his energetic treasury secretary's construction of a fiscal system finally capable of paying down the war debts and establishing the nation's credit. Hamilton's program echoed Robert Morris's program, with the passage of time convincing more people to listen. In the path to forging a new government, the Newburgh Conspiracy reminded Americans of the precarious relationship between an army and its people when the people didn't feel much attachment to each other, let alone to professional soldiers.

Washington made his final comments on the Newburgh Conspiracy in 1797 at the end of his presidency in a letter to none other than John Armstrong, Jr. The passing years—and bruising partisanship of the 1790s—softened Washington's interpretation of the incident, and he exonerated Armstrong of any ill intent. "I do hereby declare, that I did not, at the time of writing my address, regard you as the author of the said letters," Washington wrote. "And farther, that I have since had sufficient reason for believing, that the object of the author was just, honorable, & friendly to the country, though the means suggested by him were certainly liable to much misunderstanding and abuse." As Washington's remarks reveal, he later came to understand the Newburgh Conspiracy as something less than a plot and more like a misunderstanding.[1]

The Newburgh Conspiracy wasn't a conspiracy if we understand "conspiracy" to mean a concerted action among knowing participants to bring about some illicit outcome. To the extent that Philadelphia nationalists such as Hamilton and the Morrises wanted anything from the army in March 1783, it was to participate more forcefully in the political process by declaring themselves united with the other creditors through a spirited letter to Congress. Walter Stewart stirred things up when he arrived in camp, and the officers who gathered with Stewart at Gates's headquarters decided to provoke their fellow officers to action with the invitation to meet and draft an address. Armstrong, egged on by his friends as the night unfolded, produced a letter in anger, and its inflammatory talk of threats blotted out its more reasonable demands. He should have slept on it and revised in the morning. But he didn't, and the letter unleashed a crisis in the army.

Armstrong and Stewart were irresponsible. So, too, was Gates, who allowed the meeting at his house. But there's no evidence they sought to overthrow Washington and refuse to disband or abandon the country to its fate. An unfortunate piece of bad luck compounded their mistake, however. Washington had recently received letters from Hamilton and Jones alerting him to rumors of a plot to sully his reputation. Who knows where the rumors originated—probably in the fevered imaginations of overwrought politicians in Philadelphia—and Washington originally discounted them. But once Armstrong's letter appeared, Washington's eyes were opened, and he thought he saw the plot clearly. Malign influence was at work to divide civilians from soldiers. Washington was never going to react well to a meeting called outside his command, but Armstrong and his supporters had terrible timing. They released their letter not knowing the commander in chief was primed to suspect the worst.

Of course, conspiracy minded people saw the opposite: the timing was perfectly sinister. In 18th-century thinking there were no accidents, especially not in the realm of politics, and the rumors, Stewart's arrival, and the anonymous letter coincided because someone, some group, planned it that way. As much as anyone else, Washington gave a conspiratorial gloss to the events of March 1783. He said there was "something very misterious" in the affair. He said, "it is firmly believed, by *some*, the scheme was not only planned but also digested and matured in Philadelphia." He said the officers "stood wavering on a tremendous precipice." He said the army verged on "plunging themselves into a gulf of Civil horror."[2]

Though born in intemperance rather than malice, Armstrong's letter created a real crisis, because once the officers assembled and began complaining, there was no telling where it would end. Washington was right to perceive the officers standing upon a precipice. His performance at the Temple of Virtue was masterful. He defused the tension of the previous week, and he steeled the spines of any officer tempted from the path of virtue. He vanquished opposition to Congress and restored balance to civil-military relations.

For most of the Continental Army, the American Revolution had an unsatisfactory ending. Granted, it wasn't the worst ending. Independence was achieved, after all, and the men who mustered out in 1783 were alive, unlike the 25,000 who died during the war. But they returned to civilian life ignored if they were lucky and if they weren't, they were resented as corrupt pensioners. Their experience challenged the vision of the Revolution as liberty's glorious cause, a vision that emerged during the war and only strengthened afterwards. In the minds of many Americans, victory was the work of a people's army, the citizen-soldiers who sprang from their plows, intimidated the British with their righteousness, and returned home to the well-earned laurels of peace. Professional soldiers had little place in the mythology.[3]

Conspiracy thinking helped Americans of the Revolutionary generation—and beyond—avoid coming to grips with the Revolution's ambiguous ending. If a crisis like Newburgh was precipitated by designing men, however nefarious their machinations, they were easily identified as players in the same old story of power and liberty. They could be unmasked and defeated by the traditional method as well: vigilance and virtue. The world was an understandable place, and any shortcomings of the Revolution were readily explained.[4]

A more realistic approach to the Newburgh Conspiracy restores contingency to the story of how the American Revolution ended. Looking back, we know Yorktown was the last major campaign and for two years, the army mostly sat around doing nothing while Congress jawed, Robert Morris shuffled accounts, and the outcome of the Revolution rested with the diplomats negotiating in Europe. But the people of 1783 didn't know how the Revolution would end, and watching them struggle to finish the war, right the nation's finances, and disband the army shows how they confronted the very real limitations of a nation born in war with its people weakly attached to each other, jealous of their liberty, and suspicious of authority in any shape. As the events of March 1783 demonstrate, the Revolution could have easily collapsed in those final two years. The financial problems and army discontent were more than enough to allow Britain to steal a victory at the end. But the war ultimately ended in independence because of the perseverance of the army and its commander in chief, General George Washington. He was the indispensable man every bit in the war's anxious waning days as he ever was on the battlefield or, in the future, as president. Washington won the peace.

Acknowledgments

M y first encounter with George Washington probably came in
September 1984 when I was five and my family traveled to
Mount Vernon. I don't remember it, but my mom described the visit in
my baby book: "You were a good sport to trudge through Mt. Vernon
in 93° heat with a head ache & fever. Right after we left Mt. Vernon, you
threw up in a McDonald's & were a sick little boy the rest of the trip
home." I'm one of six kids, so how she had time for such chronicling I'll
never know, but all these years later, the way she recorded our family's
history makes me smile. I owe my career as a historian to her example.

This book was made possible by many people. I'd like to thank the
librarians, archivists, and editors, unknown to me, who over decades
have published the papers of the founders in wonderful volumes that
are remarkable works of scholarship. I'm especially grateful to the
National Archives and its partner, the University of Virginia Press,
for making the papers of George Washington, Alexander Hamilton,
James Madison, and others available online—and for free. Similarly,
the Library of Congress maintains online versions of key collections of
early congressional records, and Google Books, HathiTrust, and the

Internet Archive provide access to invaluable printed sources from the 18th and 19th centuries. When those repositories didn't have something, the Interlibrary Loan staff at my home institution, the University of Central Florida, found much needed collections on microfilm (helpfully filmed many years ago by some thoughtful archivist), and when I really needed something from an archive, the staff at the New-York Historical Society, New York Public Library, and the Fenimore Art Museum couldn't have been more helpful in sending materials. As a result, I did most of my research at home or in the library, a boon for a father of small children like me. I did make a couple of outings to see the sites of my story. In New York, I want to thank the New York State Parks, Recreation, and Historic Preservation staff at Washington's Headquarters State Historic Site, the New Windsor Cantonment State Historic Site, and the Knox's Headquarters State Historic Site. In Philadelphia, Karie Diethorn gave me a behind-the-scenes tour of Independence Hall and surrounding areas.

My project was supported financially by a National Endowment for the Humanities Summer Stipend and by a fellowship from the Fred W. Smith National Library for the Study of George Washington at Mount Vernon. I especially want to thank Amanda and Greg Gregory for endowing the fellowship and believing in promoting scholarship on Washington.

Being a fellow at Mount Vernon was like being an honored guest of Washington himself, except with air conditioning, Wi-Fi, and indoor plumbing. Everyone was welcoming, friendly, and supportive. A particular thank you to Dawn Bonner, Stephen McLeod, Sarah K. Myers, Mark Santangelo, Michelle Lee Silverman, Joseph F. Stoltz III, and founding director Douglas Bradburn, now president and CEO of the whole estate. No less than the staff, the other scholars I met were a font of insight into Washington, historical writing, and making a career in history. I particularly want to express my appreciation to Steven Bullock, Joshua Canale, Kevin Casey, David Hildebrand, Philip Levy, and Gates Thomas for our conversations and visits to the mansion's piazza to look out at the Potomac and see why Washington loved this place. Thank you all.

When it came time to turn my research into a book, my agent, Roger Williams, shepherded me through the transition from academic to trade publishing, and Claiborne Hancock, Maria Fernandez, and the team at Pegasus produced a handsome volume that's everything I hoped for when I dreamed of writing a work of popular history.

I've also enjoyed the encouragement of colleagues, first at Spring Hill College, where the project began, and at UCF, where it came to fruition. At UCF, I owe a debt to Rose Beiler, Barbara Gannon, John Sacher, and Amanda Snyder for reading chapters, and to Tim Dorsch, my research assistant, for wrangling the notes into shape. I received timely answers to queries from Edward Dandrow, Stephanie Lawton, Edward G. Lengel, and Jennifer E. Steenshorne. My writing was significantly improved by twice participating in the Second Book Workshop at the Society of Historians for the Early American Republic's (SHEAR) annual meetings in 2017 and 2018. Thank you to Emily Conroy-Krutz and Jessica Lepler for organizing the meetings, Amy S. Greenberg and Rosemarie Zagarri for leading discussion groups, and to my fellow group members for reading my work. Also at SHEAR, I received valuable feedback during a panel with Martha J. King and Craig Bruce Smith. Thanks also to another SHEAR person, Sam Watson of the United States Military Academy, a longtime supporter of my work.

My wife, Andrea, and our children have lived with George Washington and the Newburgh Conspiracy just as much as I have. In fact, a few days after Andrea and I learned that baby number one, Carolina, was on the way, we visited Mount Vernon and I first heard about the library's fellowship program. Then, a couple of years later, I'd just started my fellowship term when we discovered baby number two, Camila, was coming. Now, as the book is published, baby number three, Andrew, is here, too! Thanks Andrea, Carolina, Camila, and Andrew: this book is dedicated to you.

Abbreviations and Sources

T he papers of Alexander Hamilton (AHP), George Washington (GWP), and James Madison (JMP) are available through the National Archive's Founders Online website: https://founders.archives. gov/. Since online sources are most accessible to readers, I've cited the digital versions, without volume and page numbers. Search the author, recipient, and date and you'll locate any document. One caveat: the Washington papers project has not yet published the volumes for the period 1781 to 1783, and those documents are currently available in Founders Online in unannotated versions.

Three additional collections are available online, but individual documents are difficult to locate without the volume and page numbers of the print versions. As a result, I've cited *Journals of the Continental Congress, 1774–1789*, ed. Worthington C. Ford, et. al. (JCC); *Letters of Delegates to Congress*, ed. Paul H. Smith, et. al. (LD); and *The Papers of Robert Morris*, ed. E. James Ferguson and John Catanzariti (RMP) as if they were printed. You can find the digital versions at:

JCC: https://memory.loc.gov/ammem/amlaw/lwjc.html
LD: https://memory.loc.gov/ammem/amlaw/lwdg.html
RMP: https://digital.library.pitt.edu/

Other collections can be found only in manuscript, though they are microfilmed, including the Horatio Gates Papers (HGP) and Friedrich Wilhelm von Steuben Papers (VSP), both held principally by the New-York Historical Society, New York City; and the Henry Knox Papers (HKP) and Timothy Pickering Papers (TPP), both held principally by the Massachusetts Historical Society, Boston. The papers of Nathanael Greene (NGP) exist as a published collection (*The Papers of General Nathanael Greene*, ed. Richard K. Showman) and are not online. Less frequently used sources are cited fully in the notes.

INTRODUCTION

1   Charles H. Lesser, ed., *The Sinews of Independence: Monthly Strength Reports of the Continental Army* (Chicago: University of Chicago Press, 1976), 246–247; William M. Fowler, *American Crisis: George Washington and the Dangerous Two Years after Yorktown, 1781–1783* (New York: Walker and Company, 2011), 56–57; Robert K. Wright, Jr., *The Continental Army* (Washington, DC: Center of Military History, 2006), 22; George C. Daughan, *Revolution on the Hudson: New York City and the Hudson River Valley in the American War of Independence* (New York: W. W. Norton, 2016), 1–6.

2   John A. Ruddiman, *Becoming Men of Some Consequence: Youth and Military Service in the Revolutionary War* (Charlottesville: University of Virginia Press, 2014), 137–146.

3   [John Armstrong, Jr.], "To the Officers of the Army," [March 10, 1783], enclosed in George Washington to Elias Boudinot, March 12, 1783, GWP.

4   Fowler, *American Crisis*, 180.

5   Armstrong, "To the Officers of the Army."

6   General Orders, March 11, 1783, GWP.

7   Washington to Alexander Hamilton, March 12, 1783, GWP.

8   For Washington's strengths and weaknesses as a commander, see Edmund Morgan, *The Genius of George Washington* (New York: W.W. Norton, 1980), 3–25; Edward G. Lengel, *General George Washington: A Military Life* (New York: Random House, 2005), 365–371.

9   Fowler, *American Crisis*, 184, 304–46.

ONE: THE ROAD FROM YORKTOWN

1   Ralph M. Ketchum, *Victory at Yorktown: The Campaign That Won the Revolution* (New York: Henry Holt and Company, 2004), 248–255.

2   James Thatcher, *A Military Journal during the American Revolutionary War, from 1775 to 1783* (Boston: Richardson and Lord, 1823), 346; Johann Conrad Doehla, Journal, October 19, 1781, in "The Doehla Journal," trans. Robert J. Tilden, *William and Mary Quarterly*, 22 (1942), 255–259; Stephen Popp, Journal, October 19, 1781, in "Popp's Journal," ed. Joseph G. Rosengarten, *The Pennsylvania Magazine of History and Biography*, 26 (1902), 248.

3   Thomas Fleming, *The Perils of Peace: America's Struggle for Survival After Yorktown* (New York: HarperCollins, 2007), 3–4; Daniel Trabue, *Westward into Kentucky: The Narrative of Daniel Trabue*, ed. Chester Raymond Young (Lexington: University Press of Kentucky, 2004), 117–118; [Joseph Plumb Martin], *A Narrative of Some of the Adventures, Dangers and Sufferings of a Revolutionary Soldier* (Hallowell, ME: Glazier, Masters, and Company, 1830), 174.

4   Andrew Jackson O'Shaughnessy, *The Men Who Lost America: British Leadership, the American Revolution, and the Fate of the Empire* (New Haven, CT: Yale University Press, 2013), 1–2, 281.

5   Arthur Schrader, "'The World Turned Upside Down': A Yorktown March, or Music to Surrender By." *American Music*, 16 (1998),

180–216. My thanks to David Hildebrand for explaining the tune's history.

6   Ron Chernow, *Washington: A Life* (New York: Penguin, 2010), 29–30, 445–446; Annie Gittess, "Horsemanship," *Digital Encyclopedia of George Washington*, https://www.mountvernon.org /library/digitalhistory/digital-encyclopedia/article/horsemanship/; Philip G. Smucker, "Washington on the Dance Floor," George Washington's Mount Vernon, https://www.mountvernon.org /george-washington/the-man-the-myth/athleticism/on-the -dance-floor/.

7   Richard Brookhiser, *Founding Father: Rediscovering George Washington* (New York: Free Press, 1996), 107–120; Gordon S. Wood, *Revolutionary Characters: What Made the Founders Different* (New York: Penguin, 2006), 31–63.

8   James J. Graham, ed., *Memoir of General Graham* (Edinburgh, Scotland: R. and R. Clark, 1862), 63–64; Sarah Osborn, Pension Application, in Robert F. Sayre, *American Lives: An Anthology of Autobiographical Writing* (Madison: University of Wisconsin Press, 1994), 231–232; Ebenezer Denny, Journal, October 19, 1781, in *Military Journal of Major Ebenezer Denny* (Philadelphia: J.B. Lippincott and Company, 1859), 44–45.

9   Douglas Southall Freeman, *George Washington: A Biography*, vol. 5, *Victory with the Help of France* (New York: Charles Scribner's Sons, 1952), 5: 391–392.

10 Piers Mackesy, *The War for America, 1775–1783* (Cambridge, MA: Harvard University Press, 1965), 435; William Fowler, *American Crisis: George Washington and the Dangerous Two Years After Yorktown, 1781–1783* (New York: Walker and Company, 2011), 1–2.

11 Washington to Robert Morris, August 27 and September 6, 1781, GWP; Charles Rappleye, *Robert Morris: Financier of the American Revolution* (New York: Simon and Schuster, 2010), 257–263; Nathaniel Philbrick, *In the Hurricane's Eye: The Genius*

of George Washington and the Victory at Yorktown (New York: Viking, 2018), xii–xv.

12 Washington to Thomas McKean, October 19, 1781, Tench Tilghman to Washington, October 27, 1781, GWP; JCC, October 24, 1781, 21: 1071; William Brooke Rawle, ed., "A Loyalist's Account of Certain Occurrences in Philadelphia after Cornwallis's Surrender at Yorktown," *Pennsylvania Magazine of History and Biography*, 16 (1892), 103–107; Benjamin H. Irvin, *Clothed in Robes of Sovereignty: The Continental Congress and the People Out of Doors* (New York: Oxford University Press, 2011), 261; Fleming, *Perils of Peace*, 21–27.

13 Translator's note, François Jean, Marquis de Chastellux, *Travels in North-America, in the Years 1780, 1781, and 1782*, trans. George Grieve (London: G. G. J. and J. Robinson, 1787), 1: 194; Freeman, *George Washington*, 5: 401; Chernow, *Washington*, 420–421.

14 Freeman, *George Washington*, 5: 402–403; William S. Baker, *Itinerary of General Washington from June 15, 1775, to December 23, 1783* (Philadelphia: J. B. Lippincott Company, 1892), 247–248.

15 Fowler, *American Crisis*, 12–13.

16 Madison, Detached Memoranda, [January 31, 1820], JMP.

17 JCC, November 28, 1781, 21: 1142–1144; Fowler, *American Crisis*, 15.

18 JCC, November 28, 1781, 21: 1144.

19 Washington to Robert Hanson Harrison, November 18, 1781. See also Washington to Nathaniel Greene, November 16, 1781; to William Ramsay, November 19, 1781; to George Plater, November 22, 1781; to Jonathan Trumbull, Sr., November 28, 1781; to Philip Schuyler, November 28, 1781; to Thomas Jefferson, November 30, 1781; to William Lord Stirling Alexander, November 30, 1781; to James McHenry, December 11, 1781, GWP.

20 O'Shaughnessy, *Men Who Lost America*, 3–4, 76–77; Piers Mackesy, *War for America*, 434–435.

21 O'Shaughnessy, *Men Who Lost America*, 41–42.

22 *The Columbian Magazine or Monthly Miscellany Containing a View of the History, Literature, Manners & Characters of the Year 1787* (Philadelphia: T. S. Eddon, W. Spotswood, C. Cist, and J. Trenchard, 1787), 1: 392; Gillian B. Anderson, "'The Temple of Minerva' and Francis Hopkinson: A Reappraisal of America's First Poet-Composer," *Proceedings of the American Philosophical Society*, 120 (1976), 166–177; Freeman, *George Washington*, 5: 406–408; Fowler, *American Crisis*, 19; Baker, *Itinerary of General Washington*, 252–255.

23 Rappleye, *Robert Morris*, 7–14, 22–23.

24 Ibid., 27–30, 32–34, 36–38, 45–47, 69–72, 80–81.

25 Chastellux, *Travels in North-America*, 1: 202; Charles Louis Victor, Prince de Broglie, *Narrative by the Prince de Broglie of a Visit to America, 1782*, trans. Thomas Balch (Philadelphia: n.p., 1877), 15; Rappleye, *Robert Morris*, 14, 23, 26, 202–203, 206.

26 Richard Brookhiser, *Gentleman Revolutionary: Gouverneur Morris—The Rake Who Wrote the Constitution* (New York: Free Press, 2003), 10–11, 61–62; William Howard Adams, *Gouverneur Morris: An Independent Life* (New Haven, CT: Yale University Press, 2003), 3–4, 13–15, 21–29, 41–42, 47–49, 88, 121, 126.

27 Robert Morris to Matthew Ridley, October 6, 1782, RMP, 6: 513; Robert Morris to Richard Peters, January 25, 1778, quoted in Clarence L. Ver Steeg, *Robert Morris: Revolutionary Financier, With an Analysis of His Earlier Career* (1954; reprint, New York: Octagon Books, 1972), 82; Brookhiser, *Gentleman Revolutionary*, 67.

28 Rappleye, *Robert Morris*, 285–286; Robert Morris, Diary, December 3, 10, 17, 24, 1781, January 21, February 18, 1782, RMP, 3: 316–317, 3: 356, 3: 399, 3: 435, 4: 84, 4: 249.

29 JCC, November 4, 1775, 3: 322; E. James Ferguson, *The Power of the Purse: A History of American Public Finance, 1776–1790* (Chapel Hill: University of North Carolina Press, 1961), 27–28. My estimate of the number of animals is based on modern butchering

yields and the size of modern cows and pigs, which (thanks to hormones) are much larger than their colonial counterparts. See Rosie Nold, "How Much Meat Can You Expect from a Fed Steer?" iGrow: A Service of SDSU Extension, January 2, 2013, http://igrow.org/livestock/beef/how-much-meat-can-you-expect-from-a-fed-steer/; Oklahoma Department of Agriculture, Food, and Forestry, "How Much Meat?": https://www.oda.state.ok.us/food/fs-hogweight.pdf.

30 E. Wayne Carp, *To Starve the Army at Pleasure: Continental Army Administration and American Political Culture, 1775–1783* (Chapel Hill: University of North Carolina Press, 1984), 55.

31 Irvin, *Clothed in Robes of Sovereignty*, 75–96; Louis Jordan, "Continental Currency," *Colonial Currency*, Robert H. Gore, Jr. Numismatic Endowment, University of Notre Dame, Department of Special Collections, https://coins.nd.edu/ColCurrency/CurrencyText/CC.html.

32 Ferguson, *Power of the Purse*, 29–32; Stephen Mihm, "Funding the Revolution: Monetary and Fiscal Policy in Eighteenth-Century America," in *The Oxford Handbook of the American Revolution*, ed. Edward G. Gray and Jane Kamensky (New York: Oxford University Press, 2013), 331–335; Farley Grubb, "The Continental Dollar: How Much Was Really Issued?" *Journal of Economic History*, 68 (2008), 283–291; Farley Grubb, "State Redemption of the Continental Dollar, 1779–1790," *William and Mary Quarterly*, 69 (2012), 147–180.

33 Ferguson, *Power of the Purse*, 7–20; Mihm, "Funding the Revolution," 328–331.

34 Mihm, "Funding the Revolution," 334; Grubb, "State Redemption of the Continental Dollar," 150–156.

35 Mihm, "Funding the Revolution," 334.

36 Ferguson, *Power of the Purse*, 40–42, 126–127.

37 Ferguson, *Power of the Purse*, 35–40, 53–55; Mihm, "Funding the Revolution," 332.

38   Ferguson, *Power of the Purse*, 57–64; Mihm, "Funding the Revolution," 334–335; Carp, *Starve the Army*, 77–80.

39   Ferguson, *Power of the Purse*, 34.

40   Ferguson, *Power of the Purse*, 33–35; Mihm, "Funding the Revolution," 333; Grubb, "State Redemption of the Continental Dollar," 164–166; Carp, *Starve the Army*, 175–181.

41   Jack N. Rakove, *The Beginnings of National Politics: An Interpretive History of the Continental Congress* (New York: Alfred A. Knopf, 1979), 281–282; Merrill Jensen, *The New Nation: A History of the United States During the Confederation, 1781-1789* (1950; rep., New York: Alfred A. Knopf, 1965), 55–56.

42   Ver Steeg, *Robert Morris*, 79; Rakove, *Beginnings of National Politics*, 303–304.

43   Rappleye, *Robert Morris*, 216–217, 234–237; Ver Steeg, *Robert Morris*, 65–67.

44   Rappleye, *Robert Morris*, 237.

45   Ibid.

46   Ver Steeg, *Robert Morris*, 80–81.

47   Ibid., 73.

48   Carp, *Starve the Army*, 212; Rappleye, *Robert Morris*, 255–259.

49   Carp, *Starve the Army*, 211.

50   Ferguson, *Power of the Purse*, 126–127.

51   Ver Steeg, *Robert Morris*, 90–94.

52   Ibid.

53   Ver Steeg, *Robert Morris*, 93, 100–101; Rakove, *Beginnings of National Politics*, 282–283.

54   Rakove, *Beginnings of National Politics*, 285–288.

55   Ibid., 192–194.

56   Ibid., 195, 201–202.

57   *Virginia Gazette* (Williamsburg), September 25, 1779; Rakove, *Beginnings of National Politics*, 198–199, 201, 218, 224; Edmund Cody Burnett, *The Continental Congress* (1949; rep., New York: W.W. Norton, 1964), 502–503; Gordon S. Wood, *Friends*

Divided: John Adams and Thomas Jefferson (New York: Penguin, 2017), 104.

58 Rappleye, *Robert Morris*, 285–286.

59 Rakove, *Beginnings of National Politics*, 297–329; David B. Mattern, *Benjamin Lincoln and the American Revolution* (Columbia: University of South Carolina Press, 1995), 135–138.

60 Edward J. Larson, *George Washington, Nationalist* (Charlottesville: University of Virginia Press, 2016), 1–2.

61 JCC, March 20, 21, 1782, 21: 140, 141–142.

62 Robert Morris, Diary, March 22, 1782, RMP, 4: 435; Baker, *Itinerary of General Washington*, 258.

TWO: THE INSIPID CAMPAIGN

1 Hugh Hughes to William Heath, March 10, 1782, Hugh Hughes Letterbook (New-York Historical Society, New York); Janet Dempsey, *Washington's Last Cantonment: "High Time for a Peace"* (Monroe, NY: Library Research Associates, 1990), 27–28.

2 William M. Fowler, *American Crisis: George Washington and the Dangerous Two Years after Yorktown, 1781-1783* (New York: Walker and Company, 2011), 56–57; Jessie MacLeod, "William (Billy) Lee," *George Washington Digital Encyclopedia*, Fred W. Smith National Library for the Study of George Washington at Mount Vernon, https://www.mountvernon.org/library/digitalhistory/digital-encyclopedia/article/william-billy-lee/.

3 Fowler, *American Crisis*, 56–57.

4 Edward C. Boynton, *General Orders of Geo. Washington, Commander-in-chief of the Army of the Revolution Issued at Newburgh on the Hudson, 1782-1783* (Newburgh, NY: News Company, 1883), 9–10; A. J. Schenkman, *Washington's Headquarters in Newburgh: Home to a Revolution* (Charleston, SC: The History Press, 2009), 79–84; David S. Cohen, *The Dutch-American Farm* (New York: New York University Press, 1993), 49–50.

5   Tyson to Hughes, November 21, 1781, Hughes Letterbook; Fowler, *American Crisis*, 57.

6   Washington, General Orders, April 4, 1782, GWP.

7   Washington, General Orders, April 10, 1783, GWP.

8   Washington to Benjamin Lincoln, April 10, 1782, GWP; Caroline Cox, *A Proper Sense of Honor: Service and Sacrifice in George Washington's Army* (Chapel Hill: University of North Carolina Press, 2004), 55; Charles Royster, *A Revolutionary People at War: The Continental Army and American Character, 1775–1783* (Chapel Hill: University of North Carolina Press, 1979), 237.

9   Washington, General Orders, April 13, 1782, GWP.

10 Washington, General Orders, April 17, May 16, 1782, GWP.

11 Washington, General Orders, June 18, 1782, GWP.

12 Washington to Lund Washington, August 20, 1775, GWP; Royster, *Revolutionary People*, 60; Cox, *Proper Sense*, 138–140.

13 Harlow Giles Unger, *Noah Webster: The Life and Times of An American Patriot* (New York: John Wiley and Sons, 1998), 43–44; Charles Patrick Neimeyer, *America Goes to War: A Social History of the Continental Army* (New York: New York University Press, 1996), 8–26, 35–36, 49–51.

14 Royster, *Revolutionary People*, 48–50, 65–66, 131.

15 Cox, *Proper Sense*, 21–26.

16 Cox, *Proper Sense*, 22, 74; Royster, *Revolutionary People*, 71, 77–78.

17 Cox, 21–26; Gordon S. Wood, *The Radicalism of the American Revolution*, 24–30.

18 Wood, *Radicalism*, 11–24.

19 Cox, *Proper Sense*, 21.

20 Cox, *Proper Sense*, 26–27; Wood, *Radicalism*, 24–42.

21 Cox, *Proper Sense*, 23–24, 28–35; Royster, *Revolutionary People*, 84–95.

22 Washington, General Orders, June 5, 1782, GWP; John A. Nagy, *Rebellion in the Ranks: Mutinies of the American Revolution* (Yardley,

PA: Westholme Publishing, 2008), xv, 297–299; Neimeyer, *America Goes to War*, 146–157.

23 William Glanville Evelyn to William Evelyn, October 7, 1775, quoted in Cox, *Proper Sense*, xvi; Neimeyer, *America Goes to War*, 122–123.

24 Washington to Hancock, September 25, 1777, GWP.

25 Washington to Patrick Henry, October 5, 1776, GWP.

26 Cox, *Proper Sense*, 44–45; Royster, *Revolutionary People*, 50–51; Gordon S. Wood, *Revolutionary Characters: What Made the Founders Different* (New York: Penguin, 2006), 23–24; Craig Bruce Smith, *American Honor: The Creation of the Nation's Ideals during the Revolutionary Era* (Chapel Hill: University of North Carolina Press, 2018), 16–21, 98–126; Joanne Freeman, *Affairs of Honor: National Politics in the New Republic* (New Haven, CT: Yale University Press, 2001), xv–xx, 167–171.

27 Wood, *Radicalism*, 24.

28 Cox, *Proper Sense*, 47–55, 146; Royster, *Revolutionary People*, 86, 93–94.

29 Washington to William Smallwood, April 15, 1782, GWP; Royster, *Revolutionary People*, 298.

30 Royster, *Revolutionary People*, 343–344.

31 Washington to Continental Congress Camp Committee, January 29, 1778; and to Henry Laurens, March 21, 1778, GWP; Albigence Waldo, Diary, December 29, 1777, in "Valley Forge, 1777–1778: Diary of Surgeon Albigence Waldo, of the Connecticut Line," *The Pennsylvania Magazine of History and Biography*, 21 (1897), 315; William Henry Glasson, "History of Military Pension Legislation in the United States" (PhD diss., Columbia University, 1900), 15–16; Royster, *Revolutionary People*, 200–202.

32 Washington to Samuel Huntington, October 11, 1780, GWP; Glasson, "Military Pension," 17; Royster, *Revolutionary People*, 333.

33 Robert F. Haggard, "The Nicola Affair: Lewis Nicola, George Washington, and American Military Discontent during the Revolutionary War," *Proceedings of the American Philosophical*

Society, 146 (2002), 143–148; Douglas R. Cubbison, "Colonel Lewis Nicola: Soldier, Scientist and Man of Letters (Part 1)," *Journal of the American Revolution*, July 25, 2013, https://all thingsliberty.com/2013/07/colonel-lewis-nicola-soldier -scientist-and-man-of-letters/#_edn1.

34 Lewis Nicola to Washington, May 22, 1782, GWP.

35 Nicola to Washington, May 22, 1782, GWP; Haggard, "Nicola Affair," 156–158, 168.

36 Washington to Nicola, May 22, 1782, GWP.

37 William Heath to Washington, April 6 and 16, 1782, GWP; E. Wayne Carp, *To Starve the Army at Pleasure: Continental Army Administration and American Political Culture, 1775–1783* (Chapel Hill: University of North Carolina Press, 1984), 215–216.

38 Washington to Sands, May 25, 1782, GWP.

39 Fowler, *American Crisis*, 140–144; Robert Morris, Diary, July 3, 1782, RMP, 5: 521–525n13.

40 Cox, *Proper Sense*, 20, 139; Royster, *Revolutionary People*, 73–74, 131–132, 136–137.

41 Bernard Bailyn, *The Ideological Origins of the American Revolution* (Cambridge, MA: Harvard University Press, 1967), 55–93.

42 James Kirby Martin and Mark Edward Lender, *"A Respectable Army": The Military Origins of the Republic, 1763-1789* (1982; 3rd ed., Hoboken, NJ: Wiley Blackwell, 2015), 5–9; Lawrence Delbert Cress, *Citizens in Arms: The Army and the Militia in American Society to the War of 1812* (Chapel Hill: University of North Carolina Press, 1982), 15–33.

43 *Boston under Military Rule, 1768–1769, as Revealed in* A Journal of the Times, comp. Oliver Morton Dickerson (Boston: Chapman and Grimes, 1936), 93; Richard Archer, *As If an Enemy's Country: The British Occupation of Boston and the Origins of Revolution* (New York: Oxford University Press, 2010), 123–143.

44 Royster, *Revolutionary People*, 35–38, 46; Martin and Lender, *"Respectable Army,"* 19–24.

45 Cress, *Citizens in Arms*, 67–69; Royster, *Revolutionary People*, 203, 345–250.

46 Gordon S. Wood, *The Idea of America: Reflections on the Birth of the United States* (New York: Penguin, 2011), 81–123; Bailyn, *Ideological Origins*, 144–159.

47 Fowler, *American Crisis*, 44–47.

48 Guy Carleton to Washington, May 7, 1782; Washington to Livingston, June 5, 1782, GWP; Freeman, *George Washington*, 5: 415.

49 Washington to Jean-Baptiste Donatien de Vimeur, Comte de Rochambeau, June 24, 1782; Freeman, *George Washington*, 5: 414–418.

50 Freeman, *George Washington*, 5: 416; Dempsey, *Washington's Last Cantonment*, 31–32.

51 James Thacher, Diary, June 1, 1782, in *A Military Journal during the American Revolutionary War* (Boston: Richardson and Lord, 1823), 374.

52 Freeman, *George Washington*, 5: 417–418

53 Carleton to Washington, August 2 and September 12, 1782; Washington to François-Jean de Beauvoir, Marquis de Chastellux, August 10, 1782; and to John Mitchell, September 16, 1782, GWP; Freeman, *George Washington*, 5: 420–421.

54 Washington, General Orders, August 23 and 30, 1782, GWP; David Cobb to Robert Treat Paine, August 28, 1782 (Massachusetts Historical Society, Boston).

55 Washington, General Orders, September 1 and 2, 1782, GWP; Dempsey, *Washington's Last Cantonment*, 33-34.

56 Thacher, Diary, September 14, 1782, *Military Journal*, 386; Freeman, *George Washington*, 5: 422-425.

57 Washington, General Orders, October 24, 1782, GWP; Freeman, *George Washington*, 5: 425–426.

58 Arthur St. Clair to Nathanael Greene, December 22, 1782, NGP, 12: 335; Samuel Shaw to Shaw, November 13, 1782, in Josiah Quincy, *The Journals of Major Samuel Shaw, the First American*

Consul at Canton (Boston: William Crosby and H.P. Nichols, 1847), 98; Thacher, Diary, November 10, 1783, *Military Journal*, 388.

59   Washington to Lincoln, October 2, 1782, GWP.

60   Charles Louis Victor, Prince de Broglie, *Narrative by the Prince de Broglie of a Visit to America, 1782*, trans. Thomas Balch (Philadelphia, n.p.: 1877), 19–20.

THREE: THE OFFICERS' GRIEVANCES, THE FINANCIER'S FRUSTRATION

1   John Cochran to Timothy Pickering, November 4, 1782, in Morris H. Saffron, *Surgeon to Washington: Dr. John Cochran, 1730-1807* (New York: Columbia University Press, 1977), 242–244; Minutes of Conversation with M[ajor] Fish & M[ajor] Armstrong Relative to Col. Hay's Affair, January 15, 1783, TPP; Janet Dempsey, *Washington's Last Cantonment: "High Time for a Peace"* (Monroe, NY: Library Research Associates, 1990), 48–50.

2   Horatio Gates to Timothy Pickering, November 5, 1782, HGP; Dempsey, *Washington's Last Cantonment*, 49.

3   For Gates background, see Paul David Nelson, *Horatio Gates: A Biography* (Baton Rouge: Louisiana State University Press, 1976); George A. Billias, "Horatio Gates: Professional Soldier," in *George Washington's Generals and Opponents: Their Exploits and Leadership*, ed. George A. Billias (1964; rep., New York: Da Capo, 1994), 79–108.

4   Billias, "Horatio Gates," 80, 86, 90; Barbara Damon Simison, "Dr. R. Benjamin Waterhouse's Journey to Saratoga Springs in the Summer of 1794," *The Yale University Library Gazette*, 40 (1965), 24–25.

5   Nelson, *Horatio Gates*, 14–17, 34–35.

6   Ibid., 40–45, 58–88, 146–147, 157–185.

7   Ibid., 260–267; Charles Louis Victor, Prince de Broglie, *Narrative by the Prince de Broglie of a Visit to America, 1782*, trans. Thomas Balch (Philadelphia, n.p.: 1877), 21.

8   Gates to Washington, November 7, 1782, GWP.

9   François Jean, Marquis de Chastellux, *Travels in North-America, in the Years 1780, 1781, and 1782* (London: G. G. J. and J. Robinson, 1787), 2: 303; General Orders, October 28, 1782, GWP; Dempsey, Washington's Last Cantonment, 45–48.

10 Dempsey, *Washington's Last Cantonment*, 46–48; François Jean, Marquis de Chastellux, *Travels in North-America, in the Years 1780, 1781, and 1782* (London: G. G. J. and J. Robinson, 1787), 2: 303; Gates to Baron von Steuben, November 22, 1782, HGP; William Heath, Diary, October 28, 1782, in *Memoirs of Major-General William Heath*, ed. William Abbatt (1798; rep., New York: Arno Press, 1968), 329–330; Washington to John Armstrong, Sr., January 10, 1783, GWP.

11 Roger J. Champagne, *Alexander McDougall and the Revolution in New York* (Schenectady, NY: Union College Press, 1975), 157–163, 182–183.

12 North Callahan, *Henry Knox: General Washington's General* (New York: Rinehart and Company, 1958), 197, 205.

13 Mark Puls, *Henry Knox: Visionary General of the American Revolution* (New York: Palgrave Macmillan, 2008), 1–8.

14 Callahan, *Henry Knox*, 197, 271–272; Puls, *Henry Knox*, 12–20.

15 Knox's war service forms the bulk of both Callahan's and Puls's biographies. For a brief overview, see North Callahan, "Henry Knox: American Artillerist," in *George Washington's Generals*, 239–259.

16 John Patterson, John Brooks, and Richard Platt to Alexander McDougall, December 15, 1782, McDougall Papers (New-York Historical Society, New York); Puls, *Henry Knox*, 172–173.

17 William Heath to Washington, June 21, 1782, GWP; Petition of the Officers of the Massachusetts Line, August, 1782, Newburgh Papers, HKP (published out of chronological order on reel 53); Sidney Kaplan, "Pay, Pension, and Power: Economic Grievances of the Massachusetts Officers of the Revolution," *The Boston Public Library Quarterly*, 3 (1951), 29.

18 Samuel Osgood to John Lowell, September 9, 1782, LD, 19: 129–134; Osgood to Henry Knox, December 4, 1782, LD, 19: 452–454; Kaplan, "Pay, Pension, and Power," 30-32.

19 Samuel Shaw to Francis Shaw, November 13, 1782, in Josiah Quincy, *The Journals of Major Samuel Shaw, the First American Consul at Canton* (Boston: William Crosby and H. P. Nichols, 1847), 98.

20 Committee Meeting Minutes, November 16 and 20, 1782, Knox to Jeremiah Olney, December 12, 1782, Olney to Knox, December 22, 1782, Newburgh Papers, HKP, reel 53.

21 Grievances of the Fourth, Fifth, and Sixth Massachusetts Regiments, November 19 and 22, 1782, HKP.

22 Grievances of the Third Massachusetts Regiment, November 19, 1782, HKP.

23 Grievances of the Fourth, First, Seventh, Tenth, and Fifth Regiments, November 19, 1782, HKP.

24 Grievances of the Fourth Regiment, November 19, 1782, HKP.

25 Grievances of the Sixth Massachusetts Regiment, November 22, 1782, HKP.

26 Committee Meeting Minutes, November 16, December 1, December 5, 1782, HKP.

27 "Rough draught of an address to be presented to Congress," December 1782, HKP; F. W. Anderson, "Why Did Colonial New Englanders Make Bad Soldiers? Contractual Principles and Military Conduct during the Seven Years' War," *William and Mary Quarterly*, 38 (1981), 395–417.

28 Rough draught of an address," December 1782.

29 Ibid.

30 Second draft of address to Congress, n.d., HKP.

31 Ibid.

32 Ibid.

33 Ibid.

34 Ibid.

35 Ibid.

36 Committee Meeting Minutes, December 5 and December 7, 1782, HKP. The final version of the memorial presented to Congress can be found in a report submitted to Congress April 24, 1783, JCC, 24: 291–293.

37 Charles Rappleye, *Robert Morris: Financier of the American Revolution* (New York: Simon and Schuster, 2010), 290, 309–310; E. James Ferguson, *The Power of the Purse: A History of American Public Finance, 1776–1790* (Chapel Hill: University of North Carolina Press, 1961), 137–138.

38 Virginia Delegates to Benjamin Harrison, May 14, 1782, LD, 18: 516; James Madison to Edmund Pendleton, July 23, 1782, LD, 18: 661; David Howell to William Greene, July 30, 1782, LD, 18: 678–679; Rappleye, *Robert Morris*, 301, 313; Ferguson, *Power of the Purse*, 128.

39 Ferguson, *Power of the Purse*, 149; Rappleye, *Robert Morris*, 301; Introduction, RMP, 6: xxvii.

40 Robert Morris to Matthew Ridley, October 6, 1782, RMP, 6: 512; Rappleye, *Robert Morris*, 312.

41 Rappleye, *Robert Morris*, 308–309.

42 Robert Morris, Diary, June 28, 1782, RMP, 5: 495.

43 Remonstrance and Petition to Congress from Blair McClenachan, Charles Pettit, John Ewing, and Benjamin Rush, July 8, 1782, RMP, 6: 695; Rappleye, *Robert Morris*, 301–302; Robert Morris, Diary, July 9, 1782, RMP, 5: 548–549.

44 Robert Morris to the President of Congress, July 29, 1782, RMP, 6: 65, 70.

45 Patrick T. Conley, *The Makers of Modern Rhode Island* (Charleston, SC: The History Press, 2012), 77–78; Martha Mitchell, "Howell, David," *Encyclopedia Brunoniana*, (1993), http://www.brown.edu/Administration/News_Bureau/Databases/Encyclopedia/search.php?serial=H0300; Rappleye, *Robert Morris*, 319–320.

46 Charles Rappleye, *Sons of Providence: The Brown Brothers, the Slave Trade, and the American Revolution* (New York: Simon and Schuster, 2007), 216.

47 Providence *Gazette*, April 13, 1782, in Jackson Turner Main, *The Anti-Federalists: Critics of the Constitution, 1781-1788* (New York: W.W. Norton and Company, 1961), 81; Irwin H. Polishook, *Rhode Island and the Union, 1774-1795* (Evanston, IL: Northwestern University Press, 1969), 69–73.

48 Polishook, *Rhode Island*, 81–84.

49 Howell to Moses Brown, August 6, 1782, and to Nicholas Brown, September 19, 1782, LD, 19: 23–24, 173–174.

50 Howell to Welcome Arnold, August 3, 1782, LD, 19: 6.

51 Rappleye, *Robert Morris*, 322–325.

52 JCC, October 10, 1782, 23: 643; Howell to Welcome Arnold, October 9, 1782, to Theodore Foster, October 9, 1782, and to Nicholas Brown, October 12, 1782, LD, 19: 243, 245, 251.

53 Howell to Nicholas Brown, September 19, 1782, LD, 19: 173; see also, Howell to Welcome Arnold, August 23, 1782, LD, 19: 91–92.

54 Howell to John Carter, October 16, 1782, LD, 19: 268.

55 Howell to Welcome Arnold, November 17, 1782, and to Foster, November 17, 1782, LD, 19: 392, 393-394.

56 Thomas Paine to Robert Morris, November 20, 1782, RMP, 7: 88; Rappleye, *Robert Morris*, 168–171, 293–297.

57 Samuel Osgood to John Lowell, January 6, 1783, LD, 19: 540.

58 Benjamin Harrison to James Madison, January 4, 1783, JMP; Edmund Randolph to Madison, February 7, 1783, JMP; Rappleye, *Robert Morris*, 328–330; George William Van Cleve, *We Have Not a Government: The Articles of Confederation and the Road to the Constitution* (Chicago: University of Chicago Press, 2017), 87–88.

59 Madison, Notes on Debates, December 24, 1782, JMP.

60 JCC, December 6, 18, 1782, 23: 864, 868; *Continental Journal* (Boston), January 30, 1783, in Polishook, *Rhode Island*, 91. See Polishook, 88–93, for the incident generally.

61 Instructions to Committee, December 1, 1783; Committee Meeting Minutes, December 5, 1782, HKP.

62 Champagne, *Alexander McDougall*, 5–10.

63 Ibid., 11–26, 49–51, 78–81, 91–92; [McDougall], *To the Betrayed Inhabitants of the City and Colony of New-York* (New York: James Parker, 1769), 1.

64 John Adams, Diary, August 20, 1774, *The Diary and Autobiography of John Adams*, ed. L. H. Butterfield (Cambridge, MA: Harvard University Press, 1961); McDougall to Washington, November 16, 1779, GWP; Champagne, *Alexander McDougall*, 139–144.

65 McDougall to Nathanael Greene, March 24, 1779, PNG, 3: 361–362; Champagne, *Alexander McDougall*, 160–164, 166–168.

66 Nancy Isenberg, *Fallen Founder: The Life of Aaron Burr* (New York: Penguin, 2007), 6–8, 15, 21–23; Harry M. Ward, "Ogden, Matthias," *Encyclopedia of the American Revolution: Library of Military History*, ed. Harold E. Selesky (New York: Charles Scribner's Sons, 2006), 2: 857.

67 Washington to Matthias Ogden, March 28, 1782, GWP; Christian M. McBurney, "Washington Authorizes Plan to Kidnap Future King," *Journal of the American Revolution*, January 8, 2014, https://allthingsliberty.com/2014/01/washington -authorizes-plan-kidnap-future-king/.

68 Charles Brooks, *Memoir of John Brooks, Governor of the State of Massachusetts* (n.p., 1865), 1–4; "John Brooks," *Dictionary of American Biography* (New York: Charles Scribner's Sons, 1936), *Biography In Context*, http://link.galegroup.com/apps/doc /BT2310017074/BIC?u=orla57816&sid=BIC; Michael Bellesiles, "John Brooks," *Encyclopedia of the American Revolution: Library of Military History*, ed. Harold Selesky (New York: Charles Scribner's Sons, 2006), *Biography in Context*, http://link.galegroup.com/apps /doc/K3454900173/BIC?u=orla57816&sid=BIC.

69 Grievances of the Seventh Massachusetts Regiment, November 19, 1782, HKP.

70 Committee Meeting Minutes, December 1, 1782, HKP; Instructions to Delegates, December 7, 1782, McDougall Papers.

71 Committee Meeting Minutes, December 1, 1782; Note on Departure, December 21, 1782, Newburgh Papers, HKP, reel 53.

72 Washington to William Heath, June 22, 1782, GWP; "Joseph Jones," *Dictionary of American Biography* (New York: Charles Scribner's Sons, 1936), *U.S. History in Context*, http://link .galegroup.com/apps/doc/BT2310010141/UHIC?u=orla57816& sid=UHIC&xid=679b1aec.

73 Washington to Joseph Jones, December 14, 1782, GWP.

FOUR: THE DELEGATION TO PHILADELPHIA

1 Alexander McDougall to Henry Knox, January 9, 1783, HKP; editors' headnote to Thomas Paine to Robert Morris, November 20, 1782, RMP, 7: 86.

2 McDougall to Knox, January 9, 1783, HKP; Robert Morris, Diary, December 31, 1782, RMP, 7: 247; Samuel Osgood to Benjamin Lincoln, January 1, 1783, LD, 19: 529; Osgood to John Lowell, January 6, 1783, LD, 19: 544.

3 James Madison to Edmund Randolph, December 30, 1782, JMP; Andrew Burstein and Nancy Isenberg, *Madison and Jefferson* (New York: Random House, 2010), 71–78, 95–98; Lance Banning, "James Madison and the Nationalists, 1780-1783," *William and Mary Quarterly*, 40 (1983), 227–255.

4 Gouverneur Morris to Matthew Ridley, January 1, 1783, RMP, 7: 260.

5 Gouverneur Morris to John Jay, January 1, 1783, *John Jay: The Winning of the Peace; The Unpublished Papers, 1780-1784*, ed. Richard B. Morris (New York: Harper and Row, 1980), 485–486.

6 Richard Brookhiser, *Gentleman Revolutionary: Gouverneur Morris, The Rake Who Wrote the Constitution* (New York: The Free Press, 2003), 72–74.

7 Madison, Notes on Debates, January 7, 1783, JMP.

8 Madison, Notes on Debates, January 7, 1783, JMP.

9 Ibid.

10 Robert Morris to Le Couteulx and Company, September 24, 1782, RMP, 6: 424–426.

11 Editors' headnote to Robert Morris to the President of Congress (Elias Boudinot), January 24, 1783, RMP, 365.

12 Madison, Notes on Debates, January 9–10, 1783, JMP, 6: 25.

13 McDougall to Knox, January 9, 1783, HKP.

14 Ibid.

15 Madison, Notes on Debates, January 9–10, 1783, JMP.

16 George Washington to Thomas Lansdale, January 25, 1783, GWP.

17 George Washington to Hodijah Baylies, January 8, 1783, GWP; William Fowler, *American Crisis: George Washington and the Dangerous Two Years after Yorktown, 1781-1783* (New York: Walker and Company, 2011), 159–160.

18 Pickering to Washington, November 11, 1782, and January 18, 1783; Washington to Pickering, December 24, 1782, and Pickering to Washington, GWP; Timothy to Rebecca Pickering, January 19, 1783, TPP.

19 Gerard H. Clarfield, *Timothy Pickering and the American Republic* (Pittsburgh, PA: University of Pittsburgh Press, 1980), 4–10, 13, 20–22, 28–29, 35–36.

20 Ibid., 36–40, 48, 54, 56, 65, 76–77.

21 Timothy to Rebecca Pickering, January 12 and January 22, 1783.

22 Timothy to Rebecca Pickering, February 6, 1783, and to John Pickering, February 17, 1783.

23 Mary V. Thompson, "'As if I had Been a Very Great Somebody': Martha Washington in the American Revolution: Becoming the New Nation's First Lady," George Washington Symposium, Mount Vernon, VA, November 9, 2002, http://catalog. mountvernon.org/digital/collection/p16829coll4/id/2/.

24 George to Lund Washington, December 25, 1782, February 12 and 19, 1783; Lund to George Washington, January 8 and 29, 1783, GWP.

25 George to Lund Washington, February 12, 1783, GWP.

26 John A. Ruddiman, *Becoming Men of Some Consequence: Youth and Military Service in the Revolutionary War* (Charlottesville: University of Virginia Press, 2014), 134–137, 141–145.

27 Benjamin Gilbert to James Converse, September 30, 1782, in John Shy, ed., *Winding Down: The Revolutionary War Letters of Lieutenant Benjamin Gilbert of Massachusetts, 1780–1783* (Ann Arbor: University of Michigan Press, 1989), 69. For Gilbert's background, see Shy, *Winding Down*, 9–17, 65–67; Rebecca D. Symmes, ed., *A Citizen-Soldier in the American Revolution: The Diary of Benjamin Gilbert in Massachusetts and New York* (Cooperstown: New York State Historical Association, 1980), 9–19. Symmes' volume contains Gilbert's diary through March 22, 1782.

28 Benjamin to Daniel Gilbert, January 30, 1783, in Shy, *Winding Down*, 81.

29 Gilbert, Diary, January 24, 29, and 30, 1783, Manuscript Diary of Benjamin Gilbert (Fenimore Art Museum, Cooperstown, NY).

30 Gilbert to Jonathan Stone, March 1, 1783, in Shy, *Winding Down*, 86–87.

31 Madison, Notes on Debates, January 13, 1783, JMP.

32 Madison, Notes on Debates, January 13, 1783, JMP; McDougall and Matthias Ogden to Knox, February 8, 1783, HKP.

33 Madison, Notes on Debates, January 13, 1783, JMP.

34 Ibid.

35 Ibid.

36 Ibid.

37 Madison, Notes on Debates, January 13, 1783, JMP; Robert Morris, Diary, January 13, 1783, RMP, 7: 296.

38 Robert Morris, Observations on the Present State of Affairs, [January 13?], 1783, RMP, 7: 306.

39 Editors' headnote to Robert Morris to the Paymaster General (John Pierce), January 20, 1783, RMP, 7: 327–337.

40 Robert Morris to Nathanael Greene, January 20, 1783, RMP, 7: 326.

41 Editors' headnote to Robert Morris to the Paymaster General (John Pierce), January 20, 1783, RMP, 7: 327–337.

42 Robert Morris, Diary, January 18, 1783, RMP, 7: 317; Chevalier La Luzerne to Robert Morris, January 18, 1783, RMP, 7: 320.

43 Editors' headnote to Robert Morris to the Paymaster General (John Pierce), January 20, 1783, RMP, 7: 327–337.

44 Washington, General Orders, January 8, 24, and 28, February 8, 1783, GWP; John Calvin Thorne, *A Monograph on the Rev. Israel Evans, A.M., Chaplain in the American Army During the Entire Revolutionary War, 1775–1783* (1902; rep., New York: William Abbatt, 1907).

45 William Heath, Diary, October 28, 1782, in *Memoirs of Major-General William Heath*, ed. William Abbatt (1798; rep., New York: Arno Press, 1968), 329–330; Benjamin Tupper to Horatio Gates, January 10, 1783, HGP; Janet Dempsey, *Washington's Last Cantonment: "High Time For a Peace"* (Monroe, NY: Library Research Associates, 1990), 82–83, 87–88, 92–93, 96, 101–102, 105–106; Fowler, *American Crisis*, 165–167.

46 Washington, General Orders, January 29, 1783; Heath, Diary, April 19, June 11 and 19, 1783, in *Memoirs of Major-General William*; Timothy to Rebecca Pickering, February 6, 1783, TPP; Gilbert, Diary, February 6, 1783; Samuel Ball Platner, *A Topographical Dictionary of Ancient Rome*, ed. Thomas Ashby (1929; rep., Cambridge, UK: Cambridge University Press, 2015), 259; James Lloyd, "Cicero," *Ancient History Encyclopedia*, https://www.ancient.eu/Cicero/; James Fordyce, *The Temple of Virtue, a Dream* (1757; 2nd ed., London: T. Cadell, 1775); *The Temple of Virtue, a Masonic Ode* (Southampton: Linden and Hodson, 1777). My thanks to Edward Dandrow for tracking the significance of "Temple of Virtue."

47 Washington, General Orders, January 29, February 4, 5, and 6, 1783, GWP; Timothy to Rebecca Pickering, February 6, 1783, TPP.

48 Ron Chernow, *Alexander Hamilton* (New York: Penguin, 2004), 26, 37–38.

49 Ibid., 42, 72–73, 81, 84.

50 George Washington to Joseph Reed, January 23, 1776, GWP; Arthur S. Lefkowitz, *George Washington's Indispensable Men: The 32 Aides-de Camp Who Helped Win American Independence* (Mechanicsburg, PA: Stackpole Books, 2003), 8; Chernow, *Alexander Hamilton*, 85.

51 Hamilton, "The Continentalist No. I," [July 12, 1781], AHP; Chernow, *Alexander Hamilton*, 165–173.

52 Alexander Graydon, *Memoirs of His Own Time: With Reminiscences of the Men and Events of the Revolution*, ed. John Stockton Littell (Philadelphia: Lindsay and Blakiston, 1846), 149n; Chernow, *Alexander Hamilton*, 51.

53 Alexander Hamilton, Continental Congress Report on Army Memorial, January 22, 1783, AHP; Madison, Notes on Debates, January 24, 1783, JMP.

54 Madison, Notes on Debates, January 24, 1783, JMP.

55 Robert Morris to the President of Congress (Elias Boudinot), January 24, 1783; Robert Morris, Diary, January 24, 1783, RMP, 7: 368, 360.

56 Robert Morris to the President of Congress, January 24, 1783, 7: 368; Charles Rappleye, *Robert Morris: Financier of the American Revolution* (New York: Simon and Schuster, 2010), 338–340.

57 Madison, Notes on Debates, January 24, 1783, JMP.

58 Ibid.; "Theodorick Bland," *Dictionary of American Biography* (New York: Charles Scribner's Sons, 1936), Biography in Context database (accessed January 3, 2017), https://link-galegroup-com.ezproxy.net.ucf.edu/apps/doc/BT2310017623/BIC?u=orla57816&sid=BIC&xid=b79c951d.

59 Madison, Notes on Debates, January 25, 1783, JMP.

60 Madison, Notes on Debates, January 27 and 28, 1783, JMP; introduction, RMP, 6: xxviii.

61 Madison, Notes on Debates, January 27 and 28, 1783, JMP.

62 Ibid., February 4, 1783, JMP.

63 Madison, Notes on Debates, February 4, 1783, JMP; McDougall and Ogden to Henry Knox, February 8, 1783, HKP; Rhode Island Delegates to William Greene, February 4, 1783, LD, 19: 657–658; editors' headnote to Gouverneur Morris to John Rutledge, February 3, 1783, RMP, 7: 393–395.

64 Robert Morris, Diary, February 4 and 5, 1783, RMP, 7: 400, 405; editors' headnote to Robert Morris to the Paymaster General (John Pierce), January 20, 1783, RMP 327–337; Report of the Army Committee, February 8, 1783, HKP; Washington to David Rittenhouse, February 16, 1783, GWP.

FIVE: RUMORS AND GOSSIP

1 *Pennsylvania Packet* (Philadelphia), January 30, and February 11, 1783; *The Independent Gazette* (Philadelphia), February 8, and February 11, 1783; Madison to Edmund Randolph, February 11, 1783; James Madison to James Madison, Sr., February 12, 1783, LD, 19: 675, 686; John Taylor Gilman to Mesech Ware, February 12, 1783, LD, 19: 683.

2 King's Speech to Parliament, December 5, 1782, in *Journal of the House of Lords Volume 36, 1779–1783* (London: His Majesty's Stationery Office, 1767–1830), 572, British History Online, http://www.british-history.ac.uk/lords-jrnl/vol36/pp572-578; Jonathan R. Dull, *Diplomatic History of the American Revolution* (New Haven: Yale University Press, 1985), 144–151.

3 Madison, Notes on Debates, February 13, 1783, 6: 230; Elias Boudinot to Nathanael Greene, February 13, 1783, LD, 19: 688.

4 Alexander Hamilton to George Clinton, February 14, 1783, AHP.

5 JCC, February 5, 1783, 24: 110; Madison, Notes on Debates, February 4, 1783, JMP.

6 Madison, Notes on Debates, February 18, 1783, JMP.

7 Madison, Notes on Debates, February 19, 1783, JMP; Arthur Lee to Samuel Adams, January 29, 1783, LD, 19: 639.

8   Madison, Notes on Debates, February 19, 1783, JMP.

9   Madison, Notes on Debates, February 18, 19, and 20, 1783, JMP; Oliver Wolcott to Oliver Wolcott, Jr., February 19, 1783, LD, 19: 715–716.

10   Gouverneur Morris to Henry Knox, February 7, 1783, RMP, 7: 417–418; see also the editors' headnote to the letter, 7: 412–417.

11   Gouverneur Morris to Nathanael Greene, February 11, 1783, NGP, 12: 433.

12   Ibid., 433-434.

13   Greene to Gouverneur Morris, April 3, 1783, NGP, 12: 561.

14   McDougall and Ogden to Knox, February 8, 1783, HKP.

15   Knox to Gouverneur Morris, February 21, 1783, RMP, 7: 448. See also Knox to McDougall, February 21, 1783, HKP, for similar sentiments.

16   Brutus [McDougall] to Knox, February 12, 1783, HKP.

17   Knox to McDougall, February 21, 1783, HKP.

18   Baron von Steuben to Knox, February 25, 1783, HKP.

19   Hamilton to Phillip Schuyler, February 18, 1781, AHP. For the importance of this incident see Ron Chernow, *Alexander Hamilton* (New York: Penguin, 2004), 151–153; Peter R. Henriques, "The Great Collaboration: The Increasingly Close Relationship between George Washington and Alexander Hamilton," in *Sons of the Father: George Washington and His Protégés*, ed. Robert M. S. McDonald (Charlottesville: University of Virginia Press, 2013), 195–198.

20   Hamilton to Schuyler, February 18, 1781, AHP. See also Hamilton to James McHenry, February 18, 1781, 2: 569; Chernow, *Alexander Hamilton*, 151–153; Henriques, "Great Collaboration," 195–196. For a list of Hamilton's affairs of honor, only one of which involved gunfire, see Joanne B. Freeman, *Affairs of Honor: National Politics in the New Republic* (New Haven, CT: Yale University Press, 2001), 326–327.

21 For Hamilton's early military career and relationship with Washington, see Chernow, *Alexander Hamilton*, 72-93, 163-166; Henriques, "Great Collaboration," 189–209. Hamilton last wrote to Washington on March 1, 1782. See AHP.

22 Hamilton to Washington, February 13, 1783, AHP.

23 Ibid.

24 Ibid.

25 Ibid.

26 Chernow, *Alexander Hamilton*, 177; William Hogeland, *Founding Finance: How Debt, Speculation, Foreclosures, Protests, and Crackdowns Made Us a Nation* (Austin: University of Texas Press, 2012), 87–93; Merrill Jensen, *The New Nation: A History of the United States During the Confederation, 1781-1789* (New York: Alfred A. Knopf, 1965), 71; E. James Ferguson, *The Power of the Purse: A History of American Public Finance, 1776–1790* (Chapel Hill: University of North Carolina Press, 1961), 159–160; Richard H. Kohn, "The Inside History of the Newburgh Conspiracy: America and the Coup d'Etat," *William and Mary Quarterly*, 27 (1970), 201–202.

27 John Adams to Benjamin Rush, January 25, 1806, Founders Online; Henriques, "Great Collaboration," 189–190, 201-202; Chernow, *Alexander Hamilton*, 176.

28 Madison, Notes on Debates, January 28 and February 19, 1783, 6: 142, 259. Hamilton later explained his method in a letter to Washington. See Hamilton to Washington, March 17, 1783; AHP.

29 Freeman, *Affairs of Honor*, 66–67.

30 Madison, Notes on Debates, February 20, 1783, JMP.

31 Ibid.

32 Madison, Notes on Debates, February 20, 1783, JMP; Hamilton to Philip Schuyler, February 18, 1781; and to James McHenry, February 18, 1781, AHP.

33 Madison, Notes on Debates, February 20, 1783, JMP.

34 Freeman, *Affairs of Honor*, 74–78.

35 Madison, Notes on Debates, February 25, 1783, JMP; JCC, February 25, 1783, 24: 146–148.

36 JCC, February 26, 1783, 24: 149–151.

37 Madison, Notes on Debates, February 27 and February 28, 1783, JMP.

38 Madison, Notes on Debates, February 28, 1783, JMP.

39 McDougall to Knox, February 27, 1783, HKP.

40 Gouverneur Morris to Knox, February 28, 1783, RMP, 7: 480.

41 Eliphalet Dyer to William Williams, March 2, 1783, LD, 19: 753–754; McDougall to Knox, March 15, 1783, HKP.

SIX: THE ANONYMOUS LETTER

1 George to Lund Washington, December 25, 1782; and to David Rittenhouse, February 16, 1783, GWP.

2 Joseph Jones to George Washington, February 27, 1783, GWP; "Joseph Jones," *Dictionary of American Biography* (New York: Charles Scribner's Sons, 1936). *Biography In Context*; *Letters of Joseph Jones of Virginia, 1777–1787*, ed. Worthington C. Ford (Washington, DC: Department of State, 1889), iii–vii.

3 Jones to Washington, February 27, 1783, GWP.

4 Alexander Hamilton to Washington, February 24, and March 5, 1783, AHP. The text of the February 24 letter has not been found.

5 Washington to Hamilton, March 4, 1783, AHP.

6 Ibid.; "Old leaven," *OED Online*.

7 Ibid.

8 Stewart to Washington, November 17, 1782, GWP. See also Stewart to Washington, October 12, 1782, GWP.

9 Harry M. Ward, "Stewart, Walter," *Encyclopedia of the American Revolution: Library of Military History*, ed. Harold E. Selesky, 2: 1113–1114 (New York: Charles Scribner's Sons, 2006), *Gale Virtual Reference Library*; Joseph Plumb Martin attests to Stewart's nickname. See Martin, *A Narrative of Some of the Adventures,*

Dangers and Sufferings of a Revolutionary Soldier; Interspersed with Anecdotes of Incidents that Occurred within His Own Observation. Written by Himself (Hallowell, ME: Glazier, Masters, and Company, 1830), 135.

10 Washington to Stewart, January 18, 1783, GWP.

11 John Armstrong, Jr.'s son, in preparing a never-published memoir of his father, mentioned the presence of twelve to fourteen men. See C. Edward Skeen, *John Armstrong, Jr., 1758–1843* (Syracuse, NY: Syracuse University Press, 1981), 10–11. Gates revealed the attendance of Richmond, Barber, and Armstrong in Gates to Armstrong, June 22, 1783, HGP. In this letter, Gates also appeared knowledgeable of—and unapologetic about—the March 9 meeting. For Eustis's involvement, see James Thatcher to Timothy Pickering, February 5, 1826, TPP. Pickering is also sometimes mentioned as possibly present at the meeting, but there is no evidence of his attendance. He was a frequent correspondent of Gates and in the 1820s he became involved in a dispute with Armstrong over his role at the March 15 meeting. See Octavius Pickering, *The Life of Timothy Pickering* (Boston: Little, Brown, 1867), 1: 430–446.

12 No account survives of what was discussed at the March 9 meeting. I have inferred what transpired chiefly from the letter Armstrong wrote that night, as well as from reactions to that letter from Washington, Knox, Rufus Putnam, and Benjamin Walker (see below). Correspondence among Gates, Armstrong, Stewart, and Pickering in the summer of 1783, and Armstrong's later explanations of his actions, made in 1803 and in the 1820s, were also helpful. See, for example, Horatio Gates to Pickering, May 19, 1783, Pickering to Gates, May 28, 1783, Stewart to Gates, May 28, 1783, Armstrong to Gates, May 30, 1783, Gates to Armstrong, June 22, 1783, in HGP; [John Armstrong, Jr.], *Letters Addressed to the Army of the United States in the Year 1783: With a Brief Exposition, etc.* (New York: J. Buel, 1803); [John Armstrong, Jr.], "Review of Judge Johnson's *Life of General Greene*," *The United*

States Magazine, and Literary and Political Repository (1823), 3–44; Pickering, *Life of Timothy Pickering*, 1: 430–446. For Stewart's political connections, see William M. Fowler, Jr., *American Crisis: George Washington and the Dangerous Two Years after Yorktown, 1781-1783* (New York: Walker, 2011), 178.

13   Robert Morris, Report to Congress on the Continental Loan Office, June 13, 1782; Diary, June 26 and July 29, 1783; editors' headnote to Robert Morris to the President of Congress (John Hanson), July 29, 1782, RMP, 5: 398n3, 5: 483, 5: 548–549, 6: 49–50; E. James Ferguson, *The Power of the Purse: A History of American Public Finance, 1776–1790* (Chapel Hill: University of North Carolina Press, 1961), 278, 280; William Bell Clark, "That Mischievous Holker: The Story of a Privateer," *The Pennsylvania Magazine of History and Biography*, 79 (1955): 27–62.

14   Skeen, *John Armstrong, Jr.*, 1–8; C. Edward Skeen, "The Newburgh Conspiracy Reconsidered," *William and Mary Quarterly*, 31 (1974), 276–277.

15   [John Armstrong, Jr.], Letter to the Officers, March 10, 1783, enclosed in Washington to Elias Boudinot, March 12, 1783, GWP.

16   Armstrong, Letter to the Officers, March 10, 1783, in Washington to Boudinot, March 12, 1783, GWP.

17   For an analysis of Armstrong's rhetorical strategies, see Stephen H. Browne, *The Ides of War: George Washington and the Newburgh Crisis* (Columbia: University of South Carolina Press, 2016), 62–64.

18   Armstrong, Letter to the Officers, March 10, 1783, in Washington to Boudinot, March 12, 1783, GWP.

19   Armstrong, Letter to the Officers, March 10, 1783, in Washington to Boudinot, March 12, 1783, GWP.

20   Charles Royster, *A Revolutionary People at War: The Continental Army and American Character, 1775–1783* (Chapel Hill: University of North Carolina Press, 1979), 335–339.

21   Armstrong, Letter to the Officers, March 10, 1783, in Washington to Boudinot, March 12, 1783, GWP.

22 John A. Ruddiman, *Becoming Men of Some Consequence: Youth and Military Service in the Revolutionary War* (Charlottesville: University of Virginia Press, 2014), 137–139; Frankie Rubinstein, *A Dictionary of Shakespeare's Sexual Puns and Their Significance* (2nd ed.; London: MacMillan, 1989).

23 Armstrong, Letter to the Officers, March 10, 1783, in Washington to Boudinot, March 12, 1783, GWP; Royster, *Revolutionary People at War*, 341.

24 Gates to Armstrong, June 22, 1783, HGP.

25 Invitation, March 10, 1783, enclosed in Washington to Boudinot, March 12, 1783, GWP. The invitation received at West Point can be found in HKP. See also Benjamin Walker to Baron von Steuben, March 13, 1783, VSP.

26 John Chester to Joshua Huntington, March 21, 1783, in *Huntington Papers: Correspondence of the Brothers Joshua and Jedediah Huntington, during the Period of the American Revolution* (Hartford: Connecticut Historical Society, 1923), 1: 171. Chester, who was not in camp, repeated a story from Jedediah, who was. For Washington's suspicions about authorship, see Washington to Jones, February 12, 1783, and Washington to Hamilton, February 12, 1783, GWP. Some forty years later, David Cobb recalled the opinion at headquarters was that Gouverneur Morris was the author. See Cobb to Timothy Pickering, November 9, 1825, TPP. Washington later wrote Armstrong that at the time of the crisis he did not believe he was the author. See Washington to Armstrong, February 23, 1797, GWP.

27 General Orders, March 11, 1783, GWP.

28 General Orders, March 12, 1783, GWP.

29 General Orders, March 13, 1783, GWP; McDougall to Knox, February 8, 1783, HKP.

30 Washington to Boudinot, March 12, 1783, GWP.

31 Washington to Hamilton, March 12, 1783; and to Jones, March 12, 1783, GWP.

32   Ibid.

33   Ibid.

34   [Armstrong], Letter to the Officers, March 12, 1783, in Washington to Boudinot, March 12, 1783, GWP.

35   Benjamin Walker to Baron von Steuben, March 13, 1783, VSP.

36   Ibid.

37   Knox to McDougall, March 12, 1783; and to Benjamin Lincoln, March 12, 1783, HKP.

38   Harold E. Selesky, "Putnam, Rufus," *Encyclopedia of the American Revolution: Library of Military History*, ed. Harold E. Selesky, 2: 950–951 (New York: Charles Scribner's Sons, 2006), *Gale Virtual Reference Library*.

39   [Rufus Putnam], To the Officers of the Army, March [13 or 14], 1783, HKP. The precise date of composition is unknown, but it referenced the March 13 general orders and was intended to circulate in advance of the March 15 meeting.

40   Ibid.

41   Ibid.

SEVEN: GENERAL WASHINGTON IN THE TEMPLE OF VIRTUE

1   William M. Fowler, *American Crisis: George Washington and the Dangerous Two Years after Yorktown, 1781-1783* (New York: Walker and Company, 2011), 185.

2   Susan Brynne Long, "George Washington's Voice," George Washington's Mount Vernon, https://www.mountvernon.org /george-washington/the-man-the-myth/washingtons-voice. A catalogue of contemporary descriptions of Washington can be found in Paul Leicester Ford, *The True George Washington* (Philadelphia: J. B. Lippincott Company, 1905), 38–57.

3   Paul David Nelson, *Horatio Gates: A Biography*, (Baton Rouge: Louisiana State University Press, 1976), 273-274; Stephen Howard Browne, *The Ides of War: George Washington and the Newburgh Crisis* (Columbia: University of South Carolina Press, 2016), 69–70.

4 Browne, *Ides of War*, 73.

5 David Hackett Fischer, *Washington's Crossing* (New York: Oxford University Press, 2004), 313–314.

6 Henry Knox to George Washington, March 11, 1783, GWP; Knox to McDougall, March 12, 1783, HKP; Benjamin Gilbert, Diary, March 13, 1783 (Fenimore Art Museum Library, Cooperstown, NY).

7 Philip Van Cortlandt, *Memoir*, in *The Revolutionary War* Memoir *and Selected Correspondence of Philip Van Cortlandt*, ed. Jacob Judd (Tarrytown, NY: Sleepy Hollow Restorations, 1976), 1: 68; James Watson Webb, *Reminiscences of Gen'l Samuel B. Webb of the Revolutionary Army* (New York: Globe Stationery and Printing Company, 1882), 54; Frank Landon Humphreys, *David Humphreys: Soldier, Statesman, Poet, "Belov'd of Washington"* (New York: G. P. Putnam's Sons, 1917), 1: 266; William Gordon, *The History of the Rise, Progress, and Establishment of the Independence of the United States of America* (New York: Hodge, Allen, and Campbell, 1789), 3: 360.

8 Timothy to Rebecca Pickering, March 14, 1783, TPP.

9 The original manuscript is viewable at the Massachusetts Historical Society website: http://www.masshist.org/database /viewer.php?item_id=1742.

10 David Humphreys, *The Miscellaneous Works of David Humphreys: Late Minister Plenipotentiary to the Court of Madrid* (New York: T. and J. Swords), 1804), 178.

11 George Washington, General Orders, March 15, 1783, GWP. My thanks to Stephanie Lawton for explaining the significance of the Ides of March in the 18th century.

12 Benjamin Gilbert, Diary, March 15, 1783 (Fenimore Art Museum, Cooperstown, NY); John Shy, ed., *Winding Down: The Revolutionary War Letters of Lieutenant Benjamin Gilbert of Massachusetts, 1780-1783* (Ann Arbor: University of Michigan Press, 1989), 67, 98.

13 Fowler, *American Crisis*, 184–185.

14 Samuel Shaw to John Eliot, April 1783, in Josiah Quincy, *The Journals of Major Samuel Shaw, the First American Consul at Canton* (Boston: William Crosby and H. P. Nichols, 1847), 103.

15 Ibid.

16 Washington to the Officers of the Army, March 15, 1783, GWP. My interpretation of Washington's speech is indebted to the rhetorical analysis of Browne, *Ides of War*, 79–89. For another close reading, see Richard Brookhiser, *Founding Father: Rediscovering George Washington* (New York: Free Press, 1996), 43–45.

17 Ibid.; J. A. Wright to John Webb, March 16, 1783, in *Reminiscences of Gen'l Samuel B. Webb*, 60.

18 Washington, Speech to the Officers, March 15, 1783, GWP.

19 Browne, *Ides of War*, 79–81.

20 Washington to the Officers, March 15, 1783, GWP; Browne, *Ides of War*, 82.

21 John Ruddiman, *Becoming Men of Some Consequence: Youth and Military Service in the Revolutionary War* (Charlottesville: University of Virginia Press, 2014), 139.

22 Washington to the Officers, March 15, 1783, GWP; Timothy to Rebecca Pickering, March 16, 1783, TPP; Browne, *Ides of War*, 83.

23 Washington, Speech to the Officers, March 15, 1783, GWP.

24 Ibid.

25 Ibid.; Craig Bruce Smith, *American Honor: The Creation of the Nation's Ideals during the Revolutionary Era* (Chapel Hill, University of North Carolina Press, 2018), 164.

26 Washington, Speech to the Officers, March 15, 1783, GWP; Browne, *Ides of War*, 80; Fowler, *American Crisis*, 185–186.

27 Shaw to Eliot, April 1783, in *The Journals of Major Samuel Shaw*. Shaw provides the fullest description of the scene. For other accounts, see Philip Schuyler to Stephen Van Rensselaer, March 17, 1783, in Benson J. Lossing, *The Life and Times of Philip Schuyler* (New York: Sheldon and Company, 1873), 2: 427; Pickering to David Cobb, October 24, 1825; Cobb to Pickering,

November 9, 1825; Nicholas Fish to Pickering, November 30, 1825, TPP.

28 Cobb to Pickering, November 9, 1825, TPP. The sources disagree on when Washington put on his glasses: before his prepared remarks or before reading Jones's letter. I find Fowler's argument (*American Crisis*, 304–305n52) about Jones's small script persuasive. Jones to Washington, February 27, 1783, GWP.

29 The full text of Jones's letter is available as Jones to Washington, February 27, 1783, GWP. See also Ebenezer Smith, Orderly Book of the Second Massachusetts Regiment, March–November 1783 (Society of the Cincinnati Library, Washington, DC), [44–53]: https://www.societyofthecincinnati.org/collections /library/ebenezersmith; Pickering to Samuel Hodgdon, March 16, 1783, enclosure, "Copy of a Letter from a Member of Congress to General Washington," TPP.

30 Images of the original manuscript can be found at https://www .loc.gov/item/mgw433552/.

31 Pickering to Hodgdon, March 16, 1783; and to Cobb, October 24, 1825; Cobb to Pickering, November 9, 1825, TPP; Shaw to Eliot, April 1783, *Journals of Major Samuel Shaw*, 104; Edward Hand to William Irvine April 19, 1783, George Bancroft Collection, American Archives Transcriptions, volume 1, 1783, 202 (New York Public Library, New York); Schuyler to Stephen Van Rensselaer, March 17, 1783, in Lossing, *Life and Times of Philip Schuyler*, 2: 427. Schuyler's biographer rendered Washington's line as "You see, gentlemen, that I have not only grown gray, but also blind, in your service," but he doesn't mention his source. See Lossing, *Life and Times of Philip Schuyler*, 2: 426–427.

32 Proceedings of the Officers, March 15, 1783, HGP. The resolutions also can be found in GWP, though labeled as "George Washington to Horatio Gates."

33 Ibid.

34 Ibid.

35   Pickering to Hodgdon, March 16, 1783; and to Rebecca Pickering, March 16, 1783, TPP.

36   Proceedings of the Officers, March 15, 1783, HGP.

37   Timothy to Rebecca Pickering, March 16, 1783, TPP.

38   Proceedings of the Officers, March 15, 1783, HGP.

39   Ibid.

40   Ibid.; Pickering to Hodgdon, March 16, 1783, TPP.

41   Pickering to Hodgdon, March 16, 1783; to Rebecca Pickering, March 16, 1783, and March 18, 1783, TPP.

42   Schuyler to Van Rensselaer, March 17, 1783, in Lossing, *Life and Times of Philip Schuyler*, 2: 427.

43   Washington to Jones, March 12, 1783, GWP.

44   Walker to von Steuben, March 13, 1783, VSP.

45   Rufus King, Statement of Conversation with William Duane, October 12, 1788, in *The Life and Correspondence of Rufus King: Compromising His Letters, Private and Official, His Public Documents and His Speeches* (New York: G. P. Putnam's Sons, 1894), ed. Charles R. King, 1: 621–622.

46   Ibid. The reliability of King's statement is discussed in Gouverneur Morris to Knox, February 7, 1783, RMP, 7: 419n14; Nelson, "Horatio Gates at Newburgh," 146–147, Kohn's reply to Nelson, 152; C. Edward Skeen, "Newburgh Conspiracy Reconsidered," *William and Mary Quarterly*, 31 (1974), 280-281, and Kohn's reply to Skeen, 293-294.

47   John Montgars [Armstrong] to Pickering, January 20, 1820, TPP.

48   [John Armstrong, Jr.] "Review of Judge Johnson's *Life of General Greene*," *The United States Magazine, and Literary and Political Repository*, January 1823, 40.

49   Ibid.; [Armstrong] to Pickering, January 20, 1820, TPP.

50   For Gates's role in the Newburgh Affair, see Nelson, *Horatio Gates*, 267–277; Nelson, "Horatio Gates at Newburgh, 1783: A Misunderstood Role," *William and Mary Quarterly*, 29 (1972), 143–151.

51   Horatio to Elizabeth Gates, March 5, 1783, HGP.

52   "Agent," *OED Online.*

53   Samuel Johnson, *A Dictionary of the English Language: In Which the Words are Deduced from Their Originals, and Illustrated in Their Different Significations by Examples from the Best Writers: To Which are Prefixed, a History of the Language, and an English Grammar,* 6th ed. (London: J. F. and C. Rivington and others, 1785).

54   Johnson, *A Dictionary of the English Language*; "Friend," *OED Online*; Cassandra A. Good, *Founding Friendships: Friendships Between Men and Women in the Early American Republic* (New York: Oxford University Press, 2015), 2.

55   Alan Taylor, "'The Art of Hook & Snivey': Political Culture in Upstate New York during the 1790s," *The Journal of American History,* 79 (1993), 1371–1396; Joanne B. Freeman, *Affairs of Honor: National Politics in the New Republic* (New Haven, CT: Yale University Press, 2001), 74–78.

56   Robert Morris to Gates, December 3, 1782, January 28, 1783, February 25, 1783, RMP, 163–164, 377–378, 459–460; Gates to Robert Morris, December 9, 1782, RMP, 188–189; Nelson, *Horatio Gates,* 259–260, 262–263; William Hogeland, *Founding Finance: How Debt, Speculation, Foreclosures, Protests, and Crackdowns Made Us a Nation* (Austin: University of Texas Press, 2012), 89.

57   Gouverneur Morris to Philip Schuyler, August 27, 1777, September 18, 1777; Schuyler to Gouverneur Morris, September 7, 1777, in Jared Sparks, *The Life of Gouverneur Morris* (Boston: Gray and Bowen, 1832), 1: 141–146; Nelson, *Horatio Gates,* 91–92, 100–103, 106–107.

58   Alexander Hamilton to James Duane, September 6, 1780, AHP; Ron Chernow, *Alexander Hamilton* (New York: Penguin, 2004), 100–104.

59   James Wilkinson, *Memoirs of My Own Times* (Philadelphia: Abraham Small, 1816), 1: 373; Chernow, *Alexander Hamilton,* 104–105.

60   Nelson, *Horatio Gates*, 123, 131–132, 264.

61   David B. Mattern, *Benjamin Lincoln and the American Revolution* (Columbia: University of South Carolina Press, 1995), 136–142.

62   Gates to Peters, February 20, 1783, HGP; Peters to Gates, March 5, 1783, HGP; "Richard Peters," In *Dictionary of American Biography* (New York: Charles Scribner's Sons, 1936). *Biography in Context* (accessed June 25, 2018): http://link.galegroup.com .ezproxy.net.ucf.edu/apps/doc/BT2310005757/BIC?u=orla57 816&sid=BIC&xid=a6af7d57; Carol E. Brier, "Tending Our Vines: From the Correspondence and Writings of Richard Peters and John Jay," *Pennsylvania History: A Journal of Mid-Atlantic Studies*, 80 (2013): 85–111.

63   Peters to Gates, March 5, 1783, HGP.

64   Joseph Nourse to Gates, November 27, December 24, 1782, February 8, February 17, February 26, March 3, 1783, HGP; Nelson, *Horatio Gates*, 267–268; Oscar P. Fitzgerald, "'Truth, Honour, Virtue': The Life of Joseph Nourse," and Kenneth R. Bowling, "Joseph Nourse: The First American Civil Servant," in *In Search of Joseph Nourse, 1754-1841: America's First Civil Servant* (Washington: National Society of Colonial Dames of America, 1994), 1–5, 22–24.

65   McDougall to Washington, December 10, 1778, GWP; Roger J. Champagne, *Alexander McDougall and the American Revolution in New York* (Schenectady, NY: Union College Press, 1975), 135–136, 147–148, 165.

EIGHT: PEACE AND PENSIONS

1   George Washington, General Orders, March 18, 1783; GWP.

2   Washington to Elias Boudinot, March 16, 1783, GWP.

3   Washington to Boudinot, March 18, 1783, GWP.

4   Ibid.

5   Ibid.

6   Ibid.

7   Editors' headnotes to Robert Morris to the President of Congress (Elias Boudinot), December 3, 1782 and February 26, 1783, RMP, 7: 413–148, 462–470.

8   James Madison, Notes on Debates, March 4–5, 1783, JMP; Lucius to Robert Morris, March 12, 1783, RMP, 7: 559. The first Lucius letter appeared March 5 and continued through April.

9   Jonathan Arnold to David Howell, March 8, 1783, LD, 19: 777. For the possible identity of Lucius, see editors' headnote to Lucius to Robert Morris, March 5, 1783, RMP, 7: 501–504.

10   Madison, Report on Restoring Public Credit, March 6, 1783, JMP; editors' headnote to Robert Morris to the President of Congress (Elias Boudinot), March 8, 1783, 7: 518–519.

11   Robert Morris to the President of Congress (Elias Boudinot), March 8, 1783, RMP, 7: 525. See also the editor's headnote to this document, which analyzes the episode thoroughly.

12   Ibid., 7: 527–528.

13   Ibid., 7: 528–529.

14   James Madison, Notes on Debates, March 11, 1783, JMP.

15   Alexander McDougall to Henry Knox, March 15, 1783, HKP.

16   JCC, March 10, 1783, 24: 177–179; McDougall to Knox, March 15, 1783, HKP.

17   Eliphalet Dyer to William Williams, March 2, 1783, LD, 19: 753-755; Dyer to Jonathan Trumbull, Sr., April 12, 1783, LD, 20: 171–175; Madison, Notes on Debates, March 20, 1783, n4, JMP.

18   American Peace Commissioners to Robert R. Livingston, December 14, 1782, in Benjamin Franklin Papers, Founders Online; Madison, Notes on Debates, March 12–15, 1783; Madison to Edmund Randolph, March 12, 1783, JMP; Chevalier de La Luzerne to Robert Morris, March 15, 1783, RMP, 7: 586–588.

19   Madison, Notes on Debates, March 12–15, 1783, JMP.

20   Madison, Notes on Debates, March 17, 1783, JMP.

21 Ibid.; Dyer to Jonathan Trumbull, Sr., March 18, 1783, LD, 20: 43.

22 Elias Boudinot to Washington, March 17, 1783, GWP.

23 Madison to Edmund Randolph, March 18, 1783, JMP; John Francis Mercer to Henry Tazewell, March 18, 1783, LD, 20: 53.

24 Madison, Notes on Debates, March 17, 1783, JMP.

25 Dyer to Trumbull, Sr., April 12, 1783, LD, 20: 173.

26 Madison, Notes on Debates, March 20, 1783, JMP; JCC, March 20, 1783, 24: 202-203; Report on Half Pay to the Army, March 21, 1783, AHP.

27 Madison, Notes on Debates, March 22, 1783, JMP; Theodorick Bland to Baron von Steuben, March 22, 1783, LD, 20: 68.

28 Madison, Notes on Debates, March 22, 1783, n3, JMP; JCC, March 22, 1783, 24: 210.

29 Maryland Delegates to William Paca, March 18, 1783, LD, 20: 50; Washington to Boudinot, March 12, 1783, GWP.

30 Madison, Notes on Debates, March 24, 1783, JMP.

31 Boudinot to Washington, March 23, 1783, GWP; and to Lewis Pintard, March 25, 1783, LD, 20: 97.

32 Washington to Boudinot, March 19, 1783; and to the Marquis de Lafayette, March 23, 1783, GWP.

33 Washington to Jones, March 18, 1783; and to Lund Washington, March 19, 1783, GWP.

34 Washington to Robert R. Livingston, March 18, 1783; and to Lund Washington, March 19, 1783, GWP.

35 Washington to Benjamin Harrison, Sr., March 19, 1783, GWP.

36 James Madison to Edmund Randolph, March 18, 1783, JMP; Washington to Hamilton, March 12, 1783, AHP; Washington to Jones, March 18, 1783; to Harrison, March 19, 1783; and to Lund Washington, March 19, 1783, GWP.

37 Washington to Hamilton, April 16, 1783, GWP; David Cobb to Timothy Pickering, November 9, 1825, TPP.

38 Gouverneur Morris to Henry Knox, February 7, 1783, RMP, 7: 417–418. See also the editor's headnote, RMP, 7: 414. Gouverneur

Morris to Nathanael Greene, February 11, 1783, NGP, 12: 432–434.

39   Gouverneur Morris to Knox, February 28, 1783, RMP, 7: 480.

40   Robert Morris to Washington, May 29, 1783, RMP, 8: 130, 131.

41   Robert Morris, Diary, July 9, 1782, RMP, 5: 548; editors' headnote to Robert Morris to the President of Congress, February 26, 1783, RMP, 7: 462–470; Hamilton to Washington, April 8, 1783, GWP.

42   Washington to John Armstrong, Jr., February 23, 1797, GWP; Cobb to Pickering, November 9, 1825, TPP.

43   Washington to Hamilton, March 4, 1783, AHP; Douglas Southall Freeman, *George Washington: A Biography*, vol. 5, *Victory with the Help of France* (New York: Charles Scribner's Sons, 1952), 5: 429n17; Paul David Nelson, *General Horatio Gates: A Biography* (Baton Rouge: Louisiana State University Press, 1976), 276–277.

44   "Old leaven," *OED Online*.

45   Hamilton to Washington, March 17, 1783, AHP.

46   Ibid.

47   Ibid.

48   Ibid.

49   Ibid.

50   Madison, Notes on Debates, February 20, 1783, JMP.

51   Hamilton to Washington, March 25, 1783, AHP.

52   John Armstrong, Jr. to Horatio Gates, April 29, 1783, HGP; [John Armstrong, Jr.], *Letters Addressed to the Army of the United States in the Year 1783: With a Brief Exposition, etc.* (New York: J. Buel, 1803); John Montgars [Armstrong] to Pickering, January 20, 1820, TPP; [John Armstrong, Jr.] "Review of Judge Johnson's Life of General Greene," *The United States Magazine, and Literary and Political Repository*, January 1823, 41–42.

53   Washington to Knox, March 26, 1783; General Orders, March 28, 1783, GWP.

54 Benjamin Gilbert, Diary, March 27, 28, and 29, 1783. (Fenimore Art Museum Library, Cooperstown, NY)

55 Bernardus Swartwout, Diary, March 1783 (New-York Historical Society, New York); Benjamin Gilbert, Diary, March 30, 1783.

56 Washington to Nathanael Greene, March 31, 1783, GWP.

NINE: THE ARMY DISBANDS

1 Benjamin Gilbert, Diary, April 1–17, 1783 (Fenimore Art Museum, Cooperstown, NY).

2 Gilbert to Charles Bruce, March 25, 1783, and to Daniel Gilbert, March 26, 1783, in *Winding Down: The Revolutionary War Letters of Lieutenant Benjamin Gilbert of Massachusetts, 1780-1783*, ed. John Shy (Ann Arbor: University of Michigan Press, 1989), 92–93, 103.

3 Ebenezer Smith, Orderly Book of the Second Massachusetts Regiment, March–November 1783 (Society of the Cincinnati Library, Washington, DC): https://www.societyofthecincinnati .org/collections/library/ebenezersmith. The poems are undated but were clearly copied in spring 1783 after the March crisis.

4 Ibid. "The Stipulation" dated back at least as far as 1745, when it appeared in *The Gentleman's Magazine and Historical Chronicle* (London: Edward Cave, 1745), 15: 551.

5 Charles Royster, *A Revolutionary People at War: The Continental Army and American Character, 1775–1783* (Chapel Hill: University of North Carolina Press, 1979), 341–345; John A. Ruddiman, *Becoming Men of Some Consequence: Youth and Military Service in the Revolutionary Army* (Charlottesville: University of Virginia Press, 2014), 141–146.

6 Theodorick Bland to Washington, March 25, 1783, LD, 20: 98; two letters from Hamilton to Washington, March 25, 1783, AHP.

7 Richard Peters to Baron von Steuben, April 23, 1783, LD, 20: 211.

8 Washington to Bland, April 4, 1783 (official letter of that date), GWP.

9   Samuel Shaw to John Eliot, May 3, 1783, in Josiah Quincy, *The Journals of Major Samuel Shaw, the First American Consul at Canton* (Boston: William Crosby and H. P. Nichols, 1847), 107.

10 Bernardus Swartwout, Diary, April 1783 (New-York Historical Society, New York); Robert Morris, Diary, April 15, 1783, RMP, 7: 705.

11 Washington to Hamilton, April 4, 1783, AHP.

12 Hamilton to Washington, April 8, 1783, AHP.

13 Ibid. For the subtleties of defending one's honor in the 18th century, see Joanne B. Freeman, *Affairs of Honor: National Politics in the New Republic* (New Haven, CT: Yale University Press, 2001).

14 Washington to Hamilton, April 16, 1783, AHP.

15 Ibid.

16 Minor Myers, Jr., *Liberty without Anarchy: A History of the Society of the Cincinnati* (Charlottesville: University of Virginia Press, 1983), 15–19; Rob Hardy, "Cincinnatus," *George Washington Digital Encyclopedia*, Fred W. Smith National Library for the Study of George Washington at Mount Vernon, https://www .mountvernon.org/library/digitalhistory/digital-encyclopedia /article/cincinnatus/.

17 Thomas Jefferson, "Notes of a Tour through Holland and the Rhine Valley," March 16, 1788, and William Eustis, "Statement concerning the Origin of the Cincinnati," n.d., quoted in Myers, *Liberty without Anarchy*, 16, 17; Markus Hünemörder, *The Society of the Cincinnati: Conspiracy and Distrust in Early America* (New York: Berghahn Books, 2006), 15–16.

18 Knox, Rough draft of a society to be formed by the American officers, April 15, 1783, HKP; Myers, *Liberty without Anarchy*, 18–19.

19 Ibid.

20 The Institution of the Society of the Cincinnati, May 13, 1783, Society of the Cincinnati, https://www.societyofthecincinnati.org

/about/purpose/institution; Myers, *Liberty without Anarchy*, 24–28; Roger J. Champagne, *Alexander McDougall and the American Revolution in New York* (Schenectady, NY: Union College Press, 1975), 199.

21 Cassius [Aedanus Burke], *Considerations on the Society or Order of Cincinnati; Lately Instituted by the Major-Generals, Brigadier-Generals, and Other Officers of the American Army* (Philadelphia: Robert Bell, 1783), 7; Hünemörder, *Society of the Cincinnati*, 25–51.

22 Washington, General Orders, May 1, 1783, GWP; Janet Dempsey, *Washington's Last Cantonment: "High Time for a Peace"* (Monroe, NY: Library Research Associates, 1990), 172.

23 Henry Knox to Washington, April 16, 1783; Washington to General Officers, April 17, 1783; Washington to Boudinot, April 18, 1783, GWP.

24 Washington to the States, April 14, 1783; to Robert Morris, April 9, 1783; to John Pierce, April 6, 1783, GWP.

25 Washington to Boudinot, April 18, 1783, GWP.

26 Washington to the General Officers of the Army, April 17, 1783, GWP.

27 Washington, General Orders, April 18, 1783, GWP.

28 William Fowler, *American Crisis: George Washington and the Dangerous Two Years after Yorktown, 1781–1783* (New York: Walker, 2011), 192; Gilbert, Diary, April 19, 1783; Dempsey, *Washington's Last Cantonment*, 176.

29 James Madison, Notes on Debates, March 28, JMP; JCC, April 7 and 18, 1783, 24: 230–231, 256–262; headnote to Robert Morris to the President of Congress, March 8, 1783, RMP, 522–525.

30 Madison, Report on Address to the States by Congress, [April 25], 1783, JMP.

31 Alexander Hamilton to George Clinton, May 14, 1783, AHP.

32 Robert Morris to Edward Carrington, May 19, 1783, RMP, 8: 93; editors' headnote to Robert Morris to the President of Congress, March 8, 1783, RMP, 7: 525.

33 Robert Morris, Diary, April 9, 1783; and to a Committee of Congress, April 14, 1783, RMP, 7: 682–683, 702; Charles Rappleye, *Robert Morris: Financier of the American Revolution* (New York: Simon and Schuster, 2010), 354–356.

34 Robert Morris, Diary, April 22 and 24, 1783, RMP, 7: 732, 747; JCC, April 23, 1783, 24: 270–271; editors' headnote to Robert Morris to the President of Congress, May 1, 1783, RMP, 7: 770–772.

35 Robert Morris to the President of Congress, May 1, 1783, RMP: 7: 775–779.

36 Robert Morris, Diary, May 3 and 6, 1783, RMP, 7: 789, 8: 8; Rappleye, *Robert Morris*, 356–357.

37 JCC, April 23, 1783, 24: 269–270; James Madison, Notes on Debates, April 23, 1783, JMP.

38 JCC, April 23, 1783, 24: 270; James Madison, Notes on Debates, May 20, 1783, JMP; Washington to Boudinot, March April 18, 1783, GWP.

39 Madison, Notes on Debates, May 20, 23, and 26, 1783, JMP; JCC, May 23 and 26, 1783, 24: 358–361, 364; Robert Morris to a Committee of Congress, May 15, 1783, RMP, 8: 50; Rappleye, *Robert Morris*, 360.

40 Knox to Washington, May 14, 1783; William Heath to Washington, May 29, 1783; Washington to Daniel Parker, May 29, 1783, GWP; editors' headnote to Robert Morris to a Committee of Congress, May 15, 1783, RMP, 8: 48.

41 Washington to Robert Morris, June 3, 1783; Robert Morris to Washington, June 5, 1783, RMP, 8: 158, 172.

42 Washington, General Orders, June 2, 1783, GWP.

43 Dempsey, *Washington's Last Cantonment*, 209–210; Washington, General Orders, June 3, 1783; and to Thomas Lansdale, June 5, 1783, GWP.

44 Dempsey, *Washington's Last Cantonment*, 221; Charles H. Lesser, ed., *The Sinews of Independence: Monthly Strength Reports of the Continental Army* (Chicago: University of Chicago Press, 1976), 252–254.

45   Editors' headnote to Robert Morris to a Committee of Congress,
     May 15, 1783, RMP, 8: 49. The editors say the notes arrived
     June 15, but Gilbert attests to receiving his notes on June 14. See
     Gilbert, Diary, June 14, 1783. On selling notes, see Washington,
     General Orders, May 21, 1783, GWP; Royster, *Revolutionary
     People*, 342; E. James Ferguson, *Power of the Purse: A History
     of American Public Finance, 1776–1790* (Chapel Hill: University of
     North Carolina Press, 1961), 170, 172–173.

46   Heath to Washington, June 5, 1783, GWP.

47   Washington, General Orders, June 6, 1783; to Boudinot, June 7,
     1783, GWP; JCC, June 19, 1783, 24: 403; editors' headnote to
     Robert Morris to a Committee of Congress, May 15, 1783, RMP,
     8: 48–49, 59–60n23.

48   Gilbert to Bruce, June 10, 1783, *Winding Down*, 107; Gilbert,
     Diary, August 26, 1783; Gilbert to Jonathan Stone, March 1,
     1783, *Winding Down*, 87n188.

49   Royster, *Revolutionary People*, 343–346.

50   Robert Morris, Diary, June 10–19, RMP, 8: 177–178, 182–185,
     190–193; Rappleye, *Robert Morris*, 365–367.

51   JCC, June 20, 1783, 24: 406; Robert Morris, Report to Congress
     Respecting Settling of the Army Accounts, June 22, 1783, RMP,
     8: 205–206, 207n4.

52   The mutiny is described in Mary A. Y. Gallagher, "Reinterpreting
     the 'Very Trifling Mutiny' at Philadelphia in June 1783," *The
     Pennsylvania Magazine of History and Biography*, 119 (1995), 3–35;
     John A. Nagy, *Rebellion in the Ranks: Mutinies of the American
     Revolution* (Yardley, PA: Westholme Publishing), 211–229;
     editors' headnote to Robert Morris to the President of Congress,
     June 30, 1783, RMP, 8: 215–228.

53   Madison, Notes on Debates, June 13, 1783, JMP; Robert Morris,
     Diary, June 13, 1783, RMP, 8: 184–185.

54   Richard Butler to John Dickinson, June 17, 1783, in *The Diplomatic
     Correspondence of the United States of America* (Washington: Francis

Preston Blair, 1833), 1: 16; Madison, Notes on Debates, June 19 and 21, 1783, JMP.

55　John Armstrong, Jr., to Horatio Gates, May 30, 1783, HGP.

56　Washington to Boudinot, June 24, 1783, GWP.

57　Washington to the States, June 8, 1783; Washington to Boudinot, June 24, 1783, GWP; Douglas Southall Freeman, *George Washington: A Biography*, vol. 5, *Victory with the Help of France* (New York: Charles Scribner's Sons, 1952), 5: 446.

58　Editors' headnote to Robert Morris to the Paymaster General, March 15, 1783, RMP, 7: 581–582; Robert Morris, Report to Congress Respecting Settling of the Army Accounts, June 22, 1783; Diary, July 8, 1783; to Pierce, July 8, 1783, RMP, 8: 207n4, 256–257, 260; Ferguson, *The Power of the Purse*, 179–181, 186–188, 352–353.

59　Washington to Boudinot, July 17, 1783, Freeman, *George Washington*, 5: 450–451; Fowler, *American Crisis*, 214.

60　Freeman, *George Washington*, 5: 451; Fowler, *American Crisis*, 215.

61　Boudinot to Robert R. Livingston, September 16, 1783, LD, 20: 675; Robert Morris, Diary, June 24, 25, 26, and 30, 1783, RMP, 8: 214–215; Charles to Hannah Thomson, June 30, 1783, LD, 20: 383; Fowler, *American Crisis*, 216; Freeman, *George Washington*, 5: 452; Rappleye, *Robert Morris*, 366.

62　David Howell to William Greene, September 9, 1783, LD, 20: 646; Freeman, *George Washington*, 5: 452–453.

63　JCC, October 18 and 29, 1783, 25: 702–703, 753; Freeman, *George Washington*, 5: 454–455.

64　Craig Bruce Smith, *American Honor: The Creation of the Nation's Ideals during the Revolutionary Era* (Chapel Hill, University of North Carolina Press, 2018), 165; Ron Chernow, *Washington: A Life* (New York: Penguin, 2010), 448; Gordon S. Wood, *Revolutionary Characters: What Made the Founders Different* (New York: Penguin, 2006), 41–42.

65 Washington, Farewell Address to the Army, November 2, 1783, GWP.

66 McDougall to Washington, November 15, 1783, GWP; Pickering to Samuel Hodgdon, November 17, 1783, TPP; Freeman, *George Washington*, 5: 457; Fowler, *American Crisis*, 224–225.

67 Freeman, *George Washington*, 5: 458–461.

68 Fowler, *American Crisis*, 229.

69 Ibid., 230–231; James Riker, *"Evacuation Day," 1783, Its Many Stirring Events: With Recollections of Capt. John Van Arsdale* (New York: Riker, 1883), 13–17.

70 Freeman, *George Washington*, 5: 465–468.

71 Benjamin Tallmadge, *Memoir of Col. Benjamin Tallmadge* (New York: Thomas Holman, 1858), 63; Freeman, *George Washington*, 5: 467–468.

72 Freeman, *George Washington*, 5: 468–473; Fowler, *American Crisis*, 227–228, 235–236.

73 James Tilton to Gunning Bedford, Jr., December 25, 1783, LD, 21: 232; Fowler, *American Crisis*, 237–238.

74 Chernow, *Washington*, 455; Freeman, *George Washington*, 5: 475.

75 Washington to Congress, December 23, 1783, GWP; James McHenry to Margaret Caldwell, December 23, 1783, LD, 21: 221; Tilton to Bedford, Jr., December 25, 1783, LD, 21: 232; Freeman, *George Washington*, 5: 476–478.

CONCLUSION

1 George Washington to John Armstrong, Jr., February 23, 1797, GWP. My thanks to Edward Lengel for assistance considering the authenticity of this document.

2 George Washington to Alexander Hamilton, March 12, 1783, AHP.

3 John Resch, *Suffering Soldiers: Revolutionary War Veterans, Moral Sentiment, and Political Culture in the Early Republic* (Amherst, MA: University of Massachusetts Press, 1999), 1–4; Charles

Royster, *A Revolutionary People at War: The Continental Army and American Character, 1775–1783* (Chapel Hill: University of North Carolina Press, 1979), 364–368.

4   My thinking on the function of historical conspiracy theories has been shaped by David Aaronovitch, *Voodoo Histories: The Role of Conspiracy Theory in Shaping Modern History* (New York: Riverhead Books, 2010).

Index